00043063

S

AMID OUR TROUBLES

AMID OUR TROUBLES

Irish Versions of Greek Tragedy

Edited by
Marianne McDonald and
J. Michael Walton

Introduction by
Declan Kiberd

Methuen

Methuen

1 3 5 7 9 10 8 6 4 2

First published in Great Britain in 2002 by
Methuen Publishing Limited
215 Vauxhall Bridge Road
London SW1V 1EJ

Methuen Publishing Limited Reg. No. 3543167
A CIP catalogue record for this book is available from the British Library

ISBN 0-413-77142-3

Typeset by SX Composing DTP, Rayleigh, Essex
Printed and bound in Great Britain by
Creative Print and Design (Wales), Ebbw Vale

Contents

Declan Kiberd
Introduction   vii

J. Michael Walton
Hit or Myth: the Greeks and Irish Drama   3

Marianne McDonald
The Irish and Greek Tragedy   37
Appendix: Greek Tragedy in Ireland   80

Síle ní Mhurchú and Patricia Kelly
Translations into Irish of Greek Drama and of Other Works
    Concerning Greece   87

Richard Cave
'After *Hippolytus*': Irish Versions of Phaedra's Story   101

Athol Fugard
Antigone in Africa   128

Seamus Deane
Field Day's Greeks (and Russians)   148

Tom Paulin
Antigone   165

Seamus Heaney
The Cure at Troy: Productions Notes in No Particular
Order   171

Helen Vendler
Seamus Heaney and the *Oresteia*: 'Mycenae Lookout' and the
Usefulness of Tradition   181

Brian Arkins
Women in Irish Appropriations of Greek Tragedy   198

John McDonagh
'Is Medea's Crime Medea's Glory?'
Euripides in Dublin   213

Cathy Leeney
The Return of Persephone?
Missing Demeter in Irish Theatre   232

Eamonn Jordan
Unmasking the Myths? Marina Carr's
By the Bog of Cats . . . and *On Raftery's Hill*   243

Joseph Long
The Sophoclean Killing Fields: an Interview with Frank
McGuinness   263

Index   283

Introduction

Declan Kiberd

The Gaelic poets of Daniel Corkery's hidden Ireland of the eighteenth century had one aim: 'to say commonplace things superbly well'. The underlying attitude to poetry was classical, in the sense that writers were charged with the task of articulating a social consensus. This was a legacy from the glory days of the *filí*, those bards who stood second only to the chieftain in the aristocracy of Gaelic Ireland from 1200 to 1600, before the English plantations destroyed their social and cultural system. These writers put no great premium on originality of theme or thought; rather, they invested their best energies in refining an ever more complex form of metre. The more witty and ornate the quatrain, the more honour it did their chief. Truly, they anticipated by many hundreds of years those Augustan poets who took their lead from Alexander Pope:

> True wit is Nature to advantage dress'd,
> What oft was thought but ne'er so well express'd.

Bardic poetry had been filled with learned references to the texts of ancient Greece and Rome. As early as the twelfth century, the first Irish-language translation of Virgil, *Imtheachta Aeniasa*, made its appearance: and thereafter texts abounded with comparisons between local heroes and Aeneas, local beauties and Helen, local scholars and Ennius. The collapse of the bardic schools after 1600 in no way blunted this commitment to the classics. On the contrary, it gave to their study (still linked to the study of Irish) the glamour of an outlaw activity (allied to the more usual virtue of defending ancient tradition). That combination proved a potent mix in the centuries of colonial rule which followed. Analogies drawn by writers with ancient Greece often carried just the same sort of subversive implication to be later found by township audiences of Athol Fugard's plays. And just as Fugard here recalls the double layers of meaning in such works – as when Anouilh's *Antigone,* staged in occupied Paris, meant one thing to the Nazi officers and quite another to the citizens who sat behind them – so also Irish drama has a long tradition of working on more than one level of implication. In the final days of the Soviet empire, just before Gorbachev's reforms, I watched a production of Friel's *Translations,* done in Tallinn in the Estonian language: and for its audience it had all the force of a revelation about their own relationship with the Russians. Michael Walton's essay will add to the classical and dramatic background for Irish use of the classics. Further elaboration of Ireland's particular use of Greek tragedy in the anti-colonial context will be found in Marianne McDonald's essay.

Ireland, like South Africa, has known an apartheid system. Scholars as different as Maureen Wall and Conor Cruise O'Brien have called the penal laws of the eighteenth century by no other name. The study of Latin at a time when the laws gave no standing at all to Catholics must have carried a certain edge. Many of the ruined *filí* turned after 1600 to the Catholic priesthood and were educated at the great seminaries of Catholic Europe. The works that they produced posited a continuum from the ancient Mediterranean civilizations to the now-threatened Gaelic world, as in Seathrún Céitinn's *Foras Feasa ar Éirinn.*

The hedge schools established in the period of the penal laws from 1690 to the later 1700s maintained that tradition, offering an exalted pedigree to an insulted people. It survived well into the nineteenth century in the lyrics of the people's poet Anthony Raftery:

> Tá pósaidh glégeal ar bhruach na céibhe
> Agus bhuail sí Deirdre le sgéimh a's gnaoi,

'S dá n-ábrainn Helen an bhainríoghain Ghréagach
Ar thuit na céadtá dá barr 'san Traoi.

[There's a lovely posy lives by the roadway
Deirdre was nowhere beside my joy,
Nor Helen who boasted of conquests Trojan,
For whom was roasted the town of Troy.]

– and thence into the love-speeches of Christy Mahon in
Synge's *Playboy of the Western World*:

If the mitred bishops seen you that time, they'd be the like of the holy
prophets, I'm thinking, do be straining the bars of Paradise to lay eyes on
the Lady Helen of Troy, and she abroad pacing back and forward with a
nosegay in her golden shawl.

Synge's tactical use of the classics is, of course, a little more
complicated than Raftery's, for he invokes pagan Greece (as Oscar
Wilde had done) the better to mock a staid and puritanical form of
religion.

In the 'Aeolus' episode of *Ulysses*, Joyce likewise has a character
refer to ancient Greece as the Ireland of the old world, the home of
lost but noble poetic causes, which might be no match for a Roman
imperium but only because of the superior emotional and
intellectual complexity of its native people. The classics still
provided a discourse in which the contests between the various
forces contending for power in Ireland could be represented. If the
Pax Britannica was the new imperial order, it could be challenged
by the alternative use of Latin to be found in the burgeoning
schools and diocesan colleges which flourished after the relaxation
of the penal laws in the 1790s. And that newer form of *Pax
Romana* could in turn be challenged by those libertarian writers
who might turn to Greece for celebrations of the human body in all
its glory.

Ulysses provides a perfect example, for, although it begins with
the words of the old Latin Mass ('*Introibo ad altare Dei*'), it is
structured around Homer's great epic *The Odyssey* and also

around the notion of reclaiming the human body for literature after its denial in the Victorian age. The hope of hellenizing the island is to be implemented in the figure of Leopold Bloom, a man who is 'greeker than the Greeks'. The Joyce who set up his greatest book in these terms is the same author who breathed a sigh of relief, years earlier in Paris, on discovering that his young rival J. M. Synge was 'not an Aristotelian'.

Joyce in those days liked to mock *Riders to the Sea* as dwarf-drama, because of its one-act structure: but many of the play's greatest admirers have found in it traces of the Greek classics. Donna Gerstenberger, for instance, suggested that the closing lines, in which Old Maurya says that 'no man at all can be living for ever, and we must be satisfied', provide 'an echo of the conclusion of Sophocles' *Oedipus*'. Synge certainly studied that play and Gerstenberger may be right, but the more immediate source was a letter written to the playwright by a young Aran islander following the death of his sister-in-law: 'Féuc gurab brónach an sgéul é le rádh, acht má sadh féin caithfidh muid a bheith sásta mar nac féidir le aon nduine a bheith beo go deo.' ['Look, that is a sad story to tell, but if it is itself, we must be satisfied, because nobody can be living for ever.']

Síle Ní Mhurchú and Patricia Kelly in their valuable contribution to this volume point to the left affinities between the Greek and Gaelic mentality in the work of the classics professor George Thomson. He found on the Blasket what Synge had discovered on Aran: the remnants of a Homeric world in which 'fate' rather than this or that person was the tragic protagonist, often epitomized by the awesome power of the sea or by the force of nature itself. Thomson wrote a wonderful essay on Muiris Ó Súilleabháin's *Fiche Blian ag Fás* ('Twenty Years a-Growing'), in which he linked some of the epic 'runs' in Old Irish poetry to narrative descriptions of nightfall or storms in Ó Súilleabháin's book. But, most of all, the Blasket folk reminded this social radical that Homer had once been a people's poet, writing out of the experience of a common culture.

In *The Prehistoric Aegean* (1949), Thomson saluted the Blasket people at that very moment when their way of life on the island was about to end: 'The conversation of these ragged peasants, as soon as I had learned to follow it, electrified me. It was as though Homer had come alive. Its vitality was inexhaustible, yet it was rhythmical, alliterative, formal, artificial, always on the point of bursting into poetry.' In the understanding of a socialist like Thomson, such a culture offered a real alternative to the class-ridden society of imperial Britain in which he had grown up, and of course to the emerging mimic-version of it now so distressingly developing on the Irish mainland.

Synge's use of the Aran Islands had been very similar: an attempt to invoke the classic values of an old Gaelic culture as part of a radical critique of a nationalism which might only be a simulacrum of its imperial parent and not, as Seamus Deane distinguishes in his essay, a real republic (in the sense of a place devoted to that common good epitomized by the words *res publica*). Such a critique of the limits of nationalism has been often conducted through the mouths of female characters, who speak for the individual and insist that the republican discourse find room for such individuals – a theme which recurs in this volume through essays by Brian Arkins, Cathy Leeney, Richard Cave and Eamonn Jordan.

In England, the classic tradition was put to a somewhat different use, especially by the public schools, which laid great emphasis on the study of Latin as a character-forming activity. The stock justification was that Latin provided the basis of many modern languages, but this was often a thin pretext for another agenda – the implantation in schoolboys of the imperial and administrative mentality, as developed through the writings of Caesar and so on. The use of Roman numerals to describe school teams (XI or XV), the resort to such nomenclature as 'Smith major' or 'Smith minor', and the SPQR mentality were all designed to initiate students in the rhetoric of empire. A study of the past empire might strengthen the current affair, as L. A. Wilding explained in his introduction to *A Latin Course for Schools, Part 1* (1949):

The study of a foreign language is an exciting matter; it is like a key that will open many doors . . . By a knowledge of Latin we are introduced to a great people, the Romans. The Romans led the world as men of action; they built good roads, made good laws, and organized what was in their time almost world-wide government and citizenship. At their best, too, they set the highest examples of honour, loyalty and self-sacrifice.

The nervousness in that last sentence glides over the often barbaric nature of actual conquest, but Exercise 65 can leave the students in no doubt: 'At first Agricola wastes the land; then he displays to the natives his moderation.' That is Tacitus, writing of the Battle of Mons Graupius in which ten thousand Scots died. Throughout the mid-twentieth century, Scottish schoolchildren, like their English, Welsh and Irish counterparts, read textbooks like this that seemed to take it as a proper thing that the Romans slaughtered their ancestors in this way. The fact that the Romans had slaves was glossed over not just in fear of the painful light which it might cast on the heroes of schoolboys, but also lest it illuminate the current realities of a British class society. It would be left to radical playwrights such as Howard Brenton to pull the pin from this unexploded bomb – in *The Romans in Britain* he restored the full meaning of the analogy on which the British educationalists' self-image was based.

By way of contrast and perhaps by way of reaction, the emphasis in Ireland in recent decades has increasingly been placed on the Greeks – as in Friel's hedge school, which explores the Carthaginian analogy beloved of many other current playwrights like Frank McGuinness. This emphasis makes sense if we consider the peculiar fate of the 'classic' in Ireland, where it would seldom be used to underwrite empire but more often to unpick the very idea. After all, the collapse of the bardic schools after 1600 did not mark a defeat of classical ideals in Irish writing, merely a subjugation of actual classicists. The attack on those ideals had come not from within but without: it was not, as it would be in England and in other parts of Europe, the revolt of an 'unhealthy' romanticism against a 'healthy-minded' neo-classical aestheticism. In one sense, Ireland had no need of a romantic movement, for the English intervention had ensured that those who defended classical ideals would also be the rebels, the anarchists, the dissidents.

The notion of literature as the embodiment of a superior social consensus was never abandoned by the Irish through all the centuries of their colonization; if anything, that view was strengthened, as the world evoked in Gaelic poetry offered the one remaining social institution through which an underground consciousness might reveal itself. When the great modernists emerged in the wider world of the twentieth century, they found in the example of the Irish a workable model of the revolutionary use of tradition, of how the classics might be invoked as part of the hypermodernity embraced by the new experimentalists. Though T. S. Eliot might pine wistfully for the old empires, it was in those decades when Irish modernism opened up a radical 'alternative' use of the classics that the old public school version of Latin (and its clericalist Irish imitation) began to fade.

And that dialectical movement may conceal the greatest, but least tragic, paradox – that as Latin has lost its prestige and its students, the number of versions of Greek drama in modern languages has risen to an all-time high. This suggests that what is really dying is not so much classical learning as its pedagogical use for the purposes of social and political control.

Amid Our Troubles

Hit or Myth: the Greeks and Irish Drama

J. Michael Walton

'If ever there were a phase of translation in which the principle of the modernizer was incontestably to be preferred, it is in the rendering of the Greek play.'[1] So wrote Theodore Savory almost fifty years ago. Aware as he must have been of the contemporary enthusiasm for reworking the classics exhibited by such as Jean Cocteau, Jean Anouilh and Jean-Paul Sartre, Savory must also have been familiar with the more radical revision of classical themes that was to be found in the work of Hugo von Hofmannsthal, Eugene O'Neill and T. S. Eliot.

Such appropriation of classical myth to tell a modern tale was nothing new. By the time of the Roman empire the masterworks of Aeschylus, Sophocles and Euripides had virtually disappeared from the stage and retreated somewhat apologetically into the library and the classroom. They were replaced by a dramatic pabulum that was more in keeping with Roman taste. Little Roman tragedy has survived, perhaps mercifully, apart from Seneca, but then a massive proportion of the output of the Athenian dramatists has disappeared too. We are now left with a bare 10 per cent of what the greatest of the Greek playwrights wrote and, give or take a couple of disputed authorships, probably nothing from their contemporaries.

The resurrection as theatre pieces of anything remaining from the classical repertoire was left effectively till the latter end of the nineteenth century. True, there had been translations, first into Latin and then into modern European languages, from Erasmus in the sixteenth century onwards, but the potency of the texts was barely if ever tested in performance. It was not as if a knowledge of, and enthusiasm for, things Greek had disappeared, rather that everyone had been so absorbed within the acquisitive culture of Rome that Athena had become irrevocably Minerva, Odysseus Ulysses, and even Aristotle was offered the soubriquet '*divinus*' as though he had acquired his stature only through some Neronian apotheosis.

If the plays of the Athenians had ossified into literature, the myths had not. The drama of the Renaissance and after involved numbers of plots and characters that had their origins in the Trojan War, the tribulations of Thebes, the deeds of Heracles (or, rather, Hercules) and a whole host of other themes from Greek mythology. Distilled through stories of heroism and mayhem, bloodshed, pastoral and romance, they met with other chronicles and cultures without ever being overtaken by them. That, though, is the power of myth. It becomes personal by virtue of its universality, inviting decodings tied to each new occasion or circumstance. Myth can reveal you to yourself. And, as Irish writers have turned to ancient Greek material as translators, adaptors, commentators, or what you will, so in the process, through myth, they have tended to unmask themselves.

Savory, though, must have been aware how much this unmasking was already associated with the whole process of translation. In the classical revival in Britain during the late eighteenth and nineteenth centuries ancient Greece was reinvented as something pristine and Arcadian. If its drama spoke to new generations it could only be as poetry which subscribed to and reinforced eternal verities, transcending time and culture. Greek myth paradoxically had recreated its stage life in opera where the power of the word was subordinated to music; in ballet where it took second place to dance; and on the burlesque and pantomime stage where the story of Medea could be subtitled *A Libel on the Lady from Colchis*, or *The Best of Mothers with a Brute of a Husband*.[2]

The twentieth century changed this. Stutteringly, but relentlessly, the great tragedians began to emerge from the vaults to which they had been consigned, their plays, or some of them, renewed and reinvigorated through translation. It was a far from painless

4

process. In 1903 there were riots in the streets of Athens when Thomas Economou presented Aeschylus' *Oresteia* in modern rather than ancient Greek. Several people were killed.

Edward Gordon Craig re-examined the potential of the masked figure in a way that impressed and influenced W. B. Yeats, through a series of 'visions' of light and space, but he had to go and live outside his native England to find anyone who would take serious note of his ideas. In Europe Max Reinhardt rediscovered the spectacle of Aeschylus and Sophocles, but it took the Irish directors, Terence Gray and Tyrone Guthrie, to see spectacle as something to be fostered alongside subtlety and humanity.

Reinhardt relied for the most part on scripts from von Hofmannsthal which were not translations so much as 'versions' of Greek tragedy, *Elektra* (1903) – Craig did a remarkable series of designs for Eleanora Duse in the role but they were never used – *König Ödipus* (1907) and *Alkestis* (1909). 'A Version for the Modern Stage' was how Yeats was to subtitle his *Sophocles' King Oedipus* first published in 1928. All these, and the Gilbert Murray translations performed in and around the Royal Court Theatre under the Vedrenne–Barker management, were recognizable as being serious attempts to reproduce, however erratically, the essence of the original plays. Virginia Woolf was unimpressed. 'It is useless, then, to read Greek in translations. Translators can but offer us a vague equivalent; their language is necessarily full of echoes and associations.'[3] The response of T. S. Eliot was to haul the classics into the present: 'We need an eye which can see the past in its place with its definite differences from the present, and yet so lively that it shall be present to us at the present.'[4] *The Family Reunion* (1939) was a contemporary verse play based loosely on Aeschylus' *Oresteia*; *The Cocktail Party* (1949) another, based even more loosely on Euripides' *Alcestis*. He was to follow these with *The Confidential Clerk* (Euripides' *Ion*) in 1953 and *The Elder Statesman* (Sophocles' *Oedipus at Colonus*) in 1958.

However imperfect as harbingers of a revival of verse drama, never mind as representations of the Greek originals, Eliot's plays did give licence to treat situations and characters from existing plays as flexible. He may not have been the first to do this but he was the first to do so with one foot firmly in the original language, the other in the world of twentieth-century poetry. His example goes some way towards disarming the complaints of the purists and opening the door for the whole range of Irish adaptations which range from the straight translations, whatever that may mean, of Desmond Egan to the wilder excesses of Aidan Carl Mathews or Colin Teevan.

Questions of translation are knotty, not least because there is often seen to be some obligation on the writer who claims the authority and the reputation of one of the classics to serve that original as well as the self. The Greek myths may be trees with many branches, but too much parasitic ivy can destroy the trunk. The translator will never find it easy to remain neutral. The good playwright of any period will leave enough flexible for the director and the actor to bring new interpretations and fresh emphases according to the mood and sensibilities of a new occasion. Apart from linguistic equivalence, the stage translator from Greek into some modern language must leave open the 'performance door' which much literary and literal translation seems to close.

Are there ground rules for redefining or adapting for a modern audience a language that is no longer spoken, for dealing with a culture that is largely misunderstood by the vast majority of readers or theatregoers? How should an Electra or an Orestes speak? And will that be the same in a play by Aeschylus, by Sophocles, or by Euripides? As significantly, maybe more so, how does the contemporary translator tackle all those aspects of the stage play that only come alive through performance: iconography, nuance, subtext, irony? How are the plays from the classical repertoire to be made to live for an audience of today? And what licence does the translator have to nudge, tickle, or just plain sabotage the original while still laying claim to being the spirit voice of a long-dead dramatist? The medium may hold the message but who controls the seance?

Greek tragedy was born from a corpus of myth that went back to the sagas of Homer and the other composers of epic cycles. This was a pre-literary world and, accordingly, it was a flexible one. Stories evolved within an oral tradition. There was no one standard version of the past, no definitive history, no fixed time-scale. A character like Heracles or Theseus could turn up in all sorts of places and periods, significant for his heroic reputation not the accuracy of his c.v. The situations and characters of myth were a huge and pliable conglomeration of recollection, exaggeration and pure invention. For the poet and playwright they represented a series of ingredients which could be cooked up into all sorts of recipes, savoury, sweet, or sour. The stories were enduring. The stories have endured. First the Romans, then every subsequent age in which drama has flourished, were to raid and pillage the classics and introduce their own versions to suit their own tastes and their own social and political concerns: because these stories were nothing if they were not indicators of how the world worked and how the men and women of the world led and misled their lives.

Among all those who have struggled to provide the rules of engagement for translators, Walter Benjamin offered one of the more enlightening of responses when he wrote: 'While a poet's words endure in his own language, even the greatest translation is destined to become part of the growth of its own language and eventually to be absorbed by its renewal.'⁵ Though he spoke in terms of the written word, Benjamin was making a case for translation as a creative act which could equally well apply to the construction of plays. I imagine that most playwrights would be inclined to justify their personal response to the classical originals in just such a way. Most of the Irish playwrights whose work is discussed here would make no bones about their intention to follow a personal agenda whatever the direction of their source of inspiration. Any complaints about that should be referred to the originals. Personal agendas were exactly what inspired Aeschylus, Sophocles, Euripides and Aristophanes too to write what they did and in the way that they did. More, the tragedians would return again and again to the same themes, plots and characters, not in order to repeat themselves *ad infinitum* but because they found in the skeletons of the old stories more than enough inspiration to create whole new beings of infinite variety – new individuals and families, new breeds.

This malleability is perhaps what makes the Greek canon so appealing to those who want to take advantage of the distancing that a classical setting may offer. These playwrights went back and back to the same sagas from pre-history precisely because only the barest outlines were fixed. Jocasta was not going to turn out not to be Oedipus' mother, but there is a raft of possible motivations and attitudes to invest and investigate. Medea was deserted by Jason but her killing of her children may well have been a refinement dreamed up by Euripides. Why not, then, a Medea, as Franca Rame and Dario Fo envisaged her, who does kill the children, but for whom it is a metaphorical act of personal release? Or a conclusion as posited by Brendan Kennelly where the Chorus can leave the audience with the conclusion:

> And yet I wonder, and will always wonder -
> Is Medea's crime Medea's glory?[6]

What the myths have in common is their antiquity. What the myths have in common is their novelty. What the plays have in common is their attachment to issues from then. What the plays have in common is their attachment to the now. What the Greek playwrights had in common was their belief in the theatre as a serious place for ethical and political debate. As for today's playwrights, there is no paradox there. It is no accident that it is Irish settings which have given these Greek classics a new dimension: for Ireland has the last English-speaking contemporary drama that still sees the theatre as the natural place to juggle ideas. Only in Ireland, it would seem, as a former director of the Abbey Theatre has maintained, 'if you have something to say, you write a play about it'.

Perhaps that is the only link we need. What those first Greek audiences did accept was the presentation of stories, conflicts and debates in the form of dramatic parable from a deep and barely penetrable past. And so powerfully were these issues presented that audiences were moved to tears of joy or sadness. Through a sense of total artifice the playwrights developed a sophisticated stage language of mask, music and dance; of the visual and the aural; of dramatic rhythm and theatrical device. The artificiality was enhanced by the dramatic structure, the verse formations, the choice of individual words and metaphors, all in different ways according to the manner in which each playwright 'played' audience expectations.

What are Greek tragedies about? Acts of revenge, acts of treachery, acts of sacrifice, acts of resistance: so are most plays and most operas. Any of them can be generalized, inviting the audience to home in on a single issue; or they can be made specific, in a specific theatrical context, from which, again, members of the audience may draw the parallel they find most suitable. Those of us who translate are familiar with these issues and their ramifications.

Virginia Woolf was right, of course. It is useless 'to read Greek in translations'. But that is not a reason not to translate Greek plays, to rewrite them and to present them for a modern audience. Dramatic translation, either in isolation for the reader, or for a particular production, involves a reconstruction of the imagination, rooted in the original but allowing for those contributions by actor and director. And that is where adaptation comes in too. All you need for a proper climate in which to present Greek plays are the social and political conditions which demand the special enlightenment that only the theatre can offer.

Lady Gregory and Yeats initially had different ideas. Yeats seems to have felt that any concentration on Greek mythology was at the expense of Irish history. Synge too had written to Lady Gregory in 1906 implying that the only reason for the Abbey to produce classic plays such as Molière and Sophocles would be 'to illuminate the work of Irish playwrights on Irish themes'.[7] His own *Oedipus* plays, *Sophocles' King Oedipus: a Version for the Modern Stage* and *Sophocles' Oedipus at Colonus: a Version for the Modern Stage*, were presented in 1926 and 1927 but not published until 1928 and 1934 respectively. In fact, Yeats had worked for twenty-four years on his translations and the various stages through which the final version went have been carefully recorded by David R. Clark and James B. McGuire.[8] The process of 'illumination' that Synge had advocated was well illustrated in the early exchange between Oedipus and Creon in *King Oedipus*. Oedipus expresses surprise that so little is known about the circumstances of the death of Laius. He tells of the one man 'who fled in terror':

CREON: He said that they were fallen upon by a great troop of robbers.
OEDIPUS: What robbers would be so daring unless bribed from here?
CREON: Such things were indeed guessed at, but Laius once dead no
         avenger arose. We were amid our troubles.

(lines 85–91)

A Dublin audience, hearing such a phrase in 1926, would be hard put not to look for subtext when listening to the rest of this 'version'. Oedipus disarms the phrase 'amid our troubles' but draws attention to it too when he responds: 'But when royalty had fallen what troubles could have hindered [such a] search?' Creon replies: 'The riddling Sphinx put those dark things out of our thoughts', but then caps it with: 'We thought of what had come to our own doors' (lines 92–6). As it happens, these are a perfectly reasonable, straight translation of Sophocles' original text, but here, as so often, everything depends less on the text than on the context. Yeats offered us in that first loaded phrase from Creon the title for this book.

The second play, no sequel to Sophocles, but often made to seem so in modern productions of both, has the consciously Irish setting which Yeats admitted and to which Marianne McDonald draws attention elsewhere in this book (next chapter, pp. 43–4). It requires no linguistic trigger to give a taste of immediacy to a play that concerns the fear of civil war. Several plays in their first production in Athens saw this as the danger to be avoided at all costs – Aeschylus' *Seven Against Thebes*, Sophocles' *Antigone*, Euripides' *Suppliants* and *Phoenician Women* – but few can have been naturally so pointed as *Oedipus at Colonus* with a father sending a son away to his death at the hands of his own brother, a curse ringing in his ears.

Greek tragedy with its range of savage and pitiless hatreds, its victims, its losers who are losers and its winners who are losers, offers ample examples of the arbitrariness of fate. So wide-ranging is the subject-matter of even the limited amount of Greek tragedy we have that it might seem that there are metaphors here for any and every occasion. Why, one is forced to ask, did the rewriting of Greek tragedy become such a crucial part of the critical response to the political situation both north and south of the border in Ireland, particularly in the last twenty years?

The answers are given, I think, in the essays elsewhere in this book that fit the experience of Greek tragedy into a comprehensive survey of Irish engagement with classical drama: and dissect the manner in which drama in Ireland has staked out the battlefields of struggle and debate. Those best qualified, often from direct experience, draw attention to the manner in which drama has functioned as both macrocosm and microcosm. Playwrights as diverse as Synge, O'Casey and Murray are invoked as demonstrating classical themes or structures; Heaney, Kennelly, Paulin and others have all presented their fresh slants on extant plays from the Athenian canon; others whose plays are of today and set in today – Friel, Carr, Murphy – set up resonances from the Greek world that clang and clatter round the mind. What may be informative is to consider the issues from the perspective of those original playwrights whose work has been thus renewed.

Aeschylus is represented by versions of the *Oresteia* and *Prometheus*. The other plays, *Persians, Seven Against Thebes* and *Suppliants*, are less well known and certainly less frequently revived. *Persians* is parochial, dealing uniquely among surviving classical tragedies with a subject that was contemporary, or at least from living memory: the aftermath of the defeat of the Persian invading force only eight years before the first performance. Both this and the more archaic *Suppliants* might have things to say to the modern world, but their specifics would serve less well to point to predominantly Irish issues. *Seven Against Thebes* might do so, but its dramatic impact is diminished today both by being very obviously only one part of a tetralogy, and by the fact that the plot-line makes little allowance for the root causes of injustice and abuse of power that underpin, for example, Sophocles' *Antigone*, a play whose action begins effectively the same day as that when *Seven Against Thebes* ends.

Prometheus is a different story. Here is the archetypal rebel, the superhuman who defied Zeus and brought fire to mortals; whom a hostile Zeus had pegged out on a rock in the Caucasus. Prometheus is the defiant figure who suffers for refusing to tell the one secret that terrifies the lord of the gods. As a representation of the indomitability of the spirit, few images are more concentrated than the persecuted figure whose liver is pecked out daily by a vulture, only every night to be restored. For Tom Paulin, whose *Seize the Fire* is a subtle mix of classical allusion and conscious anachronism, Zeus is the authority that uses and abuses. If the broad picture invites an association between Zeus and England, Prometheus and Ireland, the play loses nothing of its power when switched to the perennial battles of capital and labour, control and freedom. This is what Aeschylus himself sets up when, right at the beginning of his play, he has Prometheus shackled to the rock by Bia, 'Power', and Kratos, 'Strength', on the orders of Hephaestus, another, and here reluctant, member of the Olympian hierarchy. Prometheus remains immobile throughout the play, his plight highlighted by the freedom experienced by Oceanus, by the Chorus of Oceanids, by the persecuted Io trying to run from the pursuing gadfly and by Hermes, the messenger god with winged sandals.

For Paulin, the fire that Prometheus brought may be both the spirit of armed rebellion and the arms themselves. The conflict remains unresolved as in Aeschylus it remains unresolved. The forecast is of 'the tanks on the lawn . . . locked doors and panic'. In Aeschylus, though, there was one more part of the trilogy to come, maybe two, leading, perhaps, to a resolution of qualified optimism. The rest has not survived. Paulin's Zeus uses tactics from bribery to physical threat which are virtually guaranteed to strengthen the resolve of his adversary. Here is the true strength of weakness, though little cause for optimism.

The revenge theme of the three plays of Aeschylus' *Oresteia* already had an overt political parallel when first presented in Athens in the middle of the fifth century BC. Progress towards democracy, albeit a democracy of limited scope and ambition, had taken the best part of fifty years after the expulsion of the last King of Athens and the struggles with Persia as he tried to win back his throne. Aeschylus' massive work, the only connected trilogy to survive the ravages of time, was on the surface, as Arthur Miller once described most plays, a story of 'the chickens coming home to roost'. Agamemnon returns victorious from the ten-year war against Troy, only to be axed in his bath by his wife Clytemnestra. In the second play of the three, revenge for the murder of a father is exacted by their son Orestes. In the third, the Furies, roused from their lair by the act of matricide, hound Orestes until, in a trial in Athens, he is acquitted and the cycle of vengeance finds resolution.

Aeschylus makes the piece work on several different levels simultaneously. The dramatized action is only one part of a saga that has carried on through generations. The present is a product of the past, the scenes of violence the latest in a long line of violations that have torn families apart. These plays are set in the world of the Trojan Wars and its aftermath, the best part of 900 years before Aeschylus was even born. But if the world of the play is the deep past, shrouded in the variations and alternatives of myth, Aeschylus' messages are set firmly in the present. There are issues of loyalty and betrayal, the conflicts of order and anarchy, the imperatives of duty and instinct. These make the *Oresteia* a set of plays that still live and breathe. Behind all this, though, in the resolution of the unresolvable – should you punish or applaud a man who avenges his father by killing his mother? – there was a specific political dimension in Athens. The judgement of Athena, patron goddess of the city, that this is too big an issue even for the gods to resolve, leads instead to the establishment of a jury system. The whole state will take responsibility for the presentation and execution of justice: and the elder deities, the Furies, whose justice was summary and unaffected by circumstance, must give way to new and younger gods with shorter memories. The *Oresteia* celebrates the final triumph of the democratic system.

There is, of course, a price and it is on that price that contemporary versions tend to concentrate. The legacy of the past cannot be so simply expunged. Louis MacNeice, in his translation of *Agamemnon*, allots to the Chorus the lines '. . . in ill fortune / The dab of a wet sponge destroys the drawing'. Virtually all classical critics give the lines to Cassandra, the prophetess doomed always to tell the truth but never to be believed. This is the last thing she says before she exits, knowingly, to her own death. She too is a victim of her past actions. MacNeice's alteration does, perhaps, make the message corporate rather than individual and may even make the immediate message stronger. The legacies of the past, attitudes as entrenched and instinctive as the power that rouses the Furies, are as easy to parallel in contemporary Ireland as they were in the Athens of Aeschylus. If the belief that *something* has to happen to break an impasse can lead to uncomfortable conclusions, that must be better than the philosophy of despair, or a Pilate-like refusal any longer to acknowledge responsibility.

Most modern adaptations of the *Oresteia* choose to treat it as a family saga. The same tends to be true for versions of the Sophocles *Electra*, which covers that part of the history of the house of Atreus that Aeschylus deals with in *Libation Bearers*, the second part of the *Oresteia*, and Euripides in his *Electra*. Frank McGuinness turned to the Sophocles *Electra* for his 'new version'. Commissioned originally by London's Donmar Warehouse Theatre in 1997, neither translation nor production made any attempt directly to invoke an Irish context. Nevertheless, the writer's patterns of speech do give resonance to particular lines – 'Is my news not good news?' / 'You're living in the land of dreams, and you don't know it.' McGuinness's work on a Greek original, as in his translations/ versions from Norwegian, Russian, Spanish and German, does no more than make the play more palatable for an audience of today. His fluency with dialogue is exemplary and, if the plays take on a wider resonance, then that is because the original makes it possible rather than that the writer has intervened with a personal agenda.

This is not true of most of the 'Irish versions' performed in the North or the South of Ireland in the last twenty years, and *Electra*, along with *Philoctetes* and *Antigone,* are the Sophocles plays which might most invite a contemporary slant. Sophocles deals with non-conformists, those who take on difficult decisions and have to learn to live with the consequences of their actions. His plays seem crammed with misfits, people who for one reason or another are in the wrong place at the wrong time and thoroughly out of sorts with the world.

Consider *Ajax*, probably the earliest of his plays. The Greek hero, cheated out of the weapons of the dead Achilles, vows vengeance on the Greek army who were his friends and colleagues. What happens to him? When we, the audience, first hear of him, it is via the goddess Athena, patron goddess of Athens where the festivals were presented and the plays first produced. She has driven him mad so that he has massacred a load of sheep and cattle believing them to be his human enemies. Has she done so simply to protect the Greeks? Well, yes, she has, but she can still boast to Odysseus, the first mortal character on the scene: 'What could be sweeter than the chance to laugh at him?' (lines 78–9).

Ajax suffers humiliation after humiliation until he decides that suicide is his only option. He leaves the scene, soon to be pursued by the Chorus, and is next seen by himself on the sea-shore where, completely alone, he falls on his sword. Madness, shame, despair, suicide: personal tragedy though this may be, it is surprising that none of the Irish writers has chosen to see his plight as having a contemporary application. It is difficult to resist the feeling that there is an Irish *Ajax* waiting to be written. Instead, it is *Antigone* and *Philoctetes*, through Seamus Heaney's *The Cure at Troy: A Version of Sophocles' Philoctetes*, which have received the exposure.

Sophocles' *Philoctetes* concerns the attempts by Odysseus and Neoptolemus to persuade or trick a man, whom they and their fellow Greeks had years ago abandoned on a desert island, to go with them to Troy. Philoctetes, marooned because his festering foot was too noxious for his shipmates to stomach, turns out to be essential if they are ever to take Troy. The reason is the bow of Heracles (or, in Heaney, Hercules). The battle becomes, though, both in Sophocles and in Heaney, a *psychomachia* over the soul of the young Neoptolemus, son of the dead hero Achilles. Philoctetes seems like the apogee of Sophoclean anguish, fainting from pain at one point but tortured too by the duplicity of the Greeks. In Heaney there is a change of tone. The pain is there, but the despair is not. The argument in *Ajax* comes down eventually to how far the man who has committed an atrocity and killed himself as a result shall be accorded posthumous honours. Heaney's approach to the Philoctetes story is to use it to offer seeds of hope for reconciliation and even redemption.

On the flyleaf of the published text Heaney quotes W. H. Auden:

> O look, look in the mirror,
>   O look in your distress;
> Life remains a blessing
>   Although you cannot bless.[9]

Heaney's Philoctetes can offer Neoptolemus some homespun advice:

> Life is shaky. Never, son, forget
> How risky and slippy things are in this world.
> Walk easy when the jug's full, and don't ever
> Take your luck for granted. Count your blessings
> And always be ready to pity other people.[10]

But his bitterness is harsh and unyielding until Neoptolemus persuades him that there is no shame 'in working for a good thing'. The Chorus, late in the play, offers a message of hope:

> Believe in miracles
> And cures and healing wells

and then themselves play Hercules, in Sophocles a *deus ex machina,* as Philoctetes is finally persuaded to leave the island.

Antigone, which bubbled up to the surface in its *annus mirabilis* of 1984, offers few opportunities for compromise. Sophocles' eponymous heroine, isolated by her resolve to bury her dead brother whatever the cost, turns against her sister for refusing to become involved, and publicly defies Creon, the figure of temporal power. She chooses to make her protest a political statement, accepting the inevitable death sentence and anticipating it by hanging herself. Here is no reconciliation, only realization when it is too late of the real cost of the rigid stance. *Antigone* has no Heaney to offer reconciliation and a change of heart, or only that exhibited by the pathetic Creon whose obduracy and innate capacity to make the wrong decisions and at the wrong time ensure he loses son and wife without even the bitter consolation of winning the argument.

Philoctetes is the only Sophocles play without a death. Of the other seven, four include suicides. *Antigone* has three, three desperate individuals, three tormented and lonely people, three self-inflicted deaths. Such is the fundamental nature of the clash between temporal power and moral stance around which this play revolves, that it is virtually impossible to detach it from whatever context the audience finds itself in. In that single scene of confrontation in Athol Fugard's *The Island* is concentrated all the futility, the absurdity and the desperation of apartheid. What remains remarkable is how in the aftermath of the overthrow of this rancid philosophy, Fugard's play and, beyond that, Sophocles' *Antigone* offer in harshly moving terms the necessary reminder of the immediate historical lesson and the hugeness of that metaphor for any government of oppressive decree in the face of the single-minded protest.

Sophocles also wrote a *Tantalus*, a *Pelops*, a *Niobe*, an *Atreus* and, apparently, no fewer than three versions of *Thyestes*. So who knows how much nightmare and misery we have been spared by not having more of his plays? From the seven plays we do have, it is clear that Sophocles dwells on physical and mental agony. Deianira in *The Women of Trachis* tries to win back the affections of her husband with a love charm which unwittingly proves as fatal as that with which Medea disposes of Jason's new wife. Deianira kills herself; so too does Jocasta in *Oedipus Tyrannus* on the discovery that her husband, the father of her children, is also her son. Only in the last and posthumous play, *Oedipus at Colonus*, does death seem to offer consolation, or, in the case of Oedipus, not death but departure from life in a transfiguration that is as mystical as it is unusual. But for those left behind the Chorus offers a dismal prospect summed up in Yeat's celebrated translation:

Death, despair, division of families, all entanglements of mankind grow,
As that old wandering beggar and these God-hated children know.
In the long-echoing street the laughing dancers throng,
The bride is carried to the bridegroom's chamber through torchlight and
    tumultuous song;
I celebrate the silent kiss that ends short life or long.
Never to have lived is best, ancient writers say;
Never to have drawn the breath of life, never to have looked into the eye
    of day;
The second best's a gay goodnight and quickly turn away.

(lines 1151–8).

This is no casual nor unfamiliar response. In Sophocles the quality of personal despair that isolation engenders is wholly unlike that to be found in Aeschylus or Euripides. It is this that makes the Sophocles originals such effective parables for any political situation where a single decision taken on moral grounds can cut the individual off from family, from friends, from established authority, from 'civilized' behaviour, from normal life, from life itself.

David Nowlan writing in the *Irish Times*[11] describes Brendan Kennelly's *Antigone* as 'probably the most substantial Irish drama since W. B. Yeats was writing . . . this is, of course, a political tragedy'. But Kennelly offers no less powerfully the family tragedy: 'I wanted to explore sisterhood, the loyalty a sister will show to a brother, against law, against marriage, against everything. There's no relation like it; it has all the passion of your whole nature, this side of incest.'[12] Sophocles' *Antigone* offers a personal but relentless exchange:

ISMENE: I want to help you.
ANTIGONE: Then save yourself. I don't want you to die too.
ISMENE: Oh, pity me. Let me die with you.
ANTIGONE: No. You chose life, and I, death.
ISMENE: I only said what I believed.
ANTIGONE: Some will think you are right; others will think I am.[13]

This becomes far more wide-reaching, softer too, in Kennelly's conciliatory:

ISMENE: Say whatever words you will.
            Let me serve you now with body and soul.
ANTIGONE: You'll serve me best by saving yourself.
ISMENE: Have I, then, no share in your fate,
            Your death.
ANTIGONE: You chose to live for fear.
            I chose to die for love.
ISMENE: At least I made a protest at your choice.
ANTIGONE: There were two worlds, two ways.
            One world approved your way,
            The other mine.
            You were wise in your way,
            I in mine.[14]

Kennelly's other two Greek 'versions' are both of plays by Euripides, *Medea* and *Trojan Women*. They too take a strongly feminine perspective, but one that is more in keeping with the sympathies exhibited in the originals. Nineteen plays by Euripides survive; one is a satyr play, another a disputed attribution; the remaining seventeen are still comfortably more than the complete legacy of Aeschylus and Sophocles combined. Of those seventeen, all but five (only four and a half if you allow *Children of Heracles* to include the hero's off-stage daughters as well as his visible sons) take their title from a woman or a group of women. Euripides' plays show an extraordinary variation in mood. The situations in which these women find themselves vary from the deeply pathetic to the frankly comic. Today, it is difficult to comprehend how

Euripides' contemporary, the comic playwright Aristophanes, could have characterized Euripides as a misogynist – still less how this could still be a common critical view as late as the twentieth century. True, many of the women in his plays – Hecuba, Phaedra, Medea, Electra, Helen, Agave – are responsible for the deaths of enemies and, in three examples, children, but what seems to concern the playwright is less the nature of such acts, however horrible, than the circumstances that have reduced the women to such measures.

Most of his plays have no history of Irish adaptation, indeed few of the less well known have much of a stage history anywhere. The ones that do remain popular are all notable for their seeming modernity. Characters in Euripides frequently display subtleties of personality and nuances of behaviour that mark them down as a spit in the eye to traditionalists and a challenge to many of the received views of myth. Euripides, the iconoclast, has enough stun guns in his armoury for him to be judged both the murderer of tragedy by making it too domestic, and the precursor of the whole European comic tradition, through his redefinition of those two prime dramatic weapons which Aristotle was later to classify as *anagnorisis* and *peripeteia,* 'recognition' and 'reversal of expecta-tion'. Maybe, in the light of the whole enthralling history of their drama, the Irish might feel entitled to appropriate an author whose juxtaposition of the pathetic and the comic is still a cause of despair to those fossilized critics who can only accept their drama cut into recognizable and properly labelled packages. In the early years of the last century Gilbert Norwood wrote an intriguing study comparing Euripides with Shaw,[15] and the mixture of the sublime, the pathetic and the ridiculous to be found in many a Euripidean scene should ring bells of recognition in the minds of those whose history has been predicated upon just such a recipe.

Any reading of Aristophanes should make us wary of finding the man within the writing. The apparent sympathy with the oppressed and frustration with entrenched social attitudes are still hard to deny when so many plays show prominent figures whose reputation is challenged by their actions. Euripides' world is peopled by those whose judgement is faulty. If the same could be said to be true for Sophocles' Creon, Odysseus and, indeed, Oedipus, the fabled heroes of Euripides frequently forfeit the right to be treated as anything other than moral cretins. It is to the savage, though sometimes comic, Euripides that Irish writers have turned: Kennelly to *Medea* and *Trojan Women*; Marina Carr to *Medea*; Aidan Carl Mathews to *Trojan Women*; Derek Mahon to *Bacchae*. All these contemporary writers, and others less successful, offer their bleak, black, farcical moments. They could all claim with justification to find such moments embedded in their source of inspiration. These, then, will be the sample plays by Euripides to consider here, plays whose sheer malleability makes them suitable for tinkering and tuning in each and every new era.

In a frontispiece to Derek Mahon's *The Bacchae: after Euripides* there is a quotation from Louis MacNeice's *The Poetry of W. B. Yeats* where he writes that 'Yeats' efflorescence in old age is perhaps unique in recent poetry. We might compare Euripides who, after a long life spent struggling with and digesting new ideas, in gradually formulating a sceptical, rationalist attitude, had in his old age the elasticity to admit that there was a case for Dionysus.'[16] MacNeice's view of Euripides as a death-bed convert to orthodoxy was a fashionable doctrine, both before and in the wake of the rationalist approach to Dionysus as a fake. Such divergent interpretations reinforce the idea of Euripides' *Bacchae* as a barometer of the current social and political moods of any era.

At the core of this play is a collision between temporal and divine authority – as in *Antigone*, several of the tragedies of Shakespeare, *St Joan*, Anouilh's *Beckett* and a whole host of other dramatic masterpieces, including, if you like, *Don Giovanni* and *Brandt*. Unlike them, though, sympathies may be much more finely tuned according to the tastes of the time. The representatives of authority and freedom are less easy fully to side with when they are delivered into the hands of Euripides' weak king and his cousin, the mocking god. In the 1960s Pentheus was identified as the fascist dictator, Dionysus as flower power, free love and the hippie culture. Ten years later and the influence of Dionysus appeared baleful. The balance had shifted within a decade and the ease with which a god used supernatural powers to befuddle and destroy his own family seemed like a ghastly whim: and at other times there have been all manner of variations, the play seeming anything from an attack on organized religion to a humanist plea for balance and understanding.

Derek Mahon's version is subtitled 'after Euripides'. Marianne McDonald wrote of it: 'This parable is suitable for Ireland. Dionysus can be regarded as a force of nature, the force of a people who are fighting to reclaim their rights – a people who are laying claim to a land that has been taken from them.'[17]

Astute as this may be, Bacchae is no Antigone, where the audience are offered a straight clash between the authority of Creon, a king trying to restore order after civil war, and the rebel Antigone who knows, without a moment's doubt, that she has to bury her brother's body whatever the law of the land happens to say. That is a relatively straightforward debate between two human beings who happen to be on different sides in every possible way: one young, one old; one female, one male; one powerless, one in authority; both stubborn unto death. In Bacchae something very different is at work. Here is a magical world, a world of miracles and marvels, of superhuman powers and delusions. Instead of a determined and stubborn girl stabbing herself after imprisonment in a cave, we have an equivocal 'stranger' who frees himself from his prison and then persuades a king to dress up in women's clothes before being torn to pieces by a mother who thinks he is a lion.

Yet both plays take place in Thebes and the battles are fought over the exercise of authority. Cadmus in the Bacchae is grandfather of the ill-starred Pentheus. He was also, the myth has it, great-grandfather of Laius, the father that Oedipus killed where three roads meet on the way from Delphi. That makes him greatgreat-grandfather to Antigone, though exactly where Pentheus and Dionysus fit into this genealogy is obscure. It may be revealing to consider what differences it makes to the quality of parable, this change from Sophocles' realistic clash of temperaments to the 'magical realism' of Euripides. One contrast stands out above all others. The Sophocles play is easy to translocate into a different time, a different culture, a different set of political circumstances. A solitary figure standing up for her beliefs in the face of all that the law of the land can throw at her can offer a dozen parallels a day from Africa to Asia, from Europe to the Americas. Antigone is the resistance icon, hence the revival of the play at moments of protest in France, South Africa, or the Ireland of 1984. *Bacchae*, though, is a play whose metaphor is both more spiritual and more theatrical. And it is far less easy either to explain what happens in it or to debate whose side you might wish to take and why.

On the surface it has one of the simplest of dramatic themes, that of the disruptive outsider who appears in a community and in a short time creates havoc before moving on. Euripides' angle is unequivocal. God though he may be, Euripides' Dionysus has been forged by the circumstances of his birth which Pentheus and the rest of the family have rejected. His mother Semele, Dionysus claims, was loved by Zeus. Then jealous Hera persuaded the pregnant Semele to get Zeus to reveal himself to her in his true nature. When he did, she was burnt to a frazzle because the true nature of Zeus is a thunderbolt. Much of this the character offers in a prologue in Mahon's version almost flippantly. Dionysus is described as 'gaily dressed', speaking in a 'light, gay voice'. In his description of what has happened and will happen in Thebes, this Dionysus poses almost no threat, except to his puritan cousin. When he leaves the scene Mahon has the Chorus describe him as 'the laughing god'. He seems at this point to be more treat than trick when they call upon the Theban men to

> shut your houses tight;
> Dionysus' women are here
> to give you all a fright.
>
> (p. 23)

But, as *Antigone*, *Bacchae* is a family drama too. Semele was one of the four daughters of Cadmus. The other three are the ones who have refused to believe the Zeus story and who will between them tear Pentheus to pieces. Dionysus, by his own admission, is only half god, half mortal. That is a major factor because the ambiguous Dionysus is determined to have it both ways, to be both god and mortal. If this is a play about persecution and repression, it is certainly open to question: who is the persecutor and who is repressed?

Tiresias, the old, blind prophet who is always consulted in times of crisis in Thebes, and usually ends up roundly abused before being proved right, is in Mahon quite childlike, trying to persuade 'the old fool' (Cadmus) 'to go to the famous ceili'. But then what an extraordinary picture Euripides does paint, two old men, one blind, one halt, dressed up for someone else's party, full of lore and blather. They might be a missing turn by Samuel Beckett: as comic too, for surely no one, however Penthean, could deny the humour in Cadmus' hoping to get a lift up the mountain to go and dance for Dionysus.

Dionysus, 'disguised as a man', has turned the women of Thebes mad. He then helps them perform miracles up in the hills; escapes from prison by deluding Pentheus; organizes an earthquake, which may or may not be an illusion too; persuades Pentheus to dress up as a woman and parade through the streets of Thebes disguised as a Bacchante; and finally convinces Pentheus' mother and the other women that this is a lion; giving them the strength to pull him apart before inspiring Agave to return to Thebes brandishing her son's head on her Bacchic wand. Mahon makes an odd decision when he takes the earthquake literally, with stage directions such as: '*The palace shakes. There is a fall of masonry within ... More falling masonry ... Dionysus appears before the palace in a cloud of smoke.*' Though the destruction of the palace prefigures the destruction of the King, another reading of the original is to treat the whole 'palace miracle' as an exhibition of Dionysus' power to deceive and delude.

One of the marks of the great play is that it will be satisfying both within the terms of reference the playwright has established – what the military call rather ominously 'the rules of engagement' – and also as a fable, as an allegory, as a debate and an argument about the human condition, the world we understand and, in this case, the world beyond, which we don't really understand. This makes it possible to speak to the future, a future that the playwright could never have envisaged in his wildest dreams. *Bacchae* does that, in a manner quite unlike any other Greek tragedy, by engaging with that wholly other world, the world of theatre.

Dionysus was, after all, apart from any functions relating to wine, nature and the irrational, the god of the theatre. And here we see the god demonstrating in his command of those he encounters, the very marrow and bone of theatre itself, that quality that made the theatre seem so dangerous and subversive to Plato and Socrates that no place could be found for it in the Utopia of *The Republic*. Here is a dramatic narrative driven by disguise, by illusion, by masquerade, deception, hallucination. Dionysus as god of the theatre may have the power to bemuse Pentheus, Agave and the women of Thebes. He also has, in his Chorus, the followers who have accompanied him from the east, a living embodiment of the Dionysiac religion, glorious, terrifying, dangerous, ecstatic – all qualities that mark the very best of theatre.

Perhaps that is why this is a play that baffles people. To those who have some garbled notion of what a Greek tragedy ought to be, *Bacchae* is a problem because it is so resistant to fitting into any category. To those who wish to find a moral message it is worse, being full of paradoxes and confusions. Whose side are you meant to take? Which character can you latch on to to help you through this moral maze? Any suggestion can only lead to further paradox: but there are some signposts. They are signposts which help to make *Bacchae* applicable to any manner of contemporary events.

The play seems to be, as are many Greek tragedies, a celebration of wisdom, '*sophia*'. There is a competition among the characters to be thought of as 'wise', 'in their right mind', 'seeing clearly'. It is not difficult in this to find today's battle for editorial approval so necessary in any contemporary political negotiation. Pentheus claims that he is the rational one. But it is Dionysus who taunts him and forces him into unreason. Tiresias similarly thinks he can explain away Dionysus and what he stands for in rationalist terms, though he does at least recognize the potential of the god. But in the last scene, when the world of the mortals – Pentheus, Agave, Cadmus – has been brought crashing round their ears, what could be less reasonable than Dionysus' lame response: 'Zeus ordained all this long ago'? The play may claim to celebrate reason but, in Dionysus, it also celebrates unreason. There are complicated moral issues in the play, but, like Brecht so many centuries later, Euripides poses them without necessarily providing any answers.

Dionysus' nature adds another ingredient that makes the *Bacchae* a very unusual soup. That is sex. Sexual attraction, perversion, abuse are part and parcel of virtually every Greek play that survives. If there is one god whose influence in the drama of classical times is more pervasive than that of Dionysus it is Aphrodite, victor in the goddesses' beauty contest, and creator of havoc wherever she turns up. Love, for the Greeks, was a madness, a source of the purest happiness and the most distilled misery. It caused the war against Troy and destroyed heroes from Agamemnon to Jason to Hippolytus, all of whose stories turn up in Irish versions. *Bacchae* is informed by licence. Freedom from restraint implies promiscuity: and it threatens the authority of the establishment, especially in the guise of a new and subversive religion. Pentheus seems obsessed by sex. Within five lines of his first entrance he is condemning the women for 'creeping off to bed down with some man in a quiet corner'.[18] When he at last confronts Dionysus he is fascinated by him: 'not so bad-looking I see, as far as women are concerned . . . not much in the sun, are you, under cover mostly, hunting Aphrodite?' (lines 452–9).

This makes it so much easier to see how Pentheus is seduced by Dionysus into doing what Dionysus wants: perhaps, Pentheus into doing what Pentheus wants. He wants to get a look at what is going on. He wants to watch the Bacchic women. This prurience is how he is persuaded to dress in women's clothes and, wholly under the influence of Dionysus, believes he can 'see them already in the bushes, at it like sparrows' (line 959).

So what lies behind this? It seems clear that what Dionysus does is release the true nature of those with whom he comes into contact. Apply this to the other characters, Cadmus, Tiresias, Agave, the first Messenger. They are all affected in different ways. For Pentheus, the exposure of his real nature is the source of his own destruction. Perhaps too it is in this revelation that the play ties in to the Nietzschean position posed in *The Birth of Tragedy*. Nietzsche is quoted in the Mahon Preface but elsewhere in *The Birth of Tragedy* he wrote: 'Every artist is an "imitator", that is to say, either an Apollonian artist in dreams, or a Dionysian artist in ecstasies, or finally, as in Greek Tragedy, at once both artist in dreams and tragedy.'[19] There's a dichotomy here, surely, that many an Irish artist would recognize?

What we have here in this last and posthumously performed play is Euripides' celebration of, and farewell to, the theatre. It can offer itself as a political allegory but it may equally be, as Mahon's version implies in his choral epilogue, a statement of what the theatre stands for and a reason for its survival as a forum of debate. The theatre is, in Michael Billington's neat term, a place 'to rearrange consciousness'. Here things can be said or hinted at that may not be said elsewhere. In Ireland issues are still debated through theatre. Problems may not be solved but at least the problems are recognized and addressed.

Of the three classical tragedians Euripides was the one who most questioned the actions of his city. Aeschylus had fought at the Battle of Marathon, Sophocles was an elected general. Euripides presumably underwent military training and fought in battle but his disillusion with the conduct of the Peloponnesian War against Sparta and the power exercised within a notional democracy by the demagogues who plagued contemporary politics, gave him a thoroughly jaundiced view of those in authority. *Trojan Women* was written in the wake of, and probably as a response to, an actual atrocity of war that his own side had perpetrated.

In 427 BC, four years after the start of the Peloponnesian War between Athens and Sparta, Mytilene, a city on the island of Lesbos, rebelled and determined to leave the Delian Confederacy which was, in effect, the Athenian empire. The issue was complicated but the 'revolt' was suppressed and the Athenians voted in Assembly for the killing of all males, and for the women and children to be sold into slavery. A boat was sent to execute the sentence but, after sleeping on their impetuous decision, the Assembly reconsidered. The debate was lengthy, sophisticated, as Thucydides records it, and cold-blooded: but the upshot was that the Assembly reversed its decision. A second boat was dispatched and, fortunately, went rather faster than the first, arriving in time to impose a less severe sentence. Aristophanes got his fingers burnt, and his bank balance, when he wrote a comedy about this indecisiveness.

Eleven years later, with the war becoming ever more ferocious, the island of Melos, which had similarly asserted the right to neutrality, was less fortunate. For the Melians there was no second boat, no reprieve. The dramatic response this time came not from Aristophanes but from Euripides who presented *Trojan Women* in 415. How the audience may have responded, many of whom would have voted for the destruction of Melos, so closely paralleled in the aftermath of the fall of Troy, there is no means of knowing. Sitting watching this play may well have been soldiers who allocated the Melian women as slaves, and killed any of the men deemed a danger. And, if they had the wit to see it, they would have recognized the sense of doom that now hung over their heads as their own war moved to what were its most desperate and damned final stages.

If Mathews opted for a modernized version of *Trojan Women* in his *Trojans*, the points of contact with the world of his audience were not hard to find. His is a vision as harsh as Euripides' own, if rather less coherent. Kennelly's *The Trojan Women: A New Version*, enhanced by striking set speeches and some wrenching phrases – 'Alone as a whisper in a sick room'; 'There's nothing more dangerous to a winner than / one seed of hope in the mind of a loser' – offers the possibility of recovery and renewal. 'The dead are not the past. The dead are the future,' says Hecuba, only for the Woman – a member of the Chorus – to respond a little later: 'If there were no forgetfulness / who would dare to continue?' For Kennelly there is hope and women offer it. If such optimism is more than a simple adjustment of Euripides, it is worth recalling that there is a romanticism in despair no less seductive than that of the will to survive.

Kennelly's *Euripides' Medea: a new version* is a different kind of work. Euripides' *Medea* gains much of its power from the fact that the situation is essentially what the police today might call 'a domestic'. From that can be extrapolated a number of possible themes, ideas, notions with which almost anyone can find a point of contact. This is one of those plays that has an air of promiscuity to it, acquiring new lovers wherever and whenever because it is so resilient. Kennelly transforms it into a dissection of 'rage' and 'the world of rage' while sticking close to the structure and dialogue of Euripides' original. Knowing at first hand, and sympathizing with, the struggles of women in Ireland, Kennelly seems to find a kind of justice in Medea's destruction of her children that places in the frame a whole stratum of Irish social history. As Medea goes indoors for the last time, she has a despairing exit line to herself; in the original this is (literally): 'For if you kill them, they are still dear. How unfortunate a woman I am'; in Kennelly it becomes the more challenging: 'Though I shall kill them, at least I loved them.'

In the light of Kennelly's change of emphasis, the Abbey Theatre production of Euripides' *Medea*,[20] with Fiona Shaw in the title role, seemed to invite a broader meaning when she said (in the translation by Kenneth McLeish and Frederic Raphael, neither of whom is Irish): 'Your "foreigner" embarrasses you.' Shaw's was the only Irish accent in the production. But any such dimension was forfeited in the unfocused mass of excess passion which so enveloped everyone else in the cast as to submerge Medea's otherness. No sense here that it was 'passion' that made Medea so different from these 'civilized Greeks'. There is, of course, no reason why a production should have a dimension that links it through to the audience's own experience, and it is the director who must choose where and when a play's stage life will start and finish.

Marina Carr's *By the Bog of Cats . . .* has about it a range and juxtaposition of the comic and the tragic which set it remarkably close to the mood of Euripides, a plausible world, the Irish Midlands, enhanced by a complex strangeness of ghosts. Perhaps it is in the rediscovery of such a strangeness, a strangeness for which Brecht too sought, that the Greeks best inhabit and illuminate the contemporary situation.

Two aspects, or issues, of translating seem worth returning to at this point, because they have an immediate resonance when dealing with a Greek text being created for a specific, and here an Irish, context.

The first of these issues is to consider whether there is really such a thing as a neutral translator. The second relates to 'translation for translocation', the adjustment of language, setting, character and situation, in order to promote a personal vision, the vision of the translator/adaptor.

The 1998 St Jerome Lecture for the British Centre for Literary Translation was given by David Constantine and an edited version was published in the *Times Literary Supplement*.[21] Much of what Constantine had to say related to poetry but his opening point is peculiarly relevant to translating a play when he talks about the need for 'vitality'. Plays and, naturally, productions are vital or they are nothing. If they do not live, they cannot hope to be read, still less to survive on stage beyond their immediate era when topicality or fashion may have awarded to them a short-lived esteem. Vitality in stage terms is far more than language and, for the translator, more than discovering a potent linguistic equivalent. It involves discovering a stage dynamic that allows objects to acquire resonance; that makes dialogue debate; that offers subtextual meaning, shared with, or, on occasions, exclusive to the audience; it means deciding whether the weight of a line in the original is better served by the same number of words in the receiving language, or more, or fewer.

Some of the best of contemporary translators from Greek, for example, have chosen ellipsis as their main dramatic weapon, curtailing the strict structure of the original, composed as it was for delivery by a masked actor to masked actors, in favour of a denser subtlety that helps the unmasked actor to become complicit with the audience. On top of this there is what Artaud described as 'the concrete language of the stage', that theatrical density where word sets up image but is subordinated to that image: as Aeschylus supplies with his red carpet for Agamemnon; Sophocles with his bow for Philoctetes or urn for Electra; Euripides with his rags for Menelaus, 'drag' for Pentheus, or casket of adornments that Medea prepares for her boys to take to the Princess.

Constantine, again, talking about poetry, referred to translation as 'an act of metaphor'. This is a useful term, because it acknowledges that translation can be no more than, in his phrase, 'a various, differentiated living equivalent of the original'. This definition, 'a various, differentiated living equivalent of the original', is one that might well prove acceptable to any of that multitude of adaptors from Seneca to Kennelly who have found the power of the original sufficient unto itself but who wish to pursue lines of thought and argument that will deck out the old play, not so much in a new set of clothes – that is the function of the director – but with a new set of brain cells, muscles, sinews and arteries to give a different life-force to the old skeleton.

All very well in theory, this gives scant guidance to the translator intrigued by the themes, situations and characters of a Greek tragedy but faced with the nuts and bolts of having to find a way of making the themes cry out to be heard, the situations leap into life and the characters jump from the page into the special world of *this* play in *this* version. Anyone who has the slightest smattering of classical Greek, or has had to endure any of that plethora of literal or appropriated translations which sound either as though the words were picked from a bran tub, or had been discovered petrified in some classics teacher's attic (his Attic attic, maybe), will know how difficult it is to find something that says what the character means: or, in a true adaptation, what you, the adaptor, want the character to mean. There may be a lot to be said for promoting the Spirit over the Letter, as have all those who have taken *Medea* or *Antigone* or *Prometheus* into other media or into the dramatic idiom of their own time, but sometimes it is also possible for the Letter to promote the Spirit.

As Yeats's phrase 'Amid our Troubles' spreads its tail like a peacock, so other resonances attach to other situations. Nurit Yaari, the Israeli scholar, has pointed out that in Israel certain phrases or situations are bound to carry a vibration with them. In Israel the phrase 'a land facing the sea', for all that it might be a literal translation of a Greek original referring to Aulis, or Troy, or Ithaca, has to be more than that. In Israel, if a character in a Greek tragedy enters the stage carrying a rifle, then the make of rifle identifies whose side he or she is on; identifies where the director is coming from. This feeling for resonance and for metaphor, in the sense in which Constantine uses it, is precisely where the power of myth resides and why Greek myth has proved so fruitful for an examination of political issues.

In '"A Bomb at the Door": Kennelly's *Medea*',[22] McDonald pointed to the way that Kennelly gave Jason the language of Cromwell and in the process turned the 'barbarian' Medea into a metaphor for Ireland. This is, of course, precisely what Euripides might himself have been doing, if not with an Irish dimension in mind. Those first Athenian audiences were watching situations which they had to treat as unreal. The world of *Medea*, Euripides' *Medea*, is a notional Corinth, a Corinth ruled by a king. Medea secures her own escape prior to any of the murders by seducing the King of Athens into guaranteeing sanctuary. Athens was on the brink of war with Sparta in 431 BC, a war in which Corinth was to be on the Spartan side. But the Athenians had thrown out the last of their kings eighty years before; and Corinth was by this time an oligarchy at loggerheads with Athens over her colonies. Was there something in the way in which Creon spoke that said more to that first audience? Or Aegeus? Or Medea herself?

The stage world of *Medea* was always, is always, a fantasy world, as was the world of all Greek tragedy, including Aeschylus' *Persians*, the only tragedy set in the knowable past. This is wonderfully liberating for adaptor, translator, director and designer. And the story of Medea is perhaps the best of all Greek myths for exploiting this freedom. The mega-myths are about the great taboos: incest, murder in the family, infanticide. Alongside them are the major injustices: exploitation, betrayal, desertion, lust for power, lust for women, lust for possessions. Apart from incest, *Medea* has got the lot. And something in addition. It has as the central figure a woman who breaks the greatest taboo of all. She murders her children: and she gets away with it, aided and abetted by divine intervention. Euripides gets close enough to accounting for, if not justifying, the act of infanticide. Medea becomes the ultimate challenge, the supreme metaphor for oppression, because it is the supreme taboo that she violates. How do you account for such an act? Face the act and face the truth behind the act. Here is Kennelly's 'rage to falsify all words ... Medea's world, the world of rage ... the world without lies': rage as a woman, rage as a country, rage as a fine line stretched until it breaks.

This leads to the second issue, 'translation for translocation', and the contribution that the translator or adaptor may make to retexturing a play within a different social milieu from that of its own time, but a milieu which has its own precise cultural parameters. Seventy years ago this tended to mean little more than Tyrone Guthrie offering Macbeth in a lounge suit and the brief but controversial 'modern dress' movement for Shakespeare. The Greeks remained Greek while everyone agreed that there were certain plays and playwrights who were so wedded to their own time that there was virtually only one way of producing them and that was strictly in period. Chekhov was one of these inviolables, until, that is, Thomas Kilroy translocated *The Seagull*. A few years ago Brian Friel followed up his forays into the classical world when he similarly transposed Turgenev's *A Month in the Country* to an Irish setting (see Seamus Deane's chapter, p. 149).

There are, no doubt, countless other examples, all of them geared not to subvert the intentions of the original playwright, but to convert them, as Athena converted the Furies, from a single, unquestioning purpose into flexible deities with a new and more versatile brief. Here resides a challenge. My impression is that Kennelly's *Medea* on radio was presented in what was clearly an English production, while his *Trojan Women* was equally clearly Irish.

These days few productions can live exclusively any more in an all-purposes classical limbo. In an essay entitled 'The Play: Gateway to Cultural Dialogue', Gershon Shaked wrote:

The past is a closed world unless we translate it into the present. The political regimes, ways of behaviour, transportation, communication, and architecture of the past are all insufficiently understood in the present. Therefore they are reinterpreted: candles become electric lights, swords and bows become rifles and mortars, human labour becomes machines, slave society becomes capitalism.[23]

One stage version of one story, the story of Hecuba, Andromache, Medea, or Phaedra, is powerful because it is specific. But the situations are more than specific. The Trojan War may be every war. It may be the Peloponnesian War. It may be the First World War. It may be NATO bombers and Kosovan refugees. The civil war of *Seven Against Thebes* or *Phoenician Women*; the right to civil disobedience of *Antigone* or Aeschylus' *Suppliants*; the demand for the bodies' return of Euripides' *Suppliants*: these are questions of human rights which transcend the parochial.

In what period and in what country would *Trojan Women* or *Hecuba* not have seemed relevant? Acts of revenge, acts of treachery, insane cruelty, sacrifice, resistance: any of these, and so many similar, form the spine of the Greek tragic canon. Any of them can be generalized, inviting the audience to home in on a single issue. Or they can be made specific, in a specific theatrical context, from which, again, the audience may draw the parallel its members find most suitable.

Irish Greek tragedy is apposite because Ireland's past is steeped in injustice and oppression. How can a stage piece confront such oppression? O'Casey found one way, Synge another, but an approach via the Greeks can focus the mind through situations that are 'givens' and characters that are 'givens' but contain within them that precious power of metaphor that David Constantine pointed to and all these fine Irish writers relish and fashion. And if this is true for plays rooted in the works of Aeschylus, Sophocles and

Euripides, how much more so when the myths that inspired those plays are revisited and renewed in contemporary situations.

Any *Medea* can be an Irish *Medea,* or a Russian *Medea*; or an Italian or an Israeli *Medea*. It does not even need to be called *Medea*. All that is necessary are the social or political conditions and these myths will work their magic. Aeschylus, Sophocles and Euripides wrote uncomfortable things for their fellow countrymen. They wrote for the Greeks they knew, 2,500 years ago. The Irish pay them homage and write for now.

Notes

1. Theodore Savory, 'Translating the Classics', in *The Art of Translation* (London: Jonathan Cape, 1957), pp. 67–8.
2. Robert Brough, *Medea; or, The Best of Mothers with a Brute of a Husband*, Royal Olympic Theatre, July 1856, and Mark Lemon, *Medea; or, A Libel on the Lady from Colchis*, Adelphi Theatre, on the same day and both with male Medeas.
3. Virginia Woolf, 'On Not Knowing Greek', in *The Common Reader*, ed. Andrew McNeillie (London: Hogarth, 1929), p. 56.
4. T. S. Eliot, 'Euripides and Professor Murray', in *Selected Essays 1917–1932* (London, Faber & Faber, 1932), pp. 59–64. See also T. S. Eliot, 'Seneca in Translation', also in *Selected Essays 1917–1932*, pp. 65–77.
5. Walter Benjamin, 'The Task of the Translator', trans. Harry Zohn, in Walter Benjamin, *Illuminations* (London: Jonathan Cape, 1970), p. 73.
6. Euripides' *Medea: a New Version by Brendan Kennelly* (Newcastle upon Tyne: Bloodaxe, 1991), p. 75.
7. A. Saddlemeyer (ed.), *Theatre Business: The Correspondence of the First Abbey Theatre Directors: William Butler Yeats, Lady Gregory, and J. M. Synge*, quoted in Fiona Macintosh, *Dying Acts: Death in Ancient Greek and Modern Irish Tragic Drama* (Cork: Cork University Press, 1994), p. 9.
8. David R. Clark and James B. McGuire, *W. B. Yeats: the Writing of Sophocles' King Oedipus* (Philadelphia, PA: The American Philosophical Society, 1989).

9. W. H. Auden, from 'As I Walked Out One Evening', in *Collected Poems* (London: Random House, 1940, renewed 1968).

10. Seamus Heaney, *The Cure at Troy: a Version of Sophocles' Philoctetes* (London: Faber & Faber, 1990), p. 27.

11. Quoted on the back cover of the printed version, *Sophocles' Antigone: a New Version by Brendan Kennelly* (Newcastle upon Tyne: Bloodaxe, 1989).

12. Brendan Kennelly, 'Q and A with Brendan Kennelly', *Irish Literary Supplement* 9(1), (Spring 1991): 22.

13. Sophocles' *Antigone*, trans. Marianne McDonald (London: Nick Hern Books, 2000), lines 552–7, p. 23.

14. *Sophocles' Antigone by Kennelly*, p. 25.

15. Gilbert Norwood, *Euripides and Shaw* (London: Methuen, 1921).

16. Derek Mahon, *The Bacchae: after Euripides* (Oldcastle: Gallery Books, 1991).

17 Marianne McDonald, 'Recent Irish Translations of Greek Tragedy: Derek Mahon's Bacchai', in *The Translation of Ancient Greek Drama into All the Languages of the World*, ed. Elena Patrikiou (Athens: Desmoi Center, 1998), p. 196.

18. Translations of *Bacchae* are by J. Michael Walton, *Euripides: Plays One* (London: Methuen, 2000).

19. Friedrich Nietzsche, *The Birth of Tragedy*, trans. Walter Kaufman (New York: Vintage Books, 1967), p. 38.

20. Directed by Deborah Warner, in 2000, and later transferred to the Queen's Theatre, London, in 2001.

21. David Constantine, 'Finding the Words', *Times Literary Supplement* (21 May 1999): 14–15.

22. Marianne McDonald '"A Bomb at the Door": Kennelly's *Medea, 1988*', *Éire–Ireland XXVIII* (2) (Summer 1993): 129–37.

23. Gershon Shaked, 'The Play: Gateway to Cultural Dialogue', in Scolnicov and Holland, *The Play Out of Context: Transferring Plays from Culture to Culture* (Cambridge: Cambridge University Press, 1989), p. 13.

The Irish and Greek Tragedy

Marianne McDonald

In the twentieth century, there seem to be more translations and versions of Greek tragedy that have come from Ireland than from any other country in the English-speaking world.[1] In many ways Ireland was and is constructing its identity through the representations offered by Greek tragedy.

The Irish first became acquainted with the classics indirectly through the Catholic Church and its love for learning (Ireland has been called the land of saints and scholars). The Irish philosopher John Scotus Eriugena (born c. 810) was fluent in Greek. The monks, as we know from Thomas Cahill, had access to, and a hand in preserving, the ancient texts.[2]

The Irish also became acquainted with the classics both in the forbidden 'hedge schools' and in the sanctioned schools that the British set up when they occupied Ireland following the Cromwellian conquest in 1650. The hedge schools taught Irish, Greek and Latin; the sanctioned schools imposed English. The Irish soon mastered English and used it for their own powerful and informed self-expression. As James Joyce said, 'The Irish, condemned to express themselves in a language not their own, have stamped on it the mark of their own genius . . .This is then called English literature.'[3]

The British occupiers thought that some of the classics would offer healthy examples of the governed accepting the power of government.[4] The Irish turned this on its head and finally used this literature in the twentieth century to feed their own subversive protests. The Irish could conceal the direct statement of their desires behind the mask of Greek tragedy. Greek tragedy in Irish hands became social critique, not only of the occupiers, but of their own comedic acquiescence or bloody squabbling among themselves.

Classics thus can provide a literature of protest, as well as acting as a literary vehicle to ensure control by an occupying government.[5] Since societies and governments appreciate the value of the classics, people who perceive themselves oppressed can use the classics to express their discontent. The Irish opt for the Greeks, while being thoroughly versed in Latin. They use Latin for their Masses, but Greek for their performances.

Declan Kiberd writes of Friedrich Engels, who 'complained that the object of British policy was to make the Irish feel like strangers in their own land; but he seriously underestimated their capacity to reformulate the culture which had been used as an instrument to "civilize" them'.[6] Kiberd goes on to say that no one thought that 'Irish students of Shakespeare' would 'treat his works like captured weapons which might one day be turned back upon the enemy'.[7] This is exactly what the Irish did with the classics they read in English; in their new treatments they eventually came to express their discontent with unjust rule. They reformulated the imposed culture on their own terms.

For the Irish, Greek classics were preferred to the English classics. In Brian Friel's *Translations*, the character Hugh responds to an English lieutenant's remark about Wordsworth, 'Wordsworth . . . No. I'm afraid we're not familiar with your literature, Lieutenant. We feel closer to the warm Mediterranean. We tend to overlook your island.'[8]

Brian Friel's *Translations* was the first play that Field Day performed after its founding in 1980. It was performed in Derry and dealt with the existential sense of the loss of Irish identity that came from the arbitrary British renaming of Irish locales. Field Day (based on the combined names of its founders Stephen Rea and Brian Friel) was established to give a Northern voice to a number of divisive issues. Like Greek tragedy, Field Day speaks the unspeakable and makes visible the invisible.

Sometimes the classics simply provided a skeleton on which new figures come to life, as Ulysses is transformed by Joyce into the wandering Bloom. Comparably, Yeats thrived on the classics and the ancient myths provided imagery for his poems. Leda was an Ireland raped by a British swan, but perhaps she 'put on his knowledge with his power / Before the indifferent beak could let her drop'. One way to put on this knowledge and power is to learn from the culture that was part of the educational agenda of the occupiers.

Pádraic Pearse made the revolutionary connection of modern Ireland with the ancients explicit when he spoke of the need for 'The divine breath that moves through free peoples, the breath that no man of Ireland has felt in his nostrils for so many centuries, the breath that once blew through the streets of Athens, that kindled, as wine kindles, the hearts of those who taught and learned in Clonmacnois'.[9] The classics are dangerous. Perhaps they always were. Plato was well enough aware of the subversive nature of drama.

Fifth-century Greek tragedy educated the citizens in democracy. Although Greek drama often featured kings, they generally consulted their subjects, and took their decisions based on their subjects' advice, like Danaus in Aeschylus' *Suppliants*, or Theseus in several plays. It is obvious why the Irish preferred the democratic vision of Athens, in contrast to other countries' classics that conveyed acquiescence to an absolute ruler.

The Irish are not unique in using Greek tragedy for political expression. Anouilh and Brecht used *Antigone* to express their condemnation of fascism. Jean-Paul Sartre used *Trojan Women* in a comparable way. Athol Fugard's *The Island* shows prisoners in South Africa performing *Antigone* in prison to express their longing for freedom and human rights, as well as condemning their jailors. As a recent review of his play said, it is 'a timeless survivors' guide for political prisoners everywhere, struggling to survive and keep despair at bay'.[10]

There are many reasons other than the political for reworking Greek tragedy: these works are masterpieces in themselves. In a translation one can simply luxuriate in selecting words, and these masterpieces provide the structure and plot, in addition to effective imagery. The original plays represent some of the greatest poetry ever written. Irish poets are naturally drawn to emulating or striving to surpass the originals. Greek tragedy with its emphasis on ethics also appealed to the Irish for religious as well as political reasons.

Early medieval translations into Irish were of Latin paraphrases of the original classics. From about 1600, both Greek and Latin were learned in schools sanctioned by the British; Irish, which was forbidden, was taught in the hedge schools. When Greek drama was first performed in Ireland it was in the original ancient language. In 1720 the Reverend Thomas Sheridan staged Euripides' *Hippolytus* in Greek at a Dublin school, and in 1723 *Oedipus Tyrannus*. Though productions were at best sporadic, they remained for the most part in the original language until the twentieth century, when translations were made into both English and Irish.

In the twentieth century the Irish made Greek tragedy their own as they progressed from translations into Anglo-English, then Hiberno-English; some authors like Monsignor Pádraig de Brún translated Greek tragedy into Irish (Sophocles' *Antigone* in 1926 and *Oedipus Rex* in 1928). The Irish authors chose specific Greek tragedies for their own purposes, and in the second half of the twentieth century the political themes take precedence over the psychological.

Oedipus Tyrannus and the *Oresteia* were initially popular as translations by the Irish, perhaps because these are plays about identity and social compromise, but the twentieth century has favoured more revolutionary subjects, where the debate is over human rights and the suffering of the oppressed: for example, *Antigone*, *Trojan Women* and *Medea*. There is an inexorable evolution towards the search for freedom, human rights for all people, and an end to conflict.

It is worth looking briefly at some of the classical ideas that inspired Irish playwrights. In Aeschylus, god can confront god and major questions are raised about conflicting rights. Prometheus opposing Zeus is an illustration and Tom Paulin's *Seize the Fire* is based on Aeschylus' *Prometheus Bound*. Sophocles shows man confronting god and a world that can never be entirely knowable, and his *Oedipus* plays inspired Yeats. Euripides shows man or woman confronting the self, and sometimes being the source of his or her own defeat. Kennelly's *Medea* well illustrates this. In Euripides' universe, the gods could be actively hostile to man. Derek Mahon found this an appropriate theme for the Irish in his version of *Bacchae*.

Sophocles presents us with the hero, and Euripides shows us the anti-hero. According to Aristotle, Sophocles claimed he depicted men as they ought to be, but Euripides as they were (*Poetics* 1460b 33–4). Euripides, who chose to be isolated from an active citizen's life, leaving Athens in old age, saw things more bleakly than Sophocles. It is difficult to find or recognize any genuine heroes in Euripides except brave women, innocent children, or honourable slaves. The main recourse man has in the chaotic Euripidean world is friendship, or human alliance. Heroism is dead, in the way it was known to Aeschylus or Sophocles, or, even earlier, Homer.

Euripides has been called the first psychological playwright. Longinus praised his depiction of madness and love (*On the Sublime*, 15.3). Euripides questions traditional beliefs and attitudes and his plays feature debates which were also popular among the sophists of his time. In these debates both strong emotions and strong intellectual positions are expressed; examples are the confrontation of Hippolytus with Theseus (*Hippolytus*) and of Hecuba with Helen (*Trojan Women*). This bothered many critics in the nineteenth century who would have preferred inspired emotionalism without philosophical debate. Nietzsche condemned Euripides for just this rationality, which he considered a debasement of the noble goals of tragedy.

Aristophanes' *Frogs,* which highlights a contest between Aeschylus and Euripides, shows the latter as an innovator and iconoclast. It is from Aristophanes that we get the dubious idea that Euripides was a misogynist. He was rather a scientist of the emotions and focused on unconventional, passionate women. It may have been his idea to have Medea kill her children, the ultimate revenge against the husband she hated. His psychological characterization is outstanding.

Although *Antigone* may be the most popular play in Ireland in the twentieth century, Euripides is the most popular playwright. Of the three great ancient Greek tragedians, there are more Irish versions of Euripides' plays than of either of the others. This is because of his psychological acuity, and also because of his celebrating the victim, and his appreciation of suffering and its effects on human beings. He is also the poet of peace.

As early as 1907 Yeats had considered staging *Antigone* in a translation by Robert Gregory (Lady Augusta's son), but opted for Synge's *Playboy of the Western World*. He also had plans for an *Oedipus Tyrannus*, a play which at the time was still banned in England because of its theme of incest. He set out to find a good existing translation, but rejected Oliver St John Gogarty's version (1905) as being too stilted. When he asked the eminent classical scholar Gilbert Murray for a new one, Murray refused, saying that Sophocles' *Oedipus* has 'no religion, not one beautiful action, hardly a stroke of poetry'.[11] For all that, Murray was to go on to translate the play for the celebrated London production in 1912 directed by Max Reinhardt.

Yeats's plans were shelved for some years. He was naturally drawn to Sophocles, the tragedian of heroism. It is significant that later Irish writers are attracted more to Euripides, who focuses more on the sufferings of the victim rather than the heroics of the victor.

Eventually Yeats translated both the *Oedipus* plays himself. Though Yeats began to translate *Antigone*, it survives only as a few lines in a poem, 'A Woman Young and Old' from *The Winding Stair* (1929). Yeats's *Sophocles' King Oedipus: A Version for the Modern Stage* was not performed until 1926, although he had finished the text ten years earlier. *Oedipus at Colonus* was produced the following year.

Yeats's adaptations were based on Sir Richard Jebb's text and commentary, and a French translation by Paul Masqueray. He added accessible language to make the play more immediately dramatic for a modern audience. He also added recognizable Irish elements.

As was typical of later Irish versions of Greek tragedy, in *King Oedipus* sexual allusions are elaborated, as in the sowing metaphor from Sophocles' lines 1211–12:

> But, looking for a marriage-bed,
>   he found the bed of his birth,
> Tilled the field his father had tilled,
>   cast seed into the same abounding earth;
> Entered through the door that had sent him wailing forth.[12]

Yeats for the most part reduced the originals, but also changed the meaning in places. He removed what he saw as difficulties in Sophocles, including much of the irony, many metaphoric or mythological allusions, and even long reflections, such as Oedipus' final despairing speech. Though he himself admitted this freedom, for many years Yeats's 'translations' served to introduce school-children to Sophocles. Misleading as this might have been, it was compensated for by the quality of his language, and his mixture of prose for the iambic sections and poetry for the choruses, which set a standard for many other translations by the Irish, including Seamus Heaney's *The Cure at Troy: A Version of Sophocles' Philoctetes* (1990).

In the *Oedipus at Colonus*, the characters were transformed into the lasses and lads of an Irish countryside or haunted woods: 'The wine-dark of the wood's intricacies, / The nightingale that deafens daylight there, / If daylight ever visit . . .' One can see how Yeats likes poetic repetitions in contrast to Sophocles' more disciplined Greek, with a nod, perhaps, to Homer, with his use of repetitions in his epic, and epithets like 'wine-dark' (sea) or 'rosy-fingered' (dawn).

Here Yeats is clearly describing Ireland rather than Colonus: 'When Oedipus at Colonus went into the wood of the Furies he felt the same creeping in his flesh that an Irish countryman feels in certain haunted woods in Galway and in Sligo.'[13] In the ode in celebration of Colonus, he also praises the intellectual and spiritual heritage of Athens, 'The self-sown, self-begotten shape that gives / Athenian intellect its mastery'. There is a reverence for Athens here barely noticeable in the original, so that Brian Arkins claims Yeats granted 'its intellect the status of a Platonic Form, by asserting that its beauty is unique, and by stressing that its power is matched only by its piety'.[14]

Antigone's lamentation at the end was severely cut to concentrate on the mystery and spirituality of Oedipus' death and transfiguration, but there seems to be a personal statement – as clear as Sophocles' own – in the way in which Yeats makes his Oedipus a proud hero who does not cling to life but, in the celebrated words of the Chorus, utters 'a gay goodnight and quickly turns away'.

Some critics have seen other Greek connections in the work of Yeats; for example, between Yeats's *Countess Cathleen* (1899) and Euripides' *Alcestis*. Greek tragedy has influenced other Irish playwrights and links have been seen between J. M. Synge's *Deirdre of the Sorrows* (1910) and Sophocles' *Antigone* and Euripides' *Trojan Women*; between his *Playboy of the Western World* (1907) and Sophocles' *Oedipus Tyrannus*; and between his *Riders to the Sea* (1902) and Euripides' *Trojan Women*. A connection has been suggested between Sean O'Casey's *Juno and the Paycock* (1924) and Aeschylus' *Agamemnon*.

In the 1930s, Lord Edward Longford and Lady Christine Longford translated Aeschylus' *Oresteia* for the Gate Theatre in Dublin. A more substantial translation by Louis MacNeice of *Agamemnon*, the first play of the trilogy, was performed in England at the Westminster Theatre in 1936, with music by Benjamin Britten.

Aeschylus' *Oresteia* appealed to MacNeice for its acceptance of authority, reverence for the gods, and respect for the state. We know Aeschylus as the father of Greek tragedy. His drama is characterized by large issues and the splendour of his choruses. His trilogies showed divine justice acting over generations. He utilized spectacle to advantage, coupling it with equally spectacular poetic words.

Both Aeschylus and MacNeice share a lack of sympathy for Helen and Clytemnestra as unfaithful wives, but this antipathy leads to felicitous poetry: the poetry of hatred can sometimes be more splendid than the poetry of love. When Clytemnestra lies to the returning Agamemnon she says, 'I know no pleasure with another man, no scandal, / more than I know how to dye metal red.' It is all too clear how this Clytemnestra will dye metal red.

MacNeice writes often of god as if he were the Christian God, and there are ritual allusions: 'To share our holy water', or 'asperging' something, or Helen as a lion cub 'sent by God as a priest of ruin'. There are class allusions too, a recurrent theme in MacNeice's work: Cassandra is called 'a fortune-teller, a poor starved beggar-woman', and Orestes, 'exile, and tramp and outlaw'.

The language is poetic and engaging, if at times dated, often echoing the Bible or Christian ritual. He speaks of the 'money-changer War' that sends back dust and ashes for what were once living men. He expresses a fear of God's justice in religious terms of mystery: 'There is something cowled in the night / That I anxiously await to hear.' Alliteration adds to the effect, notably in the passage where Clytemnestra describes Agamemnon's blood watering her like the plants in spring:

> ... he spits his life out where he lies
> And smartly spouting blood he sprays me with
> The sombre drizzle of bloody dew and I
> Rejoice no less than in God's gift of rain.
> The crops are glad when the ear of corn gives birth.[15]

All of these lines have biblical echoes.

Cassandra's final lines on the fragility of human happiness are given to the Chorus, but serve as an intriguing comment on the inconstancy of memory:

Ah the fortunes of men! When they go well
A shadow sketch would match them, and in ill-fortune
The dab of a wet sponge destroys the drawing. (p.58)

MacNeice carried on Yeats's mandate, to create poetic and dramatic renditions of the classics. And Seamus Heaney carries this forward in his brilliantly musical version of *Philoctetes*.

Up to this point plays in Ireland were written and performed mainly in what we might call Anglo-English and represent the next stage after Greek performances in British-sanctioned schools. More recent times have seen the emergence of a series of fascinating contemporary works which carry forward the influence of Greek tragic drama in a great variety of ways.

Tom Murphy's *The Sanctuary Lamp* (1976) has little of the form of Aeschylus' *Oresteia*, but thematic parallels are strong.[16] Like the *Oresteia*, Murphy's play deals with the dysfunctional family, and a final redemption from violence. He adds a religious note, as do so many of the Irish reworkings, and meditates on the Catholic Church's influence in Ireland. The human beings in this play wrest power away from the Church and put it in human hands, and particularly the human imagination. In the *Oresteia* the human lawcourt replaces divine retribution: a lawcourt is established where men determine the punishment due to murderers, rather than leave justice in the hands of the vengeful Furies. Murphy's Francisco, the Irish Catholic, prefers to imagine that no one who dies is condemned to hell, or even purgatory, but instead enjoys a tropical paradise, 'a combination of Ireland and Tahiti, untroubled by God'.[17] As in the *Oresteia*, the sanctuary lamp goes out, to be replaced by the secular sunrise.

Friel often visits the classics in his plays. Not only does he make the Irish characters trilingual in *Translations* (including Greek and Latin), but he uses myths and classical allusions freely in other plays. *Translations* ends with Hugh O'Donnell's quotation from Book I of Virgil's *Aeneid*: the analogy is drawn between Ireland as Carthage and England as the invading imperialist Roman.[18] *The Gentle Island* (1971) might be considered even closer to Hippolytus

46

than *Living Quarters: after Hippolytus*. Sarah falsely incriminates Shane who has rejected her advances. She gets her father to avenge her honour by killing Shane. *Wonderful Tennessee* (1993) also has classical references and contains a not so veiled allusion to Dionysian *sparagmos*, a ritual dismemberment, comparable with what Pentheus suffered at the end of Euripides' *Bacchae*.

Friel had written many overtly political plays, such as *The Freedom of the City* in 1973, and *Volunteers* in 1975, both probably in response to the atrocity of Bloody Sunday when thirteen unarmed Catholics in Derry (officially named Londonderry, Northern Ireland, and Brian Friel's birthplace) were gunned down by the occupying British forces (30 January 1972).[19] *Translations* in 1980 carries on this political agenda.

An early play on the Hippolytus theme was T. C. Murray's *Autumn Fire* (1924), which features an older man and a younger wife, but with an Irish slant involving convoluted family relations, suspicions and false accusations. In Friel's *Living Quarters: after Hippolytus* (1977), we are conscious of the Irish Republic's problems, since the hero of the play, Commandant Frank Butler, is in the Irish army ('OC of B Company of the 37th Battalion of the Permanent Defence Forces').[20] It is said he 'has been in the Irish army all his life'. He is located 'in a remote part of County Donegal, Ireland'.

This is a dream play in which Frank Butler's family reconstructs the circumstances surrounding his death. Nothing in Friel is simple: the political becomes familial and vice versa. The final isolation is the prison of one's own skull.

The main violence of *Living Quarters* is in the conversation as it weaves its patterns into a net which will choke the life out of the family entangled in it. The violence is not merely individual. Everyone is affected, except perhaps the priest, who drinks enough not to be aware of his own incompetence. Drink does not make him Dionysus.

Irish speech lacks American directness. It is more musical, and if there is a theme, there will inevitably be a variation before we can understand it fully. If the Irish did not have political freedom, they certainly had a compensatory linguistic ally: circling the subject for the Irish is a type of freedom. The danger is that the subject never appears and we are left with the circle. Frank in *Living Quarters* claims the Butler family use language and act in a way that is 'measured, watching, circling one another, peeping out, shying back'. This is in contrast to the direct Anna, of whom Frank says, 'Anything she thinks – whatever comes into her head – straight out – it must come straight out – just like that. So unlike us.' Anna seems never to have had an unexpressed thought. It is appropriate that she finally goes to America since she already speaks like an American.

Language is the key, and the characters assemble to reconstruct 'what was said, what was not said, what was done, what was not done, what might have been said, what might have been done; endlessly raking over those dead episodes that can't be left in peace'. It is an investigation of possibilities which all turn out to lead nowhere. Needless to say we can see the parallels with Ireland, and the failed attempts at reaching agreement or achieving peace.

The narrator, Sir, can be seen as God, as Fate, as History, and as the collective will of the people involved: 'And in their imagination, out of some deep psychic necessity, they have conceived me – the ultimate arbiter, the powerful and impartial referee, the final adjudicator . . .' One might say this man is the North's England, which, for some, if it hadn't existed, would have had to be invented. One could see this as a Unionist solution. For others it can be more complicated: because they have internalized the message of the colonizer, some Irish see England, or some such arbitrator, as what they deserve. The text of the occupier's dogma can be written so clearly in the oppressed, that they are the first to agree to its contents.

On the other hand some see 'Sir' as a Greek Chorus. The sisters and priest can also be seen to function as a Greek Chorus, witnessing and commenting on events. They act at times as if they were sources of objective truth. Unlike in Euripides, the characters in this play know the plot of their lives; we the audience must wait until it unfolds. The action does not occur chronologically, but like flower petals falling one after another, until we are left to view an empty stalk.

One specific day is described 'as if it were a feast laid out for consumption or a trap waiting to spring', an allusion perhaps to the trap of *La machine infernale*, Jean Cocteau's account of Oedipus, who is caught in a trap from which he cannot escape. Greek tragedy operates with these two seemingly contradictory assumptions: there is an overriding notion of fate, and yet man is responsible for his choices. We get the same feeling in Friel's play, which also observes the ancient unities as described by Aristotle: one place, one day and one sequence of action.

We return to the emotional violence of words *per se*. When direct speech is used it can become a violent speech act. Anna, the young second wife of Frank, addresses him and the sisters: 'I had an affair with your son, Ben – with your brother, Ben! An affair – an affair – d'you hear!' This is the climax of the cadenza, but it is ignored when first heard. The words gradually seep into the characters' psyches and they lead, like Phaedra's false accusation, to death. In this case the accusation is all too true. Anna's confession is like Phaedra's letter, but it kills the father rather than the son. Even Sir points out that the affair could have remained secret, and 'Frank's life would have stayed reasonably intact'. We remember Racine's Thésée not wanting to be 'enlightened'. This avoidance is another typically Irish solution. As Heaney said, 'Whatever you say, say nothing.' Besides the political overtones recalling the recommended response to interrogation, this is the choice of the circular dance rather than the straight and deadly winged verbal arrow.

Anna is not overcome by passion, as Phaedra is, and the gods are conspicuously absent as causal agents. It is true that she did not spend much time with Frank before he had to leave; they were married for five months but had only spent ten days together. This was indicative for Anna of how much time Frank was ready to devote to her. Yet one cannot help but think that Anna could have contrived her escape in a less destructive manner. Anna seems indifferent to any meaningful relationship. For telling his father, she is, perhaps, as Ben says, 'a heartless bitch'. This is the careless, cruel Anna, armed with the missiles of her words. Euripides was more sympathetic to Phaedra.

Frank (Theseus) is driven by guilt, and the sense of life not holding anything further for him, in spite of his promotion for his valiant action in the Middle East. Like Agamemnon, he is a man who has victories in the outside world, but returns home to be defeated by his own family. The stage direction conveys the violent act: '*Then a single revolver shot off.*' No blood is described, and the priest will not even admit it is suicide since this would prevent burial in sanctified ground. 'There was never any doubt in my mind that it was an unfortunate accident,' says the priest. Friel taps into a rich dramatic heritage: with the single shot, Hedda Gabler, and Konstantin Gavrilovitch in *The Seagull*, come to mind.

In Friel's play Phaedra and Hippolytus do not die; they just fade away. Euripides left us in Theseus a hero with a sterile past; Friel gives us Hippolytus and Phaedra with an impotent future. Several characters emigrate. One might compare *Dancing at Lughnasa* (1990), and even the stories of Joyce which end in emigration: the characters leave Ireland but cannot escape their Irishness. Seamus Deane puts it well: 'It was a world without a name; / The world we flew from and became.'[21]

The play does not end with the forgiveness between father and son, as does Euripides', although at one point there is an abortive attempt. No one in the family can fully tolerate the happiness and success of another. In a strange and haunting way this becomes a parable of Ireland with the inner strife and betrayal which occur within the family itself. Violence here is verbal and internal, and in this we see a return to Euripides. Nevertheless, this Hippolytus (Ben) is as guilty as Phaedra (Anna) of the act which destroys his father. In this case the father, instead of his son, is Aphrodite's victim. To switch myths, this Agamemnon dies from being trapped in the net of words rather than the actual net in which Clytemnestra catches him before wielding her axe. Beckett noted, 'Silence once broken will never again be whole.'

The nexus is clear. It is not simply the external enemy that one can blame. Friel uses the power of Greek myth, reinforced by the authority of the character Sir, to represent the seemingly inescapable tragedy of Irish political and family life. Enemies in the family and in oneself can be the deadliest. When one returns to the myth of Ireland, sometimes the homecoming is death itself. As we have seen in this play, both truth and fiction shatter. Frank's world is as mythical as the construct of Ireland. Like Frank, as Heaney says in 'An Open Letter', 'The whole imagined country mourns / Its lost erotic Aisling life'.[22] We can hope that some sort of truth may now emerge as the basis for *rapprochement* in the peace talks, and a communication which has failed in the past will finally take place. Perhaps in this new world both Frank Butler and Ben can live. Breaking silence in this case can make whole. Friel realizes the importance of language and communication: 'I think that is how the political problem of this island is going to be solved. It's going to be solved by language in some kind of way . . . It's going to be solved by the recognition of what language means for us on this island.'

The ancient text of Euripides' *Hippolytus* is thus like the ancient myth of Ireland, something that will only live truly if brought up to date. As Seamus Deane says, 'The only true place is that which is coincident with time. Otherwise people live in the permanent anachronism of history.'[23] *Living Quarters* has brought us firmly into Ireland's present and we must master contemporary words and language, otherwise we shall be mastered by them.

Friel's *Living Quarters* shows how words create and destroy, in the Irish context, both the country and the family. He is a master of the stage and his audience is continually enthralled until the last piece of the dramatic puzzle falls in place.

Antigone is the first, and remains, the greatest play in western literature about the consequences of individual conscience defying civil authority. Sophocles' Antigone is the first female character in drama to be a hero in the full sense of the word. She is the first voice raised in defiance of unjust law and this is a profound moment in the evolution of the human conscience. The play is often performed as veiled criticism of an abusive government to show that something is rotten in that particular state.

In her clash with King Creon, as she defends the rights of the family, Antigone invokes 'the unwritten law of the gods', whereas Creon rests his case on defending the safety and security of the state against anarchy. Familial values and duty towards the gods of the underworld conflict with state interests; personal issues confront public issues, and they radically influence each other.

Although the play is from fifth-century Athens, the issues about human rights have everlasting relevance. This play is a human drama and a tragedy that shows the price of supporting these rights. Both Antigone and Creon are passionate people who have destroyed themselves and others.

Creon opposes Antigone with the might of law on which he says personal happiness is based, namely via a well-controlled city. What Antigone does is the opposite of what Socrates did: in the Platonic dialogue *Crito*, Socrates declared that he would follow the city's laws even if the decision was unjust. With Sophocles' usual dramatic economy, Antigone is punished by the ruler and the *polis* she opposes, and Creon is punished by the loss of his own family, whose values he subordinated to those of the *polis*.

Though to treat either of the central characters as wholly right devalues the play, this is a tragedy about unrelenting passion; these protagonists do not give up. Both Creon and Antigone suffer from their inability to compromise.

Antigone is appropriate for Ireland and is the clear favourite in the twentieth century. Four versions of this myth were presented in Ireland in 1984, by Tom Paulin, Brendan Kennelly, Aidan Carl Mathews and Pat Murphy (with her film *Anne Devlin*). In 1986 Athol Fugard's *The Island* was performed at the Gate Theatre in Dublin, besides being shown on Irish television. It also toured that same year, to Limerick and Galway.

Each of the Irish playwrights has a particular approach towards Ireland's history and political situation, some more overt than others. Anthony Roche and Christopher Murray have chapters on the 1984 *Antigones* in Ireland in two books dealing with Irish literature and theatre.[24] The year 1984 was important for human rights, and the rights of women in particular. This was the year the divorce referendum was rejected, just after abortion rights had been rejected, and the year when the Criminal Justice Bill gave increased powers to the police.

Field Day Theatre first performed Tom Paulin's *The Riot Act* at the Guildhall, Derry, on 19 September 1984. It uses the language of the Irish North to place us in its modern locale, and the ideas expressed translate well into the issues that divide Derry. The words have resonance in the modern political context. Tiresias sounds the theme: 'Now so much blood's been spilt / there's none can call a halt / to those thrawn and jaggy hates / deep-rooted in your state.'[25] This idea of never-ending strife regrettably suits the Irish landscape.

Anthony Roche pointed to the Northern accents in Paulin's play: 'We hear a verbal medley of the two reigning powers in Northern Ireland, Westminster and Unionism.'[26] Westminster stands for England, which since 1972 has been dominant in Northern Ireland, and Unionism is the movement led mainly by Northern Protestants to keep Northern Ireland linked with England as a part of Britain. Roche narrows the field further by seeing Ian Paisley (the vociferous Northern Irish Protestant and Unionist) as Creon in this play, since he is introduced by the Chorus as 'the big man'. Paulin, he suggests, is rewriting Conor Cruise O'Brien's heavy-handed endorsement of Creon's role in this play as a justified representative of conservatism: status quo *über Alles*.

Paulin's Creon speaks like a typical politician:

However, let me say this, and say it plainly right at the very outset, that if ever any man here should find himself faced with a choice between betraying his country and betraying his friend, then he must swiftly place that friend in the hands of the authorities.[27]

This resonates all too aptly in the North of Ireland.

Creon's speech begins, 'In the coming months I shall be doing a very great deal of listening, sounding opinions and so forth.' It concludes, '"Thank you all for coming, and any questions just now? We have one minute" (*Flashes stonewall smile*).'[28] This is typical of the rhetoric from a whole series of political speeches delivered by newly appointed ministers in Northern Ireland. Because right is clearly not on the side of this cardboard politician, this reduces Creon's authority and his position as a valid counterbalance to Antigone.

In both Sophocles and Paulin, we find Antigone more sympathetic than Creon in her defending the rights of the individual and family against Creon's rights, namely those of government. But if you reduce Creon to the representative of an unjust occupying government, this reduces the tragedy. The tragedy returns as we realize the accurate portrayal of 'Creon's' power in the North of Ireland.

At the end Paulin cleverly echoes Yeats when the Chorus says, 'You changed your mind,' and he answers, 'I changed it, but . . . Aye, changed it utterly.' Creon homes in on Yeats's disillusionment with the Easter Rising of 1916 and its consequences, but these verbal fireworks run the risk of undermining audience sympathy.

Aeschylus' *Prometheus Bound* has been the favourite of many – Goethe, Marx, Byron, Shelley, and that most romantic of all romantics, Victor Hugo. This is a play that indicts the tyrant, in this case Zeus, who abuses man-loving Prometheus, the humanitarian. Prometheus, by stealing fire from the gods, not only saved mankind from destruction, but also brought them all the arts and sciences, from medicine to navigation to soothsaying, poetry and letters. Zeus punishes him for his defiant act and, even worse, for boasting about it. By the end of the play he will be thrown into an abyss, and an eagle will come to feed on his liver because he refuses to act subservient to Zeus, or to reveal the details of a prophecy which he knows about the fall of Zeus. He is the rebel *par excellence*. No wonder he has been a model for revolutionaries!

On the other hand, the parallels between Prometheus and Christ are obvious, from the suffering of the innocent to the pains of having hands and feet nailed. Even Prometheus' final words have a curious resemblance to Christ's complaint to his father when he is nailed to the cross. Both gave their lives for mankind. Prometheus advocates love, whereas Zeus prefers power. Prometheus is a 1960s rebel, the original flower child. But he ends up being crucified for his defiance. Prometheus and Io are also symbols for victims who suffer from slow, progressive, painful diseases such as AIDS. There are many remarks which show psychological acuity: there is reference to a 'talking cure', which characterizes talking as relief of pain, so Aeschylus anticipates Freud.

Rather than selecting a play by Aeschylus that celebrates the authority of government and the gods as MacNeice did, Paulin takes one with a more revolutionary theme, which questions authority when that authority is unjust. Paulin begins *Seize the Fire: A Version of Aeschylus's Prometheus Bound* (1989) with a quotation from Marx: 'Prometheus is the foremost saint and martyr in the philosopher's calendar.'[29] He goes on to illustrate this and marries Aeschylus to Marx; the marriage is uncomfortable at some points, binding at others.[30]

His play is a paean to liberty. Prometheus was purported to be the creator of man – and stole fire for man after Zeus took it away to punish this audacious race. Prometheus is the freedom-fighter who opposes tyranny; Zeus is the overweening tyrant.[31] Paulin transforms Zeus into an imperialist, the capitalist who will use men as tools for self-aggrandizement. He is also the England that devours Ireland for its own pleasure. Prometheus stands for all who oppose such barbaric acts. 'Seizing the Fire' can be a metaphor for regaining one's country, by the use of arms if necessary. It is a metaphor for gaining freedom not only from the tyranny of occupation, but also the tyranny of dogma, and, of course – faithful to Marx – the tyranny of class. Prometheus calls himself one who loves man too much (*Prometheus* 122). Paulin communicates the difference between Zeus the tyrant and Prometheus the democrat: 'Zeus said Exterminate! / I said Miscegenate!' (Make love not war?) Power breeds hatred, or as Aeschylus has his Prometheus say, 'There is a disease in tyranny that makes one distrust all one's friends,' (*Prometheus* 226–27). Paulin turns this into the biting line: 'Power, it clamps like a frost on those that get it.'[32]

It is ironic that Prometheus is the healer who cannot heal himself, as the Chorus points out (*Prometheus* 474–5). Paulin transforms this by having Prometheus say he cannot free himself, although he brought freedom to man (p. 31). This shows us the new emphasis, with the disease being slavery as a legacy of imperialism.

Zeus is shown to be a true tyrant, who tries to bribe Prometheus; he sends Hermes to him with an offer of awards if Prometheus will reveal the secret that only he knows: a threat to Zeus is about to be born. Other gods carry out his dirty work. Paulin's Hermes tries to bribe Prometheus with a medal, a post and a title, 'First Intellectual of the State'. The Chorus chimes in, 'The state's approval, / recognition – / that's what they'll give you!' Prometheus answers, 'Just a contradiction! / They'd let me free / but freeze my mind.' Hermes offers more bribes: a château and a place for writing, with the free time to go along with it (most writers' dream). It is the insidious bribe to an intellectual to sell himself to the state, what Julien Benda called *le trahison des clercs*. When bribes do not work, Hermes adds the threat of torture (what can be worse than having your liver consumed each day?). But the sops are not enough when a counter-revolutionary feast is possible. Hermes asks him to sign, like Michael Collins: 'It's there you'll sign / two public texts – / a recantation / and a treaty.' We think of the peace talks.

Paulin's Prometheus takes images from modern Ireland to make his points. Oceanus tells Prometheus, 'I'll see you're freed.' Prometheus answers, 'More likely you'll get kneecapped.'

The tyrant Zeus excelled in a prison system, 'a killing zone, / a meatgrinder'. Paulin's Prometheus adds, 'Had I not stole the fire / every last human body would be stacked up dead here.'

Prometheus goes on to describe a revolution that will force Zeus to come to him: 'Tanks on the lawn, new blackouts, / locked doors and panic – / those empty sinister blocked roads . . .' and immediately the North of Ireland comes to mind. Paulin continually uses the past to interpret the present, and vice versa: he interweaves the strands of history to make his tapestry.

Paulin's *Seize the Fire* is a missile aimed at the heart of Unionism.

He is a master of the colloquialisms of Northern politicians, and the way that words can mask meaning. Prometheus in this drama takes the fire and runs with it.

Paulin in his versions of the classics has created his own work, and yet at the same time has been faithful to the ideas of the original. For instance, in *The Riot Act* he retains the mythological references by Antigone and the Chorus as she goes off to die, from Danae to Lycurgus, and the daughter of Boreas, Cleopatra. These are names which are not familiar and many translators, including Kennelly, eliminate them. Other playwrights also eliminate the mythological details, perhaps considering them too foreign for the modern ear. I applaud their retention because they add colour from the ancient palette which is still bright today. Danae and Cleopatra were physically imprisoned and Lycurgus 'became sort of a hollow shell, more like a prison cell than someone living' (p. 49). They all share confinement and Antigone's personal suffering is generalized in the mythical parallels. It gives her a sort of dignity, although in another sense it reduces her to an ideological box, the common manoeuvre of a Chorus.

The mythological is retained, but the play is placed in modern times. In the chorus, 'There are many wonders on this earth / and man has made the most of them', those wonders are abbreviated, but some modern ones added:

> Fish pip inside his radar screens
> and foals kick out of a syringe:
> he bounces on the dusty moon
> and chases clouds about the sky
> so they can dip on sterile ground.
>
> By pushing harder every way,
> by risking everything he loves,
> he makes us better, day by day:
> we call this progress and it shows
> we're damned near perfect!
>
> (p. 24)

Like Kennelly, Paulin is dismayed with man's 'progress', when it risks destroying the planet. The Greek Chorus begins with the phrase, translated literally, 'There are many wonders in the world, and none more wondrous than man' (*Antigone* 332) and the word for 'wondrous', *deinos*, means 'monstrous' at the same time as 'wonderful'. Like Paulin, Sophocles was playing on the duality of man's capacity for creation, as well as for destruction.

Aidan Carl Mathews is equally political in his *Antigone: A Version* (1984).[33] The Chorus announces at the outset, 'The drama is set in Ireland in the 1980s BC, soon after Sparta had entered the war on the German side.' With allusions to Sparta and Germany, he creates a militaristic regime in a mythical and timeless Ireland. At the first performance in Dublin's Project Arts Centre, the audience was handed copies of the Criminal Justice Bill that extended the police powers to arrest and hold prisoners without charge. *Antigone* is a potent play for reminding an audience that, in the face of such violations, individuals will fight to restore their rights. The text of this bill was read at the end of the first act – and during the intermission – so the lines between past and present, audience and stage, were purposefully blurred.

Mathews's Antigone is a quiet protester. She lets others rant and rave about her, exercising their various forms of power. She is weak and inarticulate by comparison with Creon and Heman, the Jesuit-trained Chief of Police. But she knows her role: 'I know I'm colourless. I know I'm abrasive. I know I'm a bore. But I'm right, God help me, I'm right. And I have to go on being right until somebody sends help.' She brings to mind the many hunger-strikers in Ireland who joined the 'family' of others who gave their lives for their country. Her crime is to paint the letter P on walls: in this play one brother is called Peteocles and the other Polyneices. She is executed for defacing the walls and trying to stir memories. The arbitrariness of burying one brother, but not the other, brings to mind Anouilh's *Antigone* performed in France in 1944, where Creon admits that both bodies were so disfigured it was impossible to tell them apart.

In Mathews's world (as in Northern Ireland) people disappear, and fear controls. As in Friel, words can be deadly. A character enters in the role of a critic commenting on the play: 'Sophocles isn't around to defend himself, but I suspect he'd be turning in his grave if he knew what was going on . . . I think this thing tonight is in very questionable taste. It seems to me that it's basking in degradation, and that it sheds no light on – ' The lights go down and the audience hears a blow, and a cry of pain. When the lights go up, the Chorus is mopping up blood. The replacement critic must undergo a test to make sure he did not write for *The Crane Bag* (that would imply he had some ability) and that he considers *Antigone* 'a classic', the ultimate label for the ineffectual.

The ending blurs the line between audience and participant. Antigone is supposedly killed, but Heman claims she was seen in Kharkov. This may be propaganda. Creon begins to say something, then stops himself. At the end, Heman tells the audience, 'You can't do anything. You're to disperse quietly. This is a police matter.' Creon and Ismene get upset and shout at the audience, calling them 'voyeurs'. Creon has the last words: 'Go home. Go home. You can do nothing.' Mathews's play is a particularly postmodern collage of power politics.

Brendan Kennelly's *Antigone* shows us Creon as Cromwell, the man responsible for the murder of up to a quarter of the population of Ireland in the seventeenth century.[34] Kennelly has written a book of poetry called *Cromwell* and there are echoes of the earlier poems in this play. Roche notes this and points to the Chorus in the *Antigone* saying to Creon, 'You have the power to turn your words to action.' He adds, 'This same "power" is attributed to Cromwell in Kennelly's poem.'[35] In Kennelly's *Medea*, Jason is yet another Cromwell, cut from the British mould, using self-righteous rhetoric to justify his actions.

In Kennelly's *Antigone*, though, the issue is as much money as power: 'Money is the greatest evil men have known. / Maddens men from their homes / Money destroys cities / Twists decent souls till they / Will do any shameful thing.'[36] During the potato famine in the middle years of the nineteenth century the Irish starved because they had to pay exorbitant rents. Grain stored in towers for export rotted, and a Quaker gift of grain was diverted from the

Irish needy to English merchants. The English landlords went unscathed, and reports from Ireland were said to be 'greatly exaggerated'. Ireland's history is one of poverty and deprivation. The sight of a starving child renders all other betrayals insignificant. Kennelly's words resonate, as Marxism did for many of the Irish and was a feature of republicanism. Sophocles' single reference to money in Creon's speech is expanded to a lamentation, and the Irish understand all too well.

Kennelly's Antigone says that she has more love for the mistreated noble dead than for the ambitious living, bringing to mind the words of Pádraic Pearse over the grave of O'Donovan Rossa: 'The fools, the fools, the fools, they left us our Fenian dead.' These dead inspire the living to fight to make Ireland free. Antigone's acts lead to the downfall of a tyrant. She was inspired by the dead of her past. So was McGuinness's *Electra*, and as Aeschylus' Chorus says in *Libation Bearers*, 'The dead are killing the living.'

Kennelly has other concerns too, notably his particular feminism:

> What man
> Knows anything of woman?
>
> If he did
> He would change from being a man
> As men recognize a man.[37]

There is also the sense of awe and mystery that we find in Yeats's and MacNeice's versions of Greek tragedy, and man is seen as subject to god and his own fears:

> To be wise is to be almost happy.
> The god's laws
> Are the laws we must observe.
> Our little strength is nothing
> Set against their might
> And the ringing words of proud men
> Are children's frightened whispers in the night.[38]

Words are repeated as in a litany, as if they were prayers. The Catholic Church colours much of the language in Kennelly's plays, as it does in those of Mathews, and Heaney. Gods become God, and prayers, curses and blessings resonate from antiquity to modern times.

Euripides' *Medea* shows a woman who takes vengeance on a husband who has abandoned her. She kills the ruler and his daughter, and finally her own children, while perfectly sane, and escapes to lead a new life. The thought of her would make most philandering husbands writhe. Besides this, the whole idea of child killing taps into the primal horror of a mother slaying rather than nurturing, coming with a knife instead of milk.

Medea is a Sophoclean (or even Homeric) hero. Like heroes in Homer, she says that she acts as she does so that her enemies cannot laugh at her. Help your friends and harm your enemies was an ancient Greek maxim, and Medea does just that.

Jason's quest for the Golden Fleece is a theme for epic. He was successful, with Medea's help, and married her. He brought her from her native Colchis (the Caucasus region) to Corinth after a series of adventures. While their two sons were still young, he decided that it would be best for them all if he marry the royal princess of Corinth. This is where Euripides' play begins. He investigates how happy 'ever after' is, following the marriage of the prince and princess.

Medea has calculated the worst possible vengeance. A Greek man wanted fame, fortune and offspring. She arranges that Jason has no offspring, not only by killing their own children, but by destroying the possibility of future offspring from the princess. Then she predicts that his death will be inglorious. He, the once glorious hero, will be killed by a piece falling from the ship *Argo*, in which he sailed on his quest for the Golden Fleece. She destroys the fame that he has worked so hard to earn, besides his children, and his fortune. Why does Medea decide to kill the children? Creon says he fears Medea because of the danger to his daughter. Jason says that he will benefit their own children by giving them royal brethren. Aegeus tells Medea he consulted an oracle on how he might have children. Medea sees how important children are to Creon, Aegeus and Jason, so they show her how this is the best way to destroy her husband. The sons are in the image and likeness of their father. When Medea looks at them she sees Jason. One wonders if Medea would have killed daughters.

All our sympathy is on Medea's side at the beginning. She has been victimized by Jason who owes her everything. She has no place to return to because of the crimes she committed on his behalf. But by the end, we cannot accept her killing the children. We can even make arguments for Jason. How many men have left wives for other women? Is it worth killing the children in response?

Medea is heroic and deadly, sympathetic and appalling. She uses the devices which the Greek playwrights traditionally ascribe to women: lies, deceit and plots. These devices are sufficient to destroy the rulers and the man who oppressed her. This play is often performed to express the discontent of those who perceive themselves as abused. A victim can be victimized only so long before fighting back. That fight can be successful. There have been many productions where Medea is played by a black actress.

For Kennelly the past impinges on the present. In his *Medea* there is not only the rage of woman against man, but parables of another rage: Jason exploited and victimized Medea, just as England exploited and victimized Ireland. Medea gave everything to Jason, but he was unworthy because he lied and cheated.[39] In vengeance she killed her own children, and Ireland is known for killing her children in her own agony of vengeance. Kennelly talks about betrayal as 'the ripest crop in this land'. The betrayal is not only found among the enemy but also – worse – among friends: the informer co-opted in the service of the enemy.

In Kennelly's *Medea* we find that 'God's laws' or 'heaven's laws' are what Jason has violated, and whereas Euripides has Jason mention prayer once in his reply to Medea, Kennelly expatiates on prayer. Jason tells Medea: 'Pray to make sense of the swirling world.' She answers:

Your prayer for sense –
the commonest of common sense –
is an insult. Prayer is not
a way of coping with fools.
Prayer is for dealing with the injustice caused by fools . . .
Prayer, my plausible friend, is
anger at what is, and a longing
for what should be.
Prayer is a bomb at the door of your house.[40]

Prayer inevitably returns us to the Irish question. Prayer can lead to acts. As the Nurse says, 'Medea knows the meaning of prayer. / She knows the meaning of revenge.' In this play we find the opposite of Heaney's *Cure at Troy*, which urges the cure of the wound: 'Believe in miracles, believe in healing wells and cures.' Here Medea/Ireland takes poison from her wound so that she can accomplish her revenge.

Kennelly's Medea speaks of exile as 'the worst form of living death'. So many Irish were exiled, either because their land was confiscated, or because of their poverty. Jason throws in Medea's face: 'Your savage language has guaranteed your exile . . . / Exile is hard.' Medea's savage language, like the Irish language itself, can be dangerous: it was legally forbidden for a time in Ireland.

Medea is the eternal exile, like Marina Carr's Hester in *By the Bog of Cats . . .* (1998), an outcast, a 'tinker' ostracized by those better off.[41] Her solution to her problems is to burn her house down and then kill herself after she kills her daughter. How often the Irish solution is a living suicide in drink, or other forms of self-destruction. Self-hatred and self-mutilation can result from an internalization of the colonizer's negative construction of the colonized. In Carr's play death is a refuge for the mother and daughter, a place where they can be free.

The next play to consider is *Trojan Women*, which has been called the greatest anti-war play ever written. Some will deny this and cite Cassandra's speech which praises the fame that follows war. She advocates fighting back. Hecuba also says that later generations will make songs about their sufferings:

And Hector, your son. A hero with a chest full of medals, and only because our country was attacked! If the enemy had stayed at home, no one would ever have heard of Hector . . . this war made us famous. A wise man will avoid war, but if war comes, it's best to die fighting for those you love and for what you believe. Better to die with honour.[42]

Even in the martial arts one is taught only to respond when attacked, and these words from the play suggest that one only fights if one is invaded. This is not total pacifism; it does not support 'turning the other cheek', but neither does it support a war of aggression. I think with these qualifications one can accept *Trojan Women*'s being characterized as an anti-war play. One cannot condone the horrors that are seen on stage. The final vision is of desolate women, their destroyed city and a grim future. This play is a warning; war is to be waged only as the last horrible choice left when one has lost freedom and all other reasons for living.

From Aeschylus to Euripides there is a shift in focus. Aeschylus wrote with the glory of the Persian wars vividly in mind, whereas Euripides was overwhelmed by the horrors of the Peloponnesian War (431–404 BC), in which Greek fought Greek. The names of Marathon and Thermopylae are synonymous with Greek bravery, but the name of Melos is synonymous with the oppression that comes from empire. In the year before this play was produced (415 BC), the Athenians killed all the males and enslaved the women and children on Melos. This is vividly described by Thucydides, who reveals the Athenian *Machtpolitik* ('might makes right'). In the same year the Athenians made the disastrous decision to invade Sicily, the first step towards their final defeat in 404 BC.

Trojan Women, as bleak a play as Euripides ever wrote, proved a stimulus to both Mathews and Kennelly.[43] Mathews's *Trojans*, like his *Antigone*, contains allusions to the Second World War and is set in Germany. In Mathews's play, there is little emotional involvement with the characters. This is more intellectual exercise than drama. Astyanax dies, but the announcement to Hecuba is almost perfunctory. The women at the end assume the pose of statues, all equally lifeless, those condemned to life and those to death.

Mathews's play is more about German history than Irish history, yet some of the abuse of the women was certainly comparable with what happened in Ireland. The gods are not taken seriously, even though God appears as a character, but the Catholic allusions are there: 'I do not want to be safe in the arms of Jesus,' says one woman, 'I want to be safe in the arms of my husband.' When Cassandra drinks from a wine bottle, she says, 'Let this chalice never pass from me.' There are other Irish references. Menelaus says he enlisted 'to get drunk. To get laid. Bushmills and pussy.' Like Joyce saying, 'History is a nightmare from which I'm trying to wake,' Mathews says, 'History is a fucking forced march. They don't want to be History.' Overall this piece offers little poetry or song, but much violence.

Trojan Women: A New Version by Brendan Kennelly (1993) is filled with poetic meditations. His poetry gives emotional dimensions to the words: 'The day wears pain like a black jewel.' When Poseidon asks Athena if he's to let the ships flounder, she answers, 'I want them to know that home / is what is always in the mind and always out of reach.'

Unlike Mathews, Kennelly does offer mystery and poetry, and Hecuba reaches a true epiphany, seeing God in her suffering: 'I heard the music of our hearts / I knew the everlasting beauty of the song of earth and heaven. I kissed God's hand! I am real. I am so real / I am not afraid to look into the eyes of God.' Here again is God, enhanced by a Christian transfiguration. But what she says accords with the Greek claim that the gods teach man through suffering. There are references to song and magic: 'Beware the song of Helen's beauty . . . I've seen the very air seduced / by magical ripples of her sweet manipulating voice. / Her voice is her best song, song of beauty, song of hell!' Sometimes he uses rhyme in the poetry: 'Dance like the happy light, let earth and heaven sing / here where I make this bright and fiery ring.'

The greatest overall difference is that Kennelly offers more hope than Euripides: 'The living must forget the dead . . . Let the dead rest in peace. In peace let the dead rot.' This contradicts the Irish belief that the dead are always with us, as one sees in Joyce's

Dubliners, or indeed in the claims of Pearse about the Fenian dead.

Both Kennelly and Euripides write about suffering. Captive women are hauled off to slavery, and when they feel they can suffer nothing worse than the loss of their country, they learn there is more: they can lose their life-blood – their children. This is a story for Ireland: it is well understood there because they have lived it.

The history of Ireland validates many observations:

> Freedom is like health –
> you never know it until you've lost it . . . (p. 8)

> People of my heart, do everything you can
> to banish war
> from the lives of women, men and children.
> But if war comes to the land
> like a murderous brute into your house
> and you find that you must fight
> then fight like people who have found
> their special light,
> there's no evil in that fight . . . (p. 25)

> There's nothing more dangerous to a winner
> than one seed of hope in the heart of the loser. (p. 71)

Euripides' Hecuba says, 'Where there's life, there's hope.'

Kennelly plays on Paris as a firebrand. He knows his mythology. This was Hecuba's dream, that she gave birth to a torch. It is also a poetic image, given the fire of passion which brought about the torching of Troy.

Kennelly uses another phrase from Yeats ('The Fiddler of Dooney'):

> A wave of the sea!
> Natural and fearless!
> That is what I want –
> I want to live without fear

> and I will, I will,
> no matter where I happen to be,
> Hecuba, a woman, Hecuba,
> a natural, fearless wave of the sea. (p. 79)

Woman here is a force of nature. Kennelly's play is a seething indictment of man's cruelty. It is a fitting conclusion to his trilogy. He endorses women and endorses Ireland: woe to the man or country that would enslave either. Who can enslave the waves of the sea? The play ends in hope. Hecuba says, 'The waves are free. The war is over. The war begins – for me! ' We know that Hecuba will prevail. As for Ireland, freedom is her battle cry.

Brendan Kennelly's poetry in *Trojan Women* dances like a wave of the sea. From his play we see that Ireland like Hecuba will never be tamed. Who can tame the sea?

Kennelly's play has humanity and thereby follows Euripides closely, although it polishes some sharp edges. It ends in an upbeat way, understanding what Hölderlin said in an epigram to Sophocles, '*Manche versuchen umsonst, das freudigste freudig zu sagen, hier spricht endlich es mir, hier in die Trauer sich aus.*'[44] ('Many try in vain to express happiness in terms of happiness; here, finally, I discover happiness through grief.') One thinks of Aristotle's catharsis, that strange feeling of elation when we leave the theatre.

Philoctetes is a late play by Sophocles (409 BC), and the only Greek tragedy with all-male characters. Seamus Heaney, in his artfully crafted *The Cure at Troy: A Version of Sophocles' Philocetes* (1990), makes his Chorus women as a contrast to the dominant male characters.[45] Here Heaney emphasizes the cure, and compromise, rather than the aggression that an all-male cast suggests.

Sophocles' genius is to show us Neoptolemus trying to compromise his nature. Only after experience and reflection does he see that the loss of self – or self-betrayal – is worse than the loss of Troy. His dilemma is like Antigone's, and his loyalty to himself and the ideals that constitute his character is more important than loyalty to those in power, particularly when his allegiance involves a loyalty to a higher truth.

The issue of truth vs falsehood is important here. In the *Iliad*, Achilles, the father of Neoptolemus, says words to the same effect, 'More hateful to me than the gates of Hades is a man who says one thing and conceals another thing in his heart.' Achilles lives a short life, and gains honour; Odysseus lives a long life because of his lying. He also knows when it is in his own best interest to be a coward, and the scene where the blustering Odysseus runs away when Philoctetes regains his bow and tries to kill him is largely comic. This is typical of Odysseus. He is true to himself, and he is a survivor. Such cowardice would have been unthinkable for Achilles.

Theme upon theme is repeated in Sophocles, as he replicates the hero in his strange majesty. Philoctetes and Neoptolemus are like two sides of Achilles: one, the irascible and wild nature of the devoted warrior; the other, his virtue and integrity. When they are divided they lose; together, they defeat Odysseus. Heracles brings about this powerful fusion by dragging them back on to the mythological track.

Both Odysseus and Philoctetes fight to gain the soul of Neoptolemus. Neoptolemus ultimately opts for the truthful Philoctetes, who most resembles his father. During the course of the drama he matures.

Philoctetes, like Prometheus and Io, intermittently suffers agonies sent to him by a divine source. He is representative of all those victims who suffer from chronic illness. The bow itself is a prominent and magical symbol. It never fails. It is both a provider of life, and a destroyer. Philoctetes says he cannot survive without it. The destruction that it will bring to Troy will also lead to peace.

The Cure at Troy proceeds from, and ends, in optimism. It is a version that truly urges and believes, and hopes 'for a great sea-change / On the far side of revenge /. . . that a further shore is reachable from here'. 'Sea-change' can remind us of Shakespeare's *The Tempest*, and the forgiveness urged by Prospero, likewise an island-bound victim, saying, 'The rarer action is / In virtue than in vengeance' (V.i.27–8). Ariel misleads Ferdinand about his father, saying he 'doth suffer a sea-change / Into something rich and strange' (I.ii.400). Heaney was reading *The Tempest* at the time he made this translation.

The Chorus at the beginning and end of Heaney's play puts us in the middle of the Irish problem:

> Heroes. Victims. Gods and human beings.
> All throwing shapes, every one of them
> Convinced he's in the right, all of them glad
> To repeat themselves and their every last mistake,
> No matter what . . .
>   Licking their wounds
> And flashing them around like decorations.
> I hate it, I always hated it, and I am
> A part of it myself.
>   And a part of you,
> For my part is the chorus, and the chorus
> Is more or less a borderline between
> The you and the me and the it of it. (pp. 1–2)

This is an exposition that not only locates the Chorus in its mediating function, but lays out the theme of the play: a focus on the wound, rather than the cure. The play is about a man with a wound, and he will be cured at Troy.

Heaney has said in a letter that he was inspired by 'Edmund Wilson's essay, "The Wound and the Bow", and a fascination with the conflict between the integrity of the personal bond and the exaction of the group's demands for loyalty. A sense that pride in the wound is stronger than the desire for a cure.'

Heaney's optimism shines at the end in a speech delivered by the Chorus leader. These words are not in Sophocles, but in modern Ireland:

> Human beings suffer,
> They torture one another,
> They get hurt and get hard.
> No poem or play or song
> Can fully right a wrong
> Inflicted and endured.

The innocent in gaols
Beat on their bars together.
A hunger-striker's father
Stands in the graveyard dumb.
The police widow in veils
Faints at the funeral home.

History says, *Don't hope*
On this side of the grave.
But then, once in a lifetime
The longed-for tidal wave
Of justice can rise up,
And hope and history rhyme. (p. 77)

The sufferings on both sides are mentioned. The hope is for a peaceful settlement, and a healing of the wound of hate.

We can see Yeats's image from 'Easter 1916', 'Too long a sacrifice can make a stone of the heart', in Heaney's 'Human beings suffer, / They torture one another / They get hurt and get hard'.

Heaney polishes some of Sophocles' rough edges. Now Philoctetes shows sympathy for others in Heaney's play: 'Count your blessings and always be ready to pity other people.' Heaney's own humanity appears in his Philoctetes, who in the original referred only to himself. This Philoctetes wants an end to curses, whereas for the original, curses were a way of life.

In Heaney, Philoctetes' farewell to his island shows that he identifies with it, and that he will carry it inside himself, rather as Heaney himself carries the memory of growing up in the North now that he lives in the Republic:

I'll never get over Lemnos; this island's going to be the keel under me and the ballast inside me. I'm like a fossil that's being carried away, I'm nothing but cave stones, and damp walls and an old mush of dead leaves. The sound of waves in draughty passages. A cliff that's wet with spray on a winter's morning. (p. 80)

It also shows Heaney's love for the land. His father was a farmer and he grew up appreciating man's dependency on land with its times of plenty and famine. In Sophocles, Philoctetes delivered a mournful farewell to his island, but objectified it. Heaney has Philoctetes derive his identity from it, as many an Irishman has identified himself with his land.

Heaney again, I think, sympathizes when he has Philoctetes say, 'I feel I'm a part of what was always meant to happen, and is happening now at last. Come on, my friends.' This warm address to his friends is another affirmation of confidence in the process of peace. Heaney's emphasis here is not on the brutal taking of Troy, but on forgetting wounds, doing one's duty towards others, and finally securing a lasting peace. This is advocated by the god Hercules, who appears at the end, played by a Chorus woman, a good symbolic choice. Heaney said he wanted the presence of women in his play.

Heaney has his Hercules say,

> Go, with your bow. Conclude the sore
> And cruel stalemate of our war.
> Win by fair combat. But know to shun
> Reprisal killings when that's done.
>
> Then take just spoils and sail at last
> Out of the bad dream of your past. (p. 79)

He adds, 'Show gods respect.' There are few that would fault this message. He may be playing on the title of his next book of poetry *Seeing Things* (1991), when he has Neoptolemus say, 'Stop just licking your wounds. Start seeing things.' Heaney made a poetic masterpiece of his own, filled with what he believes.

Greek tragedy can be reworked in poetry and not simply drama. Heaney's 'Mycenae Lookout' (a poem in *Spirit Level*, 1995) gives a grim picture of war and its recurrent cycle, but it celebrates life, and the lessons learned from suffering. It is a poetic version of the *Oresteia*, and, if recited, close to a play. Just as life and fertility go in cycles, so Heaney sees death and war returning in regular patterns. He begins the first section, 'The Watchman's War', with a vigorous rhythm, apt for marching in war or sexual intercourse, with its climax in 'Clytemnestra's love-shout'. It is typical of Heaney that he gives us the Watchman's point of view, not Agamemnon's. We the audience are all watchpeople, and as he says, no one is innocent. We are Rosencrantz and Guildenstern, and we affect Hamlet much more than we think.

Cassandra in the next section is seen as a virgin violated not only by her captors but by 'bystanders', who want 'to do it to her'. The sexual attraction of war is clearly expressed in the figure of this child. The lines 'No such thing / as innocent / bystanding' apply to the Irish, as well as any observer of war. We watched the war in Iraq on television as if it were a video game and cheered the hits. Heaney applies Cassandra's final lines, 'A wipe of the sponge, that's it', to the destruction of Troy itself, and light. In the original the image of man's happiness overturned was of writing erased, here it is of light extinguished. Light and darkness play throughout this poem, besides dawn and night. Other images are beacon, holocaust of Troy and dawn, followed by what extinguishes fire, water.

'The Dawn Vision' is of Romulus and Remus, in their endless dance of death, murder and power, history without hope. Typical of Ireland it describes territorial conflict, 'a man / Jumped a fresh earth-wall and another ran / Amorously, it seemed, to strike him down'. Heaney describes the love-lust of the personal duel and local wars which implicate the world: 'Our war stalled in the pre-articulate', and 'I felt the beating of the huge time-wound / We lived inside'. The wound was what Heaney's *The Cure at Troy* was meant to address, the wound from which memory continually picks the scab. The North and commitment to it reappears, and Heaney seems to describe himself in his being

> . . . far less
> Focused on victory than I should have been –
> Still isolated in my old disdain

Of claques who always needed to be seen
And heard as the true Argives. Mouth athletes,
Quoting the oracle and quoting dates,
Petitioning, accusing, taking votes. (p. 33)

'The Nights' is a section filled with sex: 'real life was the bed'. Clytemnestra carries on in the same rhythm as the gods and goddesses do in their lovemaking. Troy is also a locus for sex: 'When the captains in the horse felt Helen's hand caress / its wooden boards and belly / they nearly rode each other.' From the blood-bath, peace is born. The after-birth of water mixed with blood, besides cleansing ablutions, is described in the last section, 'Reverie of Water'. There is first a bath that cleanses the wounds of a hero; then a well under Athens' Acropolis is a lifeline, and fought over as Greek meets Greek (read again Irish vs Irish, and the fight is territorial). Finally a well is described, the 'healing well' from *The Cure at Troy*, which sustains life and which teaches the men who went in: 'deeper in themselves for having been there ... finders, keepers, seers of fresh water / in the bountiful round mouths of iron pumps / and gushing taps'. Water can be baptismal water, or the water in which Orestes was finally purified. Or the internal moisture which makes intercourse possible, a source of new life. All life is said to have come from the ocean. Water is more life-evoking than the fire in the torches at the end of the *Eumenides*. The objects are common, a bath and a well, and the water is priceless to man, a source of life and witness to his death. It cleans, purifies and sustains. Here it also educates, and inspires, like water from the Castalian spring.

Heaney's words are wielded like a fencing foil by a master. The Watchman describes the dawn of 'victory' over Troy:

I balanced between destiny and dread
And saw it coming, clouds bloodshot with the red
Of victory fires, the raw wound of that dawn
Igniting and erupting, bearing down
Like lava on a fleeing population... (p. 30)

Here we have the major themes, water and fire, water and blood, destiny/history determining the return of war and the dread the people feel. The water is only in the clouds, dried out by the fires of victory; lava is the semen of war, generating only stillbirths; only in the final section does water overwhelm the fire, and one hopes that people prefer the bath to the battle.

Heaney took his pen, dug into the past, and mined light from words of love and war. The poem offers hope that man can learn from his past.

In Derek Mahon's *The Bacchae: after Euripides* (1991) we also find the Catholic Church and here, as it did during the Crusades, it sanctions a Holy War. Politics and the Church have always had an uneasy alliance in Ireland, as elsewhere. Dionysus is associated with Christ as 'Lord of the Dance'.[46] One remembers the popular Irish song 'Lord of the Dance', describing Christ coming to earth to save mankind and to lead them in the dance of salvation.

Mahon's Dionysus speaks like a rather hip, charismatic leader from the 1960s. He describes miracles – his birth by lightning, and Hera's fiery revenge (Hera is 'the jealous bitch') – and the attendant effects are conveyed by suggestive onomatopoeia such as 'Whoosh!' and 'Pow!' It sounds a bit like a comic strip (p. 11). Dionysus could easily be mistaken for a member of the Dublin rock group 'The Commitments'.

This play is also a parable suitable for Ireland. Dionysus can be regarded as a force of nature, the force of a people who are fighting to reclaim their rights. There is a chorus in the *Bacchae* in which the Asian Bacchantes describe the pleasure of holding one's hand over the head of a conquered foe (877–81):[47]

> What pleases best, what grand
> gift can the gods bestow
> more than the conquering hand
> over the fallen foe?
> It's still the same old story,
> a fight for love and glory,
> and every heart admits that this is so!
> (pp. 41, 42 and 62)

Mahon places this appeal within his play in a position corresponding to where Euripides placed it, but it also concludes Mahon's play. Euripides concluded *his* play with a formula that he has used to end the *Medea, Helen, Alcestis* and *Andromache* in addition to the *Bacchae*. Except for the *Alcestis*, each of these plays involves vengeful murders in excess of the crime first committed. Mahon does not allow Euripides' rather didactic, and formulaic, ending to have the last word. Instead, the note of vengeance, as sounded in the earlier chorus, and pleasure in vengeance is what is stressed. Part of the tragedy is history itself, and Mahon's lines beat with the life-blood of passion.

Sophocles' *Electra* is another play used in political contexts, put on by people who see themselves oppressed. At a conference on Sophocles' *Electra*, Fiona Shaw, the actress who had recently played this role, described how she had lost a brother, and this I am sure added to her moving performance, particularly during the urn scene. Zoë Wanamaker, also, had just lost her father when she played Electra in Frank McGuinness's version. A Hellenistic actor who played the role of Electra had his own son's ashes in the urn that was said to hold Orestes' ashes. Their tears were real.

When Shaw played the part in Derry, no one applauded, simply because they were so moved. But they all stayed to discuss the issues, because these were issues which everyone knew. Mary Holland wrote of this performance:

At one level, last week was an awesome vindication of those who believe that this is what the arts should be about, and where they should be – close to the cutting edge of political argument. Fiona Shaw said: 'I do believe we must use the theatre to debate these dangerous issues – justice, retribution, violence.'

Holland continues:

One woman spoke of the actress's performance as Electra: 'I thought of Mrs Kelly, whose son was killed on Bloody Sunday, and the way they would find her, even years afterwards, lying on his grave with her face smeared with earth.' Another talked of Electra's sister begging her to bow to the inevitable: 'I kept remembering the hunger-strikers, when their families were trying to persuade them to give up the fast and accept the prison system.'[48]

I think Frank McGuinness carries this on in his version of this play (1997).[49] It was performed in London and Broadway, directed by David Leveaux. It showed vengeance in full swing, along with the consequences of that vengeance. The image invoked by the New York set suggested Bosnia and Zoë Wanamaker played Electra as mad with grief, tearing her hair, wandering distractedly and menacingly around the stage. After the murder of Clytemnestra she licked the blood off Orestes' arm. McGuinness wanted to show the madness of vengeance, as he himself had seen it in Northern Ireland.

McGuinness not only has the poetic vocabulary necessary, but a dramatic sense that many other Irish translators of Greek drama do not have. He includes all the things that characterize Irish translations. His language is up-to-date yet follows the original for the most part. There are lovely poetic phrases: 'The day is breaking to the birds' voices. / The stars have shrunk, / The night is nothing.' He makes Electra's pleas poetic, but keeps a dramatic terseness. His repetitions are emotive, as Electra repeats the word 'pain' five times over the urn she thinks contains her brother's ashes, besides mourning with elaborate and apt words. There are Irish turns of phrase as Electra says to Chrysothemis, 'You'd be a coward as well as a victim, would you?'

Religious tones emerge, besides the mystery:

> May I not bear false witness,
> But through the darkness,
> I see the workings of Justice. (p. 19)

Gods become God and Electra says, 'I swear by the Virgin.' We find ourselves in the Catholic world. Prayers occur in the litany form:

Let me live a life unharmed.
Let me rule the house of Atreus and this kingdom.
Let me live among friends.
Let my days be prosperous.
Let the children who wish me no pain prosper too. (p. 25)

This is Clytemnestra's prayer, and McGuinness has made her even more sympathetic than Sophocles did.

There are folk sayings: 'I'll never darken their door again,' and 'Who would battle with such a mighty man? / If you do you will be eaten without salt.'

Sophocles reworked Ajax's claim, 'It is noble to either live with honour or die with it,' by having Electra say, 'It is base for nobles to live basely.' This McGuinness renders, 'Shame is truly shame to a noble soul.' He also makes statements succinct, as in Chrysothemis' claim, 'Sometimes being right is wrong.' This is translating 'It is terrible for a good speaker to be wrong [in what she says].'

There are specifically Irish turns of phrase, and the one-woman Chorus could well be giving advice in some Irish village. This is a dramatist who listens to country folk showing their reverence for God:

God is still great in his heaven, and he sees everything.
Offer up to him what is eating you inside.
Don't go on fire with hatred.
Remember this – time's a gentle god, he heals.
Agamemnon's son may wander the plains of Crisa,
But he will not forget his father,
And the God of Death will not forget either.[50]

Note the mixture of blessings for friends and curses for enemies. McGuinness's Electra is stronger even than the original: she is the republican woman whose loss has inflamed her to action (as in the film *Some Mother's Son*, 1996). Yeats and MacNeice minimized the role of women, but Kennelly, McGuinness and other modern Irish playwrights have made their women stronger than their Greek originals, even at the risk of upsetting the balance between the sexes.

McGuinness eliminates Sophocles' final lines given to Orestes, saying that if more crime were dealt with like this, there would be fewer criminals. It seems McGuinness wants us to see the violence in a more ambivalent light than Sophocles saw it, namely as a means of enforcing justice. This brings us again to Ireland and to the fact that he is a writer from the North and has himself seen so much violence that he abhors it. Sophocles' clarity ends with McGuinness's question mark.

McGuinness writes drama which sparkles and sets the stage on fire. His *Electra* seared the souls of many who attended performances both in Europe and America.

In Marina Carr's *By the Bog of Cats . . .* death is a refuge for the mother and daughter, a place where they both can be free. Anouilh also had his Medea kill herself. We understand how Hester, Carr's Medea, kills her daughter, Josie. Her daughter begs her mother to take her with her, and Hester remembered how she spent her life longing for her own mother who had abandoned her. Hester kills Josie to keep them together for eternity. The belief in an afterlife is typically Irish, and Carr often populates her plays with ghosts. She does not kill her daughter to avenge herself on Jason. She kills her daughter for her daughter's sake and, she thinks, benefit. Hester also does not kill the new bride. She feels that Jason's having to live with the new bride (she is somewhat of a simpleton) is punishment enough. We have total sympathy for all that she does. It is only reinforced by the ending.

Carr's play sparkles with dialogue, and Carr well conveys the Irish Midlands with their land struggles. Local language is used. She also uses names that are suggestive, Hester for the unmarried Medea stand-in, right from *The Scarlet Letter*, complete with an illegitimate daughter. Jason is Carthage and we remember Cato's *Carthago delenda est*. Xavier's name is evocative of a Catholic saint, and ironic given his villainy. It also may be a slap at the impotence of the Church to control some of the atrocities the audience sees.

The abusive and self-absorbed mother-in-law Mrs Kilbride contributes to the humour of many scenes. Kilbride is another obvious name that anticipates the future. This mother would kill any bride that came between her and her son.

Father Willow with his admiration for Catwoman rather redeems the Church. Both he and Catwoman are the 'seers' that we find in so many Greek plays. They have the ability to bless and curse, and Catwoman can predict the future. Tiresias has wandered into *Medea*.

This Medea has crimes to her credit like Euripides' protagonist, but the psychological overtones are stronger in Carr's play. Hester murders her brother more out of sibling rivalry than to benefit Carthage. By the use of ghosts there is a chance for at least verbal reconciliation between brother and sister. The mother remains stubbornly absent, as she did in life. But it seems that the tradition of witchcraft was passed on.

Carr adds an element of incest. There is a suggestion that Xavier was involved with his daughter, besides Hester's own mother. This rampant sexuality is typical of many rural areas in Ireland, where jokes abound about the similar appearance of the children. Carr's recent play *On Raftery's Hill* (2000) is about incest in the Irish Midlands.

Carr makes her Jason weak and dependent. The Creon stand-in (Xavier) is the more powerful. Both are like the original in their concern for property and station. But neither of them is a match for Hester/Medea, who is powerful from the beginning of the play.

Carr's play has lively action, and exciting witty dialogue, more than many of the playwrights here whose forte is more in the poetry. This play is a good example of how thoroughly Greek tragedy can be assimilated into the Irish countryside, and can add to the local stories a dimension of timelessness.

Marina Carr's version of *Medea* celebrates women as Kennelly does. She shows that even death cannot overcome a woman. In her play, it is a viable way to escape oppression, even another type of freedom. Her masterful use of the dialect of the Midlands proves yet again that language is as vital to Ireland as its land. Language is its curse and its blessing.

Some of the characteristics that distinguish these Irish versions of the classics are almost formulaic: Irish-English; allusions to Irish history; anachronisms; poetry; philosophy; folk sayings; humour; at times sexual explicitness and scatological language; references to drink and drunks; colloquialisms; literary allusions and wordplay; repetition of words; rhyme and rhythm; the use of music and song; references to a Christian God; rituals; prayers; a sense of mystery, the inexplicable, and the spiritual; memory; 'ordinary' people rather than nobles; gravitation towards human rights and freedom; and struggles over or identification with the land. Most of these plays feature strong women who represent Ireland: the mothers, the daughters, the freedom-fighters and the victims. These characteristics show that the Irish do not abstract themselves when they use the classics to express their joys and sorrows, their sincerest wishes besides their most profound fears.

Each of these plays shows the power of Greek tragedy as interpreted by the Irish. The ancient plays provide 'the force that through the green fuse drives the flower'.[51] The Irish make the flower bloom.

Appendix: Greek Tragedy in Ireland

Originally performed in Greek

1720: Performance of Euripides' *Hippolytus*, put on by Rev. Thomas Sheridan, Dublin School production. Jonathan Swift wrote the prologue.

1723: Performance of Sophocles' *Oedipus Tyrannus*, by Rev. Thomas Sheridan, King's Inns, Dublin.

English translations and versions of Greek tragedy

J. M. Synge, *Shadow of the Glen* (1903; Euripides' *Alcestis*); *Deirdre of the Sorrows* (1910; *Antigone* and *Trojan Women*).

George Bernard Shaw, *Major Barbara* (1905; *Bacchae*).

Sean O'Casey, *Juno and the Paycock* (1924; Aeschylus' *Agamemnon*).

Christine Longford, *Aeschylus' The Furies* (c. 1934; *Eumenides*).

Lord Longford, *Aeschylus' Agamemnon, Drink Offerings* (1933;

Euripides' *Bacchae*).

W. B. Yeats, *Sophocles' Oedipus the King* (1926); *Oedipus at Colonus* (1927); *Antigone* (survives only as a few lines in a poem, 'A Woman Young and Old', from *The Winding Stair*, 1929); *Deirdre* (1906), a possible version of the myth of *Helen*; *Countess Cathleen* (1899; a possible version of Euripides' *Alcestis*).

Louis MacNeice, *Aeschylus' Agamemnon* (1937).

Brian Friel, *The Gentle Island* (1971; *Hippolytus*); *Living Quarters, after Hippolytus* (1977); *Wonderful Tennessee* (1993; *Bacchae*).

Tom Murphy, *The Sanctuary Lamp* (1976; after the *Oresteia*).

Sidney Bernard Smith, *Sherca* (after Sophocles' *Philoctetes*).

Ulick O'Connor, *The Oval Machine* (after *Hippolytus*, unpublished).

Mary Elizabeth Burke-Kennedy, *Oedipus* (unpublished).

Tom Paulin, *The Riot Act* (1984; based on Sophocles' *Antigone*); *Seize the Fire* (1989; based on Aeschylus' *Prometheus Bound*).

Aidan Carl Mathews, *Antigone* (unpublished, 1984) and *Trojans* (1994, unpublished, based on Euripides' *Trojan Women*).

Brendan Kennelly, *Antigone* (1985); *Medea* (1991); *The Trojan Women* (1993).

Seamus Heaney, *The Cure at Troy: A Version of Sophocles' Philoctetes* (1990).

Desmond Egan, *Medea* (1991; a translation) and *Philoctetes* (1998; a translation).

Derek Mahon, *The Bacchae* (1991); *Racine's Phaedra* (1996).

Colin Teevan, *Iph after Euripides' Iphigeneia in Aulis* (1996).

Frank McGuinness, *Electra* (1997).

Marina Carr, *The Mai* (1994; Sophocles' *Electra*); *By the Bog of Cats . . .* (1999; following Euripides' *Medea*).

Greg Delanty, *Orestes* (1999).

Michael Scott, *Agamemnon* (1999).

Declan Donnellan, *Antigone* (2000).

Translations of Greek tragedy in Irish

Pádraig de Brún, *Sophocles' Antigone* (1926); *Oedipus Tyrannus* (1927; 1928); *Oedipus at Colonus* (1927; 1929); *Euripides' Iphigenia in Aulis* (1935).

George Thomson, *Euripides' Alcestis* (1932); *Aeschylus' Prometheus Bound* (1933).

Suibhne Geilt, *Euripides' Trojan Women* (1938).

Fr Art C. Mac Giolla Eoin, *Euripides' Iphigenia in Tauris* (1950).

Notes

1. I have addressed some of this material before: Marianne McDonald, 'Thomas Murphy's *The Sanctuary Lamp*: The Light at the End of the Night', in my *Ancient Sun, Modern Light: Greek Drama on the Modern Stage* (New York: Columbia University Press, 1992); ' "A Bomb at the Door": Kennelly's *Medea*, 1988', *Éire-Ireland* XXVIII (2) (Summer 1993): 129–37; 'Seamus Heaney's *Cure at Troy*: Politics and Poetry', *Classics Ireland* 3 (May 1996): 129–40; 'Medea as Politician and Diva: Riding the Dragon into the Future,' in *Medea: Essays on Medea in Myth, Literature, Philosophy and Art*, ed. James J. Clauss and Sarah Iles Johnston (Princeton: Princeton University Press, 1997); 'When Despair and History Rhyme: Colonialism and Greek Tragedy', *New Hibernia Review* 1(2) (Summer 1997): 57–70; 'Recent Irish Translations of Greek Tragedy: Derek Mahon's *Bacchai*', in *The Translation of Ancient Greek Drama into All the Languages of the World*, ed. Elena Patrikiou (Athens: Desmoi Center, 1998), pp. 191–200; 'Violent Words: Brian Friel's *Living Quarters*: after *Hippolytus*', *Arion* (Spring/Summer 1998): 35–47; 'Classics as Celtic Firebrand: Greek Tragedy, Irish Playwrights, and Colonialism', in *Theatre Stuff: Critical Essays on Contemporary Irish Theatre*, ed. Eamonn Jordan (Dublin: Carysfort Press, 2000), pp. 16–26.
2. Thomas Cahill, *How the Irish Saved Civilization: The Untold Story of Ireland's Heroic Role from the Fall of Rome to the Rise of Medieval Europe* (New York, London, Toronto, Sydney: Doubleday, 1995), pp. 160–4, 209.
3. Quoted in Richard Ellmann, *James Joyce*, revised edn. (Oxford: Oxford University Press, 1983 [1959]), p. 217.

4. See W. B. Stanford, *Ireland and the Classical Tradition* (Dublin: Irish Academic Press, 1976).

5. Kiberd quotes Ronan Fanning: 'ruling regimes always seek to control the presentation of the past in such a way as to buttress and legitimize their own authority', in *Inventing Ireland* (Cambridge, Mass.: Harvard University Press, 1996), p. 644. The Irish on the other hand invented Ireland 'By performing their own acts of translation and retranslation ... by writing their own history and then rewriting it', p. 629. See also Victoria Tietze Larson, 'Classics and the Acquisition and Validation of Power in Britain's "Imperial Century" (1815–1914)', *International Journal of the Classical Tradition* 6 (2) (Fall 1999).

6. Fanning, *Inventing Ireland*, p. 271.

7. Ibid.

8. Brian Friel, *Translations*, in *Selected Plays of Brian Friel* (London: Faber & Faber, 1984), p. 417.

9. *Collected Works of Pádraic H. Pearse*, Vol. III, *Political Writings and Speeches* (Dublin and London: Maunsel, 1922), p. 50, cited by Fiona Macintosh, *Dying Acts: Death in Ancient Greek and Modern Irish Tragic Drama* (Cork: Cork University Press, 1994), p. 14.

10. Nicholas de Jongh, *Evening Standard* (27 January 2000).

11. J. M. Hone, *W. B. Yeats: 1865–1939* (London: Macmillan, 1942), p. 257.

12. W. B. Yeats, *Sophocles' King Oedipus'* in *The Collected Plays of W. B. Yeats* (London: Macmillan, 1934), pp. 510–11.

13. *The Letters of W. B. Yeats*, ed. A. Wade (London: Macmillan, 1954), p. 537.

14. Brian Arkins, *Builders of my Soul: Greek and Roman Themes in Yeats*, Irish Literary Studies, 32 (Gerrards Cross: Colin Smythe, 1990), p. 138.

15. Louis MacNeice, *The Agamemnon of Aeschylus* (London: Faber & Faber, 1936), p. 61.

16. See McDonald, *Ancient Sun, Modern Light*, pp. 172–200.

17. Tom Murphy, *The Sanctuary Lamp* (Dublin: Gallery Press, 1976), p. 54.

18. Aeneas was a Trojan refugee, but became identified with Roman imperialism. We remember that Cato under the Republic recommended Carthage's destruction, which occurred in 146 BC.

19. The following quotation is from Simon Winchester's account in the *Guardian*: 'Four or five armoured cars appeared at William St, and

raced into the Rossville Street square, and several thousand people began to run away . . . Paratroopers piled out of their vehicles, many ran forward to make arrests, but others rushed to the street corners. It was these men, perhaps 20 in all, who opened the fire with their rifles. I saw three men fall to the ground. One was still obviously alive with blood pumping from his leg. The others, both apparently in their teens, seemed dead . . . Army snipers could be seen firing continuously towards the central Bogside streets and at one stage a lone army sniper fired two shots at me as I peered around a corner.' Quoted in Tim Pat Coogan, *The Troubles: Ireland's Ordeal 1966–1996 and the Search for Peace* (Boulder, Co: Roberts Rinehart, 1996).

20. *Selected Plays of Brian Friel*, pp. 171–246.

21. Seamus Deane, 'A World Without a Name', in *History Lessons* (Dublin: Gallery Press, 1983), p. 33.

22. A dictionary entry on the Aisling begins, 'As a result of the disaster of Kinsale, and of their failures in the Confederate War (1641–1649) and in the Williamite War (1688–1691), the Old Irish were completely overthrown. Historians have called eighteenth-century Ireland the Protestant nation, for the Protestant planters possessed nine-tenths of the land, formed the government and Parliament, to neither of which any Catholic was admitted, controlled industry and the professions with the single exception of medicine, and enjoyed every privilege in the state. The Catholics, on the other hand, had no right in law. Their position was defined clearly by Lord Chancellor Bowes and Chief Justice Robinson, who laid it down from the bench that the law does not suppose any such person to exist as an Irish Roman Catholic. The old Gaelic aristocratic society had perished . . . But poetry itself was not dead . . . A new poetic convention arose in the eighteenth century, that of the political aisling, or vision poem . . . From earliest times we have stories in which Ireland is represented as a beautiful lady, and the myth of the lady from the síodh, the fairy-mound, uttering prophecies about the sovereignty of Éire is common.' *Macmillan Dictionary of Irish Literature,* ed. Robert Hogan (London: Macmillan, 1979), pp. 45–6. The vision of the Aisling is a poetic narcotic to assuage the pain of political impotence.

23. 'Brian Friel: The Name of the Game', in *The Achievement of Brian Friel*, ed. A. Peacock (Gerrards Cross: Colin Smythe, 1993), p. 111.

24. Anthony Roche, 'Ireland's *Antigones*: Tragedy North and South', in *Cultural Contexts and Literary Idioms in Contemporary Irish Literature,*

ed. Michael Kenneally (Gerrards Cross: Colin Smythe, 1988), pp. 221–50; Christopher Murray, 'Three Irish *Antigones*', in *Perspectives of Irish Drama and Theatre*, ed. Jacqueline Genet and Richard Allen Cave, Irish Literary Studies 33 (Gerrards Cross: Colin Smythe, 1991), pp. 115–29.

25. *The Riot Act: A Version of Sophocles' Antigone* (London/Boston, Mass.: Faber & Faber, 1985), p. 54.

26. Roche, 'Ireland's *Antigones*', p. 24.

27. Paulin, *Riot Act*, p. 16.

28. Ibid., p. 17.

29. Tom Paulin, *Seize the Fire: A Version of Aeschylus's Prometheus Bound* (London: Faber & Faber, 1990).

30. See G. Thomson's Marxist study *Aeschylus and Athens* (New York: Haskell House, 1972).

31. Aeschylus' Kratos says that no one is free except Zeus (*Pro.* 50). Euripides in the *Helen* makes a comparable claim for the barbarian tyrant, saying, 'Among barbarians, all are slaves but one.'

32. Io in Aeschylus's *Prometheus Bound* is the female-counterpart to Prometheus: both are victims of Zeus. They are also related in that both are descended from Oceanus, who figures also in this play, as do the Oceanids.

33. Dublin, July 1984, unpublished.

34. Brendan Kennelly, *Sophocles' Antigone: A New Version by Brendan Kennelly,* written 1984, performed 1986 (Newcastle upon Tyne: Bloodaxe, 1996).

35. Roche, 'Ireland's *Antigones*', p. 240.

36. Kennelly, *Antigone*, p. 16. Later Creon will apply these same epithets to disobedience, p. 29.

37. Ibid., p. 35.

38. Ibid., p. 48.

39. Brendan Kennelly, *Euripides' Medea: A New Version by Brendan Kennelly* (Newcastle upon Tyne: Bloodaxe, 1991).

40. Ibid., p. 42.

41. *By the Bog of Cats* . . . (following Euripides' *Medea*) in *Marina Carr: Plays,* Vol. 1, (London: Faber & Faber, 1999).

42. This is my translation, performed at the Old Globe Theatre in San Diego in autumn 2000.

43. Matthews' *Trojans*, 1994, unpublished; *Euripides' Trojan Women: A New Version by Brendan Kennelly* (Newcastle upon Tyne, Bloodaxe, 1993).

44. Quoted by Albin Lesky, *A History of Greek Literature*, trans. James Willis and Cornelis de Heer (London: Methuen, 1966).

45. Seamus Heaney, *The Cure at Troy: After Philoctetes by Sophocles* (Derry: Field Day, 1990); 'Mycenae Lookout' in *The Spirit Level* (London/Boston, Mass.: Faber & Faber, 1996).

46. Derek Mahon, *The Bacchae: After Euripides*, (Loughcrew, Oldcastle, Co. Meath: Gallery Press, 1991), p. 47.

47. See my article about this chorus, 'Vengeance is Mine, ll. 877–81: *Philia* Gone Awry in the Chorus of Euripides' *Bacchae*', in *Proceedings of the Third International Meeting of Ancient Greek Drama* (Athens: European Cultural Centre of Delphi, 1989), pp. 170–87.

48. *Irish Times* (13 February 1992).

49. Frank McGuiness, *Sophocles' Electra: A New Version* (London/Boston, Mass.: Faber & Faber, 1997).

50. Ibid., p. 7.

51. Dylan Thomas.

Translations into Irish of Greek Drama and of Other Works Concerning Greece

Síle Ní Mhurchú and Patricia Kelly*

This enquiry is confined to the nineteenth and twentieth centuries, the only period when translations from Greek made directly into Irish were published. The medieval 'translations' are, in fact, translations into Irish of Latin paraphrases of Greek materials.[1] The only serious twentieth-century translators of Greek into Irish are Fr (later Monsignor) Pádraig de Brún and George Thomson alias Seoirse Mac Tomáis (lecturer in ancient classics, a Gaelic-Hellenic scholar and a very fine classicist). Only Pádraig de Brún seriously attempted the literary translation of Greek drama.

The work of these two men, each in background and philosophy quite at variance with the other, converges in their total immersion in the literary and linguistic culture of ancient Greece and their total commitment to the culture of the Irish language as they discovered it in the early decades of the twentieth century, and in their confidence in the viability of the language as a literary medium. De Brún (1889–1960), from Grangemockler, Co. Tipperary, received his Doctorat-ès-Sciences in mathematics from the Sorbonne in 1912. He was ordained a priest in 1913, and was appointed to the chair of mathematics in Maynooth the following year, a post he held until he was elected president of University College Galway in 1945. He had been made foundation chairman of the Dublin Institute for Advanced Studies in 1940. During the Irish revolutionary period, he was an ardent nationalist and republican, and was imprisoned briefly in 1923 on suspicion of

*The introductory essay is by Síle Ní Mhurchú alone; the list of texts is the work of both authors.

87

revolutionary conspiracy.[2] A great classicist – his niece, Máire Mhac an tSaoi, the distinguished poet and woman of Irish letters, recalls his reputation, as a student, for being able to take up, at any line, *The Odyssey* and recite by memory to the finish[3] – he also had a masterly command of the major European languages. Some time before 1925, he got a house in West Kerry, and in the 1920s, 1930s and 1940s he immersed himself in the Irish dialect of Dún Chaoin. He developed an individual style and powerful literary medium which manifested itself in both his original writings and translations. While, from the 1930s, his views on the development of Irish literature were eclipsed to a certain extent by those of the far less talented polemicist, Daniel Corkery,[4] it seems that de Brún's reputation is now likely to enjoy a revival. His translation of *The Odyssey* appeared in 1990[5] and his editor, Ciarán Ó Coigligh, is now preparing for the press his translations of the *Paradiso* and *Purgatorio* of Dante's *Commedia*. All of de Brún's work in Irish is characterized by his retempering of *caint na ndaoine*, 'the language of the people', and fashioning it into a powerful intellectual tool.

By contrast, the classicist, Thomson, was a product of the socialist ferment that took place in Cambridge in the 1920s. His mother was from a Northern Irish Protestant family of republican sympathies, and she it was who turned the young George in the direction of the Irish language. On the advice of Robin Flower (Celtic scholar and manuscriptologist) and others, he visited the Great Blasket for the first time in 1924. His relationship to that Irish-speaking island community almost from the beginning took on a quasi-symbiotic character. He is best remembered now for the influence he exercized over the Blasket writer Muiris Ó Súileabháin, acting twice as his editor and general literary mentor.[6] What he detected as a form of pre-capitalist society on the Blasket Island modified his communist opinions.[7] It needs to be stressed, too, that the speech rhythms and folk poetry of that community had a deep influence on his thinking on Greek metre and on the entire Homeric question.[8] He lectured on Greek, through the medium of Irish, in University College Galway, in the period 1929–34. His excellent spoken Irish overcame the inevitable prejudice that might have denied him that position. His written Irish, both original and translated, has qualities of crispness and elegance that make for great readability, even if it lacks the power of de Brún's language, but he published no translations of Greek drama.[9]

The other translators were attempting to provide (and scantily) textbook material for the teaching of Greek through Irish in a small minority of the secondary schools in the first half of the twentieth century or basic reading material in translation for the emerging Gaelic reading public in the early years of the century.

At best, translations from the Greek were peripheral to the main thrust of revivalist writing and, in consequence, bibliographical data are difficult to track. In any case, bibliographical guides to modern Irish literature are very limited. While one, therefore, cannot claim completeness for the present enquiry, it is likely that nothing of significance has been passed over.

Drámaí Gréigise
Greek Drama[10]

Aeschylus

1 *Promethus Bound*

Prométheus fé Chuibhreach le h-Aeschylus, ar a chur in eagar Gaodhluinne le Seoirse Mac Tomáis. vi + 160 pp. Baile Átha Cliath: Oifig Díolta Foillseacháin Rialtais, 1933.

[*Prometheus Bound* by Aeschylus, edited in Irish by George Thomson. vi +160 pp. Dublin: Government Publications Sales Office, 1933.]

Greek text with textual and other notes in Irish.

Euripides

2 *Alcestis*

Alcéstis le h-Eurípidés, ar a chur in eagar Gaodhluinne le Seoirse Mac Tomáis. 239 pp. Baile Átha Cliath: Oifig Díolta

Foillseacháin Rialtais, 1932.

[*Alcestis* by Euripides, edited in Irish by George Thomson. 239
    pp. Dublin: Government Publications Sales Office, 1932.]
Greek text with textual and other notes in Irish.

3 *Iphigenia in Aulis*

Íodhbairt Ifigéine, dráma le Euripides. Pádraig de Brún d'aistrigh.
    49 pp. Baile Átha Cliath: Oifig Díolta Foillseacháin Rialtais,
    1935.

[*The Sacrifice of Iphigenia*, a play by Euripides. Translated by
    Pádraig de Brún. 49 pp. Dublin: Government Publications Sales
    Office, 1935.]

4 *Iphigenia in Tauris*

Iphigenia in Tauris le h-Eoirpid. Ar n-a chur i n-eagar i nGaedhilg
    ag an Athair Art C. Mac Giolla Eoin. Téacs Gréigise le
    brollach, nótaí agus foclóir Gréigis-Gaeilge. xiv + 228 pp. Baile
    Átha Cliath: Oifig an tSoláthair, 1950.

[*Iphigenia in Tauris* by Euripides. Edited in Irish by Rev. Art C.
    Mac Giolla Eoin. Greek text with introduction and notes in
    Irish; and Greek-Irish vocabulary. xiv + 228 pp. Dublin:
    Government Publications Sales Office, 1950.]

5 *Trojan Women* 799–818

'Traoi ["I Sálamis chumhra na mín-bheach . . ."]'. Suibhne Geilt
    d'aistrigh ó'n *Troades*, le Euripides.

['Troy'. Translated by Suibhne Geilt [pseudonym] from *Troades*
    by Euripides.]

In *Ireland To-Day* 3(3) (March 1938): 239–40.

Sophocles

6 *Antigone*

Aintighoiné, dráma le Sofoicléas. Pádraig de Brún d'aistrigh ó'n
    nGréigis. 43 pp. Baile Átha Cliath: Ponsoinbi agus Gibbs,
    Clódh na hOllscoile, 1926.

[*Antigone*, a play by Sophocles. Translated from Greek by
    Pádraig de Brún. 43 pp. Dublin: Ponsonby & Gibbs, University
    Press, 1926.]

7 *Oedipus at Colonus* 668–719

'Dán molta na hAittiche ["Fód rí-chapall an tír, a dheoraidhe . . ."].
As *Oidiopús i gColón*, dráma le Sofoicléas.' Pádraig de Brún
[d'aistrigh].

['Poem in Praise of Attica. From *Oedipus at Colonus*, a play by
Sophocles.' Translated by Pádraig de Brún.

In *The Nation* (2 April 1927): 5.

8 *Oedipus at Colonus*

Oidiopús i gColón. Dráma le Sofoicléas. Pádraig de Brún
d'aistrigh. 52 pp. Magh Nuadhat: Cuallacht Chuilm Cille,
1929.

[*Oedipus at Colonus*. A play by Sophocles. Translated by Pádraig
de Brún. 52 pp. Maynooth: Cuallacht Chuilm Cille [The
League of St Colomba], 1929.]

Contains a revised version of lines 668–719, translated in 7,
above.

9 *Oedipus Rex* 1110–1415

'*Sliocht as Rí Oidiopús* ["A shinnsir, muran misde dhom
baramhail . . ."], dráma le Sofoicléas.' Pádraig de Brún
d'aistrigh ó'n nGréigis.

[An excerpt from *King Oedipus*, a play by Sophocles. Translated
from Greek by Pádraig de Brún.]

In *Irisleabhar Muighe Nuadhad* [*Maynooth Journal*] 23 (1927):
6–12.

10 *Oedipus Rex*

Rí Oidiopús, dráma le Sofoicléas. Pádraig de Brún d'aistrigh. 44
pp. Magh Nuadhat: Cuallacht Chuilm Cille, 1928.

[*Oedipus Rex*, a play by Sophocles. Translated by Pádraig de
Brún. 44 pp. Maynooth: Cuallacht Chuilm Cille [The League of
St Colomba], 1928.]

Contains a revised version of lines 1110–1415, translated in 9,
above.

Saothair Eile Gréigise
Other Greek Texts

Aristotle, *Nicomachean Ethics*

1 *Leabhar Aristodeil dá nglaetar Béasgna Nichomhach.* Leabh. a
  1. Tomás Ua Nualláin do chuir Gaedhilg ar Ghréigis Ariostodeil.
[The Book of Aristotle entitled Nicomachean Ethics. Book I.
  Translated into Irish by Tomás Ua Nualláin.]
In *An Claidheamh Soluis* [The Sword of Light] 6, 13, 20, 27
  January, 3, 10, 17 February, 2, 9, 16, 23, 30 March, 6, 20
  April, 4, 11, 18 May 1912.

Herodotus

2 'An seana-shaol Gréagach: Scéalta ó stair Herodotus'. Seoirse
  Mac Laghmainn do chuir i nGaoluinn.
['Life in Ancient Greece: Stories from Herodotus'. Translated into
  Irish by Seoirse Mac Laghmainn (= George Thomson).]
In *An Phoblacht/The Republic*, 21, 28 January, 11 February, 10,
  17, 31 March, 14, 28 April, 19 May 1928.

Homer, *Iliad*

3 *Iliad* i 225–50
'A mheisgeóir thréith ó fhíon, tá lán dimiadh . . .', translated by
  John O'Donovan. In Owen Connellan, *A Dissertation on Irish
  Grammar*. Dublin: 1834, pp. 38–9.
Reprinted as 'Dr John O'Donovan's translation of the speech of
  Achilles'.
In *Irisleabhar na Gaedhilge/The Gaelic Journal* ii (21) (1885):
  287–8.
4 *Iliad* i–viii
An t'Íliad air chogadh na Tróighe ro chan Homear.
  Aisdríghthe ó Ghréag-Bhéarla go ran [sic] Gaoidhilge le
  Seághan, Árd-easbog Thúama. 478 pp. Baile Átha Cliath:
  Gudmhain agus a chómh-chuideacht, 1844–71.
[*The Iliad on the War of Troy which Homer sang*: Translated
  from the Greek into Irish verse by John (Mac Hale),

Archbishop of Tuam. 478 pp. Dublin: Goodwin, Son &
Nethercott, 1844–71.]

Published in eight separate parts from 1844 to 1871: i (1844), ii
(1846), iii (1851), iv (1857), v and vi (1860), vii (1869), viii
(1871).

Modern edition, in standardized spelling:

Seán Mac Héil, *Íliad Hóiméar*. Leabhair I–VIII. Réamhaiste le
Breandán Ó Doibhlin. xvi + 241 pp. Gaillimh: Officina
Typographica, 1981.

[John Mac Hale, *Homer's Iliad*. Books I–VIII. Preface by
Breandán Ó Doibhlin. xvi + 241 pp. Galway: Officina
Typographica, 1981.]

5 *Iliad* vi 407–502

'Address of Andromache to Hector ["A dhuine dhána faraoir tá
air tí . . ."]. From the original Greek of Homer's *Iliad*, Book 6,
by Archbishop McHale.'

In *An Gaodhal/The Gael* (July 1890): 971–3.

Book vi 565–690 of Mac Hale's translation.

6 *Iliad* vi 369–502

'Scaradh Hectoir le hÁndromaché. ["Sin mar adubhairt, 's
annsoin d'fhág Hector lonnra-chathbhárrach . . ."].' Pádraig de
Brún [d'aistrigh].

['The Parting of Hector and Andromache'. Translated by Pádraig
de Brún.]

In *Irisleabhar Muighe Nuadhad* [*Maynooth Journal*] 22 (1926):
12–15.

7 *Iliad* i 1–52

'Véarsaí as leabhartha Hómér. I. Tosach na hIléide. An Fiúnach
["Abair, a dhia-bhean an bhéil bhinn-bhriathraigh, fiúnach
Achilléis . . ."].' An t-Athair Pádraig de Brún d'aistrigh.

['Verses from Homer. I. The Beginning of the Iliad. The Wrath'.
Translated by Rev. Pádraig de Brún.]

In *Humanitas* ii (1) (March 1931): 14–15.

8 *Iliad* vi 390–465

'Véarsaí as leabhartha Hómér. II. Scaradh Hechtóir le
hÁndromaché ["Labhair a bhanóglach leis amhalaidh, 's amach

ón dteaghlach le Hechtor . . .".' An t-Athair Pádraig de Brún
d'aistrigh.

['Verses from Homer. II. The parting of Hector and
Andromache'. Translated by Rev. Pádraig de Brún.]

In *Humanitas* ii (1) (March 1931): 15–16.

Revised version of some lines from 6, above.

9 *Iliad* i

'Fuíoll Léinn Sheoirse Mhic Thomáis, II. An tIliad le Hóiméar.
Leabhar a hAon'. In eagar ag Pádraig Ó Fiannachta.

['The Scholarly Remains of George Thomson, II. The Iliad by
Homer. Book One'. Ed. Pádraig Ó Fiannachta.]

In *Léachtaí Cholm Cille* 18 (1988): 169–82.

A prose translation.

Homer, *Odyssey*

10 *An Odaisé*. An Monsignor Pádraig de Brún a d'aistrigh. Ciarán
Ó Coigligh a chuir in eager. Máire Mhac an tSaoi a scríobh an
brollach. xix + 462 pp. Baile Átha Cliath: Coiscéim, 1990.

[*The Odyssey*. Translated by Monsignor Pádraig de Brún. Edited
by Ciarán Ó Coigligh. Introduction by Máire Mhac an tSaoi.
xix + 462 pp. Dublin: Coiscéim, 1990.]

Lucian of Samosata

Dialogues of the Gods

11 'Agallamh na ndéithe ó Lúcián'. Peadar Ua Laoghaire
d'aistrigh.

[*Dialogues of the Gods* by Lucian. Translated by Peadar Ua
Laoghaire.]

In *Journal of the Ivernian Society* i (1908–9): 47–51, 119–25;
189–93; 247–52; ii (1909–10): 49–53, 111–17, 161–71,
236–42; iii (1910–11): 49–55, 113–19, 135–41, 207–13; iv
(1911): 3–9, 65–72, 129–35, 193–9; v (1912–13): 1–6, 65–70.

Republished as a single volume:

Lúcián. An t-Athair Peadar Ua Laoghaire, Canónach, S. P.
d'aistrigh. iv + 185 pp. Baile Átha Cliath: Brún agus Ó Nóláin,
1924.

[*Lucian*. Translated by Rev. Peadar Ua Laoghaire, Canon and parish priest. iv + 185 pp. Dublin: Browne & Nolan, 1924.]

12 *Vera Historia*, I and II

Vera Historia; scéal ainspianta a chéad-cheap Lucian san Ghréigis. Domhnall Ó Mathghamhna a chuir i nGaedhilg. vi + 79 pp. Baile Átha Cliath: Oifig Díolta Foillseacháin Rialtais, 1931.

[*Vera Historia*, a preposterous tale written originally in Greek by Lucian. Translated into Irish by Domhnall Ó Mathghamhna. vi + 79 pp. Dublin: Government Publications Sales Office, 1931.]

Originally published in the *Sunday Independent*, 21 June 1925 – 25 April 1926.

Plato

Apology

13 'Socratés ghá chosaint féin.' Uilliam Ó Rinn do thiontuigh i nGaedhilg.

['The Apology of Socrates', translated into Irish by Uilliam Ó Rinn.]

In *Irish Freedom* (October, November, December 1913; January, February, March 1914).

14 'The Apology of Socrates' (translated by) D(omhnall) Ó M(athghamhna).

In the *Sunday Independent*, 17 March–1 December 1929.

Apology, *Crito* and *Phaedo*

15 *Breith báis ar Eagnuidhe*. Trí cómhráidhte d'ár cheap Platón (*Apologia*, *Critón*, *Phaedón*). Seoirse Mac Laghmhainn do chuir i nGaodhluinn. 173 pp. Baile Átha Cliath, C. S. Ó Fallamhain Teo. i gcomhar le hOifig an tSoláthair, 1929.

[*Sentence of Death on a Sage*. Three dialogues written by Plato (*Apology*, *Crito*, *Phaedo*). Translated into Irish by Seoirse Mac Laghmhainn [= George Thomson/Seoirse Mac Tomáis]. 173 pp. Dublin: C. S. Fallon Ltd. in association with the Stationery Office, 1929.]

Critias

16 *Inis Atlaint*, scéal a chéad-cheap Platón 'san Ghréigis.

Domhnall Ó Mathghamhna do chuir i nGaedhilg. 79 pp. Baile
Átha Cliath: Brún agus Ó Nualláin, 1935.
[*The Island of Atlantis*, a story written originally in Greek by
Plato. Translated into Irish by Domhnall Ó Mathghamhna. 79
pp. Dublin: Browne & Nolan, 1935]
Originally published in the *Sunday Independent*, 5 April–2
August 1931)

Crito

17 '*Crito*, or the Duty of a Citizen.' (Translated by) D(omhnall)
Ó M(athghamhna).
In the *Sunday Independent*, 8 December 1929–30 March 1930.

Symposium

18 'Fuíoll Léinn Sheoirse Mhic Thomáis, III. An Suimpóisiam'. In
eagar ag Pádraig Ó Fiannachta.
['The Scholarly Remains of George Thomson III. The
Symposium'. Ed. Pádraig Ó Fiannachta.]
In *Irisleabhar Mhá Nuad* [*Maynooth Journal*] (1988): 161–89;
(1989): 76–102.

Plutarch, *Lives*

19 *Saoghal-ré na nGracchi*. Plutarchus do chéad-cheap 'san
Ghréigis. Domhnall Ó Mathghamhna do chuir i nGaedhilg. 64
pp. Baile Átha Cliath: Oifig Díolta Foillseacháin Rialtais, 1933.
[*Lives of the Gracchi*. Written originally by Plutarch in Greek.
Translated into Irish by Domhnall Ó Mathghamhna. 64 pp.
Dublin: Government Publications Sales Office, 1933.]
20 *Démostenés agus Cicero: tuairisc a mbeathadh*. Plútarc do
chéad-cheap 'san Ghréigis. Domhnall Ó Mathghamhna
d'aistrigh go Gaedhilg. 116 pp. Baile Átha Cliath: Oifig Díolta
Foillseacháin Rialtais, 1935.
[*Demosthenes and Cicero: an Account of their Lives*. Written
originally by Plutarch in Greek. Translated into Irish by
Domhnall Ó Mathghamhna. 116 pp. Dublin: Government
Publications Sales Office, 1935.]
21 *Beathaí Phlútairc*. Pádraig de Brún d'aistrigh ón nGréigis. 272

pp. Baile Átha Cliath: Oifig Díolta Foillseacháin Rialtais, 1936.
[Plutarch's *Lives*. Translated from Greek by Pádraig de Brún. 272
pp. Dublin: Government Publications Sales Office, 1936.]

Theocritus, *Idylls* XV

22 'Fuíoll Léinn Sheoirse Mhic Thomáis, I. An Lá Féile ["An
bhfuil Praxinoé istigh? . . ."].' In eagar ag Pádraig Ó Fiannachta.
['The Scholarly Remains of George Thomson, I. The Festival'. Ed.
Pádraig Ó Fiannachta.]
In *Léachtaí Cholm Cille* [*Colomban Lectures*] 18 (1988):
164–9.

Thucydides

23 *The Peloponnesian War*, Book ii, Chapters 34–46
Óráid Caointe Phericléis. Domhnall Ó Mathghamhna d'aistrigh
ó'n mbun-Ghréigis. 23 pp. Baile Átha Cliath: Brún agus Ó
Nóláin, 1930.
[*The Funeral Oration of Pericles*. Translated from the original
Greek by Domhnall Ó Mathghamhna. 23 pp. Dublin: Browne
& Nolan, 1930.]
Originally published in the *Sunday Independent*, April–June
1930.
24 *The Peloponnesian War*, Book iv, Chapters 1–49
Tuicid. Leabhar IV, Caib. 1–49. Pádraig Ó Meachair a chuir in
eagar. xxviii + 191 pp. Baile Átha Cliath: Oifig an tSoláthair,
1964.
[*Thucydides*. Book iv, Chapters 1–49. Edited by Pádraig Ó
Meachair. xxviii + 191 pp. Dublin: Stationery Office, 1964.]
Greek text with introduction and explanatory notes in Irish.

Xenophon, *Anabasis*

25 Csenophón *Anabasis* II. An t-Athair Cathal Mac Giobúin do
chuir in eagar. xx + 121 pp. Baile Átha Cliath: Oifig an
tSoláthair, 1944.
[*Anabasis* II. Edited by Rev. Cathal Mac Giobúin. 121 pp.
Dublin: Stationery Office, 1944.]

Greek text with introduction, summary and notes in Irish.
26 *Anabasis* VII, 4
' "An fhairrge! An fhairrge". Csenofón Aitéanach d'aithris.'
Maud Joynt d'aistrigh.
[' "The Sea! The Sea!" by Xenophon the Athenian.' Translated by
Maud Joynt.]
In *Celtia* iii (5) (May–June 1903): 86–7.

Saothair Ilghnéitheacha
Miscellaneous Works

1 *Stair na Gréige*. An Monsignor ró-oirmhidneach Pádraig de
Brún do chuir Gaeilge ar *A History of Greece*. le J[ohn]
B[agnell] Bury. Cuid a hAon: Ón tosach go claoi na bPeirseach.
Cuid a Dó: Fás, bláthú agus meath impireacht na nAtaenach.
Cuid a Trí: Ó chreachadh na nAtaenach go bás Alastair Mhóir.
914 pp. Baile Átha Cliath: Oifig an tSoláthair, 1954.
[John Bagnell Bury's *A History of Greece* translated into Irish by
the Very Rev. Monsignor Pádraig de Brún. Part One: From the
Beginning to the Defeat of the Persians. Part Two: The Growth,
Rise and Decline of the Athenian Empire. Part Three: From the
Downfall of Athens to the Death of Alexander the Great.
Dublin: Stationery Office, 1954.]
2 Seoirse Mac Tomáis, *Tosnú na Feallsúnachta*. 76 pp. Baile
Átha Cliath: Oifig Díolta Foillseacháin Rialtais, 1935.
[George Thomson, *The Beginnings of Philosophy*, 76 pp. Dublin:
Government Publications Sales Office, 1935.]
3 M. A. North and A. E. Hillard, *Bun-chúrsa Ceapadóireachta
Gréigise*. Mairghéad Ní Éimhthigh d'aistrigh ón mBéarla. 376
pp. Baile Átha Cliath: Oifig an tSoláthair, 1941.
[M. A. North and A. E. Hillard, *Greek Prose Composition*.
Translated by Mairghéad Ní Éimhthigh from English. 376 pp.
Dublin: Stationery Office, 1941.]
4 E. A. Sonnenschein, *Graiméar Gréigise*, le E. A. Sonnenschein,
Mairghéad Ní Éimhthigh M.A. d'aistrigh ó'n mBéarla. Cuid I:

Deilbh-eolaidheacht. Cuid II: Cóimhréir. 472 pp. Baile Átha Cliath: Oifig an tSoláthair, 1942.

[E. A. Sonnenschein, *Greek Grammar*. Translated by Mairghéad Ní Éimhthigh from English. Vol. I: *Morphology*. Vol. II: *Syntax*. 472 pp. Dublin: Stationery Office, 1942.]

5 An t-Athair Pádraig Ua Duinnín, *Aistí ar litridheacht Ghréigise is Laidne*. 162 pp. Baile Átha Cliath: C. S. Ó Fallamhain Teo. i gcomhar le hOifig an tSoláthair, 1929.

[Rev. Patrick Dinneen, *Essays on Greek and Latin Literature*. 162 pp. Dublin: C. S. Fallon in collaboration with the Stationery Office, 1929].

Notes

1. W. B. Stanford, 'Towards a History of Classical Influences in Ireland', *Proceedings of the Royal Irish Academy* (C) 70 (1970): 13–91; W. B. Stanford, *Ireland and the Classical Tradition* (Dublin: 1976); Frederick Ahl, 'Uilix mac Leirtis: The Classical Hero in Irish Metamorphosis', in R. Warren (ed.), *The Art of Translation* (Boston, MA: 1989), pp. 173–98; Ludwig Bieler, 'The Classics in Celtic Ireland', in R. R. Bolgar (ed.), *Classical Influences on European Culture AD 500–1500: Proceedings of an international conference held at King's College Cambridge April 1969* (Cambridge: 1971), pp. 45–49; W. Berschin, 'Griechisches bei den Iren', in Heinz Löwe, *Die Iren und Europa im früheren Mittelalter* (Stuttgart: 1982), pp. 501–10; Bernhard Bischoff, 'Das griechische Element in der abendländischen Bildung des Mittelalters', in B. Bischoff, *Mittelalterliche Studien*, Vol. II (Stuttgart: 1967); Mario Esposito, 'The Knowledge of Greek in Ancient Ireland', *Studies* [Dublin] 1 (1912): 665–83, repr. in Mario Esposito, *Latin Learning in Mediaeval Ireland*, ed. M. Lapidge (London: 1988), Chap. 8; Whitley Stokes (ed. and trans.), *Togail Troi: The Destruction of Troy* (Calcutta: 1881); Whitley Stokes (ed. and trans.), 'The Destruction of Troy', in W. Stokes and E. Windisch (eds), *Irische Texte*, series 2 (1) (Leipzig: 1884), pp. 1–142; Kuno Meyer (ed. and trans.), *Merugud Ulix maicc Leirtis: the Irish Odyssey* (London: 1886); George Calder (ed. and trans.), *Togail na Tebe: The Thebaid of Statius* (Cambridge: 1922); Leslie Diane Myrick, *From 'De excidio*

Troiae historia' to the *'Togail Troí': Literary-Cultural Synthesis in a Medieval Irish Adaptation of Dares' Troy Tale* (Heidelberg: 1993); Barbara Hillers, 'Ulysses and the Judge of Truth: Sources and Meanings in the Irish *Odyssey', Peritia* 13 (1999): 194–23.

2. Diarmuid Breathnach and Máire Ní Mhurchú, *Beathaisnéis a ceathair: 1882–1982* (Dublin: 1994), pp. 23–26.

3. Monsignor Pádraig de Brún a d'aistrigh, Ciarán Ó Coigligh a chuir in eagar, Máire Mhac an tSaoi a scríobh an brollach, *An Odaisé* (Baile Átha Cliath: 1990), p. vi [Monsignor Pádraig de Brún (trans.), *The Odyssey*, ed. Ciarán Ó Coigligh (Dublin: 1990), p. vi (in preface by Máire Mhac an tSaoi)].

4. Máire Mhac an tSaoi, 'Pádraig de Brún agus an Ghaeilge: Saol agus Saothar in Aisce?' ['Pádraig de Brún and the Irish Language: A Life and Work in Vain?'], in Pádraig Ó Fiannachta (ed.), *Maigh Nuad agus an Ghaeilge* ['Maynooth and The Irish Language']; Léachtaí Cholm Cille 23 (Maigh Nuad: 1993), pp. 140–60 (141).

5. De Brún, *An Odaisé.*

6. Muiris Ó Súilleabháin, *Fiche Blian ag Fás* ['Twenty Years a-Growing'] (Dublin: 1933). This is the autobiography of Ó Súilleabháin whom Thomson encouraged and helped to write.

7. Eoin Ó Murchú, 'George Thomson agus an Cumannachas' ['George Thomson and Communism'], in Máire Ní Chéilleachair (ed.), *Ceiliúradh an Bhlascaoid* [*Celebrating the Blasket Island*] 4. *Seoirse Mac Tomáis 1903–87* (Dublin: 2000), pp. 105–11.

8. Margaret Alexiou, 'George Thomson: the Greek Dimension', in Ní Chéilleachair, *Ceiliúradh an Bhlascaoid*, pp. 52–74.

9. For a brief survey and appreciation of Thomson's works in Irish, see Seán Ó Lúing, 'George Thomson', *Classics Ireland* 3 (1996): 141–62.

10. Entries are listed alphabetically, according to author and title, then chronologically, according to date of publication.

'After *Hippolytus*':
Irish Versions of Phaedra's Story

Richard Cave

The story of Semele might seem a curious point of entry into a discussion about Irish dramatizations of the myth of Phaedra and Hippolytus, but it does have a relevance to my larger purpose. Semele, as Ovid tells the tale in *Metamorphoses* (Book III), was hated by Juno for attracting the attentions of Jove; disguising herself as an aged crone, the goddess prevailed on Semele, largely through flattery, to persuade Jove to appear to her in all the majesty of his godhead. Semele played on Jove's infatuation for her to trick him into agreeing to grant her a favour as proof of his esteem without his knowing precisely what that favour entailed; as instructed by Juno, she then asked Jove to visit their next union with none of his celestial radiance dimmed, as had previously been his habit out of respect for her mortal vision. Reluctantly he fulfilled the bargain and the intensity of his brilliance and of her raptures burned Semele to ashes. None of the mortals loved by Jove (Europa, Leda, Danae, Alcmene) seems to have met a comfortable fate, but none fared as cruelly as Semele in being totally consumed by the divine passion. Her selfhood was not marginalized like theirs before the imperative of the god's lust but utterly obliterated. If the others fared somewhat better, it was because Jove chose to appear to them in disguise: he undertook a metamorphosis (into a bull, a swan, a shower of gold, a double of the woman's husband): the terror of his divinity was at once revealed yet subdued through a process of transformation.

These stories (Semele's in particular) offer a useful analogy for the dangers of attempting to dramatize situations that through sheer age and the respect accorded by repeated artistic use have become archetypal. A playwright takes on a peculiarly difficult challenge in choosing to handle such material: it is a process fraught with hazards. James Hillman, the Jungian analyst, defines archetypes as metaphors, images for 'the *deepest patterns of psychic functioning*' (the italics are his); and, to further justify the argument of that opening paragraph above, he continues: 'By setting up a universe which tends to hold everything we do, see and say in the sway of its cosmos, an archetype is best comparable with a god.'[1] Archetypes in this view are fecund with potential meaning and as such are infinitely complex, inclusive: they tap a basic root structure of experience and so are to be seen as 'a necessary universal with consequents'.[2] One danger in dramatising an archetypal situation is the risk of reductionism, a limiting of the inclusivity to which Hillman refers, to the point where the resulting play seems trivial to an audience, banal by contrast with the paradigm that has inspired it.[3] Closely allied to this is the dramatization that reveals too readily its shaping source to the audience so that all subsequent developments of the situation become easily predictable, which rapidly loses that audience's imaginative engagement except at a limited and chiefly cerebral level.

This is the problem that, for example, Eugene O'Neill never adequately negotiates with much of *Mourning Becomes Electra* (first staged in 1931). The closer the American tragedy patterns itself on its Greek source in the *Oresteia*, the more an informed audience concentrates on the ingenuity that went to the devising of the modern parallels at the expense of focusing on any thematic life that might lie behind the surface of the drama, which would invite a fuller engagment with the performance. If this criticism does not hold true for the final part of *Mourning Becomes Electra*, it is because O'Neill there chooses to depart significantly from his source by marginalizing Orin/Orestes as weak, debilitated, neurasthenic and suicidal, thus allowing his forceful and ever-resilient Lavinia/Electra the better to command our attention. O'Neill's heroine steadily and implacably throughout Part Three (significantly called 'The Haunted') *internalizes* all that creates the action of Aeschylus' *Eumenides*, accepting as her fate the past that has determined her genetic and emotional inheritance and sitting in judgement on herself for those actions of her own which have of necessity compelled her to adopt the harsh discipline demanded by such a stoical mind-set. There are here no intervening and controlling deities the like of Athena or Apollo; no rule of law for the general community is established; no vengeful Furies are first propitiated and then honoured in a new guise as chastening and tutelary guardians. They are all instead sensed as presences at work in the depths of Lavinia's psyche, where consciousness and the unconscious do battle behind the mask-like composure that O'Neill's directions insist should set hard into the actress's face as the play closes. In that last act of *Mourning Becomes Electra* Aeschylus' tragic cycle has not been adapted, plagiarized, or imitated but rather it has been creatively reworked: the substance has undergone a transformation (a credible metamorphosis) from classical Greece to post-Freudian America. While the archetype is all-too-visible in the opening acts, O'Neill's creativity seems virtually subsumed within Aeschylus' genius; but in the final scenes he finds his independence, though not at Aeschylus' expense: the theories defining Freudian and Jungian analytical practice allow O'Neill comfortably to embrace Aeschylus' archetype as a metaphor with distinct resonances relating to his own psychological concerns. *Mourning Becomes Electra* is in many ways an object lesson for the modern dramatist, demonstrating in equal measure, as it does, the challenges, the risks and the potential for innovation to be found in taking one's inspiration from Greek myth and classical tragic dramaturgy.

The first of the Irish engagements with the myth of Phaedra and Hippolytus that I wish to examine, Brian Friel's *Living Quarters* (first staged at the Abbey Theatre, Dublin, in March 1977),[4] seems by its very nature to be the work of a playwright alert to the many dangers inherent in such an enterprise. This is implicit in the careful description of the play as 'after *Hippolytus*'. Tyrone Guthrie, the theatre director, was an early mentor to Friel; and Guthrie had achieved by the time of his death an illustrious record of revivals of

Greek tragedy in the modern theatre. The strengths of these productions at London's Old Vic, in Minneapolis and at the Edinburgh Festival lay in their exploratory use of masks and a resultant ritualized style of acting, and in the deployment of massed movement for the Choruses (manipulating crowds within varying sizes of stage space repeatedly won Guthrie considerable praise). None of these qualities is directly to be observed in Friel's tragedy, although attending Guthrie's rehearsals for a period taught him a great deal about proxemics and stage space; and he deploys in this play a remarkable freedom by requiring a divided setting, showing hallway, living-room and garden, which allows him to bring together a group within one area while isolating one or two characters to poignant effect in another. This account, however, suggests a naturalistic deployment of the playing space and it is here that the problems in staging *Living Quarters* begin: they all focus on the issue of an appropriate style of performance in the theatre.

The action may be described as following the story-line of Euripides' play: Commandant Frank Butler has been away from Ireland for some months leading a peace-keeping force for the United Nations and returns a celebrated hero of the campaign only to learn that in his absence his young second wife, Anna, has had a brief affair with his estranged son, Ben. But this 'plot' is wholly marginalized; the affair is now over; the issue of who seduced whom is treated as negligible in marked contrast to either Euripides' focus of interest or Racine's (in his *Phèdre* of 1677) on the illicit nature of the passions which generate the action. With *Living Quarters* the past has to be pieced together by the audience often through tangential inferences (until the final moment of outright revelation). The characters, composed of Butler's family and a friend of long standing, are, we discover, all too familiar with the events and seem determined to downplay them, since the outcome is the Commandant's suicide (a departure from the classical source) in which they all feel implicated. Where the guilty passion of stepmother for stepson is examined by Euripides and Racine with scrupulously balanced attention to the inner torments of both suffering characters, scarcely any stage-time is devoted by Friel to motivating the affair in depth (Anna feels used, abandoned and bored; Ben has a deep-seated but largely unconscious urge to punish his father for his mother's death). Instead the subject of Friel's play would appear to be not individuals in conflict but a family group coping with the intricate workings of guilt within it in the wake of Butler's death.

To achieve the particular effect he is after, Friel would appear to be taking up a concept (borrowed from Japanese Noh drama) that furnished Yeats with a structure and dramatic impetus for many of his later plays: the idea of a process of 'dreaming back' (usually undertaken by a dead soul or ghost), of retracking one's way through one's past in an effort to discover some moment of choice, some hidden motive, some now-forgotten impulse to action that might explain how one's course became implacably directed towards tragedy and guilt. The hope motivating the search through memory is of finding through this 'significant moment' some degree of atonement. Yeats first recognized the possibilities of such a theme in his draft versions of *The Countess Cathleen*, but it does not begin completely to structure the dramatic action until *The Dreaming of the Bones* (written in 1916–17; first staged in 1931) and *Calvary* (written in 1918), two of his four *Plays for Dancers*.[5] The most developed expression of the concept, however, is to be found in three of his late works: *The Words upon the Window-Pane* (staged 1930), *Purgatory* (staged 1938) and *The Death of Cuchulain* (first staged posthumously in 1945).[6] Beckett was to take up and transform the 'dreaming back' structure into the nightmarish purgatorial experiences that, in particular, shape *Krapp's Last Tape* (staged 1958), *Play* (written in 1962–3, first staged in England in 1964), *Not I* (written in 1972, first staged in England in 1973), *That Time* (written in 1974–5, staged 1976), and *Footfalls* (written in 1975, staged 1976). It is worth rehearsing the dates of composition and staging in this way since they readily demonstrate the frequency with which this acutely existentialist mode of drama captured the imagination of two theatrical predecessors within the Irish tradition whom Friel has acknowledged as potent influences on his work. Such a listing of examples also shows what a widely diverse range of subjects can be addressed and tones achieved with this structural technique.

The 'dreaming back' in *Living Quarters* has one notable feature which marks a departure from its usage by Yeats and Beckett: where in their works there is a single dreamer who, as always in the Noh drama, searches the deeps of mind in quest of release from the overwhelming torment that accompanies the acceptance of responsibility for a tragic event, in Friel's play it is the family, severally and corporately, who seek atonement.[7] We, as audience, have to accept as a 'given' (and it requires a massive suspension of disbelief) the premise that the Butlers have contrived to draft their experiences into a script, a playtext which enshrines and confirms their every move and word during the period of time that led from the father's return till his death. Their 'dreaming back' must, therefore, be played out exactly as the script dictates; and so the potential for free will on anyone's part is constricted, however much at times they may individually try to resist its determining power. The effect that this device has in performance (particularly for any spectator familiar with *Hippolytus*) is to suggest that the characters are all endeavouring to break away from the power of the dramatic (but, more importantly, the psychological) archetype to shape their lives to a given schematic pattern. They do not want to conform to 'type'; and only Frank, the father-figure, finds a way out of the dilemma by breaking the accepted ordering of events in committing suicide. By refusing to imitate Theseus, his prototype in the story, he brings not destruction on the son-figure but a death of the heart and spirit to everyone in the family circle, since all feel implicated in Frank's death. No one foresaw the inevitability of that death, though they all sense its inexorable progress in retrospect; and so no one moved to direct the action towards a different resolution while they all had time and the freedom of will to do it. To keep them to the demands of their scripted text (it exists materially on stage in the form of a ledger) the characters have invented an individual, whom they have named 'Sir'; his function (and his existence in the play is confined entirely to that function) is to direct their performances to accord with absolute precision to the 'book'. Significantly, Sir refuses ever to take on the further role of Judge, who would assign to them precise degrees of culpability and related punishments. There is to be no means of assuaging either their private or their shared knowledge of remorse.

Again there is a precedent within the tradition of Irish drama for Sir, this largely silent watcher and controller of events.[8] In the fifth season (1931–2) of Edwards and MacLiammoir's Gate Theatre they staged the first and what proved the most popular of Mary Manning's plays, *Youth's the Season – ?* It is a brilliant satire on the 'bright young things' (Manning's own, recognizable contemporaries) then peopling Dublin's partying middle classes. MacLiammoir, who played in it, described it as 'a curious mixture of Cowardly influences and unfinished Joycean symphonies', which nicely evokes the quality of the dialogue.[9] Edwards, who directed it, not surprisingly chose to recall the difficulty the play posed for him in relation to style:

'Youth's the Season – ?' departs from the naturalistic only by the inclusion of one character who is apparently perfectly rational and accountable, but whose function is something more than his place in the story. Completely silent throughout, a clouded mirror in which the vague reflection of something more than the surface of things is seen, Egosmith is the silent reflection of another self.[10]

Egosmith, like Sir, hardly quits the stage and he acts indeed as a mirror to the other characters, one to whom each addresses in confidence some insight into a deeper self, normally kept firmly hidden behind a nonchalant façade. He represents to some degree the moral probity on which the social satire rests. Wholly passive as a listening presence, Egosmith is the means by which the other characters sit in judgement on themselves. Sir is a more developed conception in being allied closely by the characters in *Living Quarters* with the workings of fate (as distinct from judgement); but, like Egosmith, his role and function render him magisterial, unemotional, steely.

The premise of the script and the attendant implication that Sir, who possesses the 'book', is directing the characters through a rehearsal (more pointedly *une répétition*, as the French term it) takes the process of dreaming back away from an exclusively Yeatsian or Beckettian inspiration towards Pirandello and his existentialist preoccupations with identity, which he chose to investigate through the medium of theatre and its need to create 'credible' illusions. The linking of Yeats with Pirandello is not far-fetched: *The Words upon the Window-Pane* stages the dreaming back through a seance in which the angry ghost of Jonathan Swift possesses the medium, Mrs Henderson, displacing the ghostly presences she had intended to invoke; the members of the audience then experience a play for voices ventriloquized by the medium and imagine one play taking place in the spirit world, even as they watch another in the form of a realistic drama (the representation of the seance and its own attendant audience, which is situated in a Dublin tenement). Passion and its workings on the spectator's imagination make the play-within-the-play (Swift's reliving the anguish of his relations with Stella and Vanessa) seem more 'real', though not in any conventional sense 'embodied', than the framing drama set in Dublin in 'present time'. Yeats's play pursues a profoundly metaphysical argument by exploring the nature of acting, of *inhabiting* a role while *performing*. During the time of the play's composition Yeats's letters on several occasions refer to Pirandello's explorations of illusion and appearance; and Pirandello's *Henry IV*, *The Pleasure of Honesty* and *The Rules of the Game* had been staged at the Abbey Theatre over the preceding six years by the Dublin Drama League under Lennox Robinson's direction at times when Yeats was resident in Dublin. Yeats, well versed in the best of contemporary modern theatre, would seem in *The Words upon the Window-Pane* to be offering a very personal exercise in Pirandellian metatheatricality.[11]

The same observation might be made of Friel's *Living Quarters*. He would appear to be setting his drama deliberately within the context of a rehearsal in order to examine the conflict in the actor between the demands of the role (as determined by all the conventions that go to the creating of a performance) and those of the intervening self. This is to enter the same territory as Pirandello's *Six Characters in Search of an Author*; but Pirandello, like Yeats in *The Words upon the Window-Pane*, deploys the device of the play-within-the-play the better to distinguish for his audience between different levels of representation: the acted role, the constructed and carefully projected social identity, and the deep inner core which may be defined as the passionate self. The context of rehearsal allows Pirandello to show the layers of masks any actor learns to deploy and to use that process of layering as a metaphor through which to analyse his more philosophical preoccupation with existential anguish. The characters of *Living Quarters* are by contrast allowed only one dimension of reality in which to exist on stage before us as audience: the dimension occasioned by the scripted play. While we sense this is a performance of their devising, we are allowed access to no alternative dimension of reality which might serve as a frame through which to make the kinds of discrimination that Yeats and Pirandello's metatheatrical devices encourage us to pursue. This, one might argue, is a play-within which has no further play in which to situate itself. Alternatively, one might argue, perhaps, that *Living Quarters* presents us with the framing play and that we have to imagine that Euripides' *Hippolytus* is the play-within-that-play which Friel's characters are resisting having to perform, being reluctant to conform to archetypal patterns of behaviour. Either way we are left with only half the theatrical equation so that the metaphysical ramifications of Friel's drama are left largely unrealized. It is this deficiency which poses an insurmountable hurdle for cast and director when trying to determine an appropriate style with which to interpret *Living Quarters*. At first view, as was argued above, the play's dialogue, setting and rhythms would seem to invite a Chekhovian naturalistic staging; but how is a director to reconcile that naturalism with action and intimations of ritual that are palpably 'after' Euripides, with metaphysical imperatives that are 'after' Yeats and Beckett, and with metatheatrical questioning that is 'after' Pirandello (not to mention a surreal structural device that is 'after' Mary Manning)? It is as if Friel is so aware of the dangers and difficulties of writing a play 'after' a Greek classical archetype that he has chosen to write a play out of and about that very consciousness of the hazards confronting him, which in consequence are left wholly unresolved.[12] In trying to avoid predictability in shaping his dramatic action 'after' an archetype, Friel has created a drama in *Living Quarters* which lacks any definable centre; a maelstrom of ideas circles about a thematic void.[13]

Such criticisms cannot be levelled against an earlier Irish deployment of the Phaedra myth in T. C. Murray's *Autumn Fire* (first staged at the Abbey in September 1924).[14] Murray's first encounter with any form of drama had significantly been his reading of Racine's *Phèdre* while training to be a teacher at St Patrick's College, Drumcondra. He had been impressed by the intensity that develops in Racine's tragedies when a group of characters are brought together within a constricting space, where passions are for much of the action suppressed in the interest of preserving an agreed decorum of behaviour but erupt finally from their restraint with devastating consequences. In Racine's works Murray also experienced drama that fearlessly addresses archetypes, classical and biblical; indeed his plays demonstrate the enduring power of archetypes and the need to respect that power even within as seemingly regulated a society as the court of Louis XIV. Murray's inspiration within his best plays was the rural peasant community of County Cork where he had grown up; he returned there from Drumcondra to become a village schoolmaster until 1915 when he moved to Dublin. These were people who could not afford the luxury of a civilized decorum; their lives were patterned to the harsh, energy-sapping rhythms of a working farm or smallholding; the sheer pressure of time that of necessity had to be devoted to securing a basic living gave them no chance to expatiate on their sentiments or develop subtleties of expression or feeling. Unlike Synge's vagabonds, tinkers and travellers, they were prisoners to the demands of working the land; but they were Murray's own people and, for all the material bleakness of their lives, they were in his representation of them not without dignity or passion. Much as he admired Synge's lyrical wordplay, Murray eschewed such a self-conscious stylization of speech. He favoured the realism of a darker, more prosaic diction coloured only by the effortful experience of the round of rural tasks. Such duties circumscribe the lives of his characters as rigorously as decorum constrains the existence of Racine's; the farmhouse kitchen (a particularly limited space on the old Abbey stage) became in Murray's plays as a consequence a credible site of tragedy.

If Murray's attention to detail brings a scrupulous realism to his representations of the Cork peasantry, it is a meticulous control of the pacing of dramatic episodes that brings a similar degree of scruple to his handling of archetypal situations and characters. He carefully takes time to establish complexities of characterization, lingering to clarify emotional tensions and differences in sensibility between his characters without disturbing his evocation of the rhythms of Irish rural existence which creates the surface of each play. The archetype is deeply rooted in this particular, precisely observed world and its presence emerges gradually to deepen the tragic climax, only when Murray has judged that that first dimension of reality is fully established. Only in the final stages of a play's reception or, perhaps, later still in retrospect does the shaping force of the archetype affect a spectator's perception. Its presence does not intrude itself to control response, but rather is *found*; and its discovery enriches one's insight and understanding. Often that understanding is deepened by Murray's technique of subtly overlayering archetypes which also ensures that no one pattern asserts a dominant and a potentially limiting control over one's interpretation of a play.

To take Murray's first attempt at tragedy as an example: *Birthright* (staged at the Abbey in October 1910) examines the roots of conflict between two brothers for the inheritance of their father's meagre property; one (Hugh) is genial, socially gregarious, but lacking in innate, concentrated attention to the demands of running a farm; the other and younger brother (Shane) is surly, a loner, but possessed of the necessary gifts of good, thrifty husbandry. The father, Bat, favours Shane but respects the traditions of primogeniture; against his will he arranges for Shane's passage to America (a trunk bearing Shane's name and clothing is a focal symbol of the action) but, out of rage at Hugh's thoughtlessness which results in the loss of the family's mare (a mainstay of their market-centred economy), he substitutes his older son's name on the label as a gesture of disinheritance: 'Hugh Morrissey, Passenger Queenstown to Boston, *via* Campania'.[15] A conflict between the brothers (each accuses the other of being a 'grabber') escalates into a fight in which Hugh is killed (originally Shane's action was deliberate; but Murray succumbed to critical pressure and revised the ending, making the death an accident). In that conclusion one detects a retelling of the story of Cain and Abel. But the conflict, growing apace throughout the play, is focused on the future ownership of Bat's farmstead; land-hunger, that recurring passion that fuels so much Irish tragic culture, ownership-as-power through mastery of the soil, overlays the biblical archetype with resonances of the myth of Polyneices and Eteocles, Oedipus' sons, who fought to their mutual destruction for possession of the city of Thebes. The long, opening sequence of the second act (in which the boys' mother, Maura, breaks the news of his enforced departure to Hugh) establishes, however, a profound emotional bond between mother and elder son, showing the extent to which she has favoured him over Shane (Shane's accusing her of this precipitates the brothers into their fight); and here a third archetype, the tale of Jacob and Esau, divided from each other by their mother's unashamed favouring of the latter, fuses with the other two. (The title of the play invokes this biblical parallel.) Long before Shane's outburst against his mother, Maura's cherishing of Hugh has been intimated in her repeated defence of his conduct when Hugh becomes the subject of Bat's wrath and criticism. Initially all the tensions in the household are contained by the need of the group to sustain the livelihood of the farm on which they all depend. The scene between Hugh and Maura, where an increasing intimacy between the two carries troubling Oedipal overtones, is twice disrupted at intervals by Bat's needing more light to assist him and Shane in delivering a cow outside in the byre; the threatened loss of cow and calf and Bat's sheer physical exhaustion heighten his coarse derision of Hugh later in the scene. Motivations grow like this out of the particular verisimilitude Murray establishes for his play; they are not factitiously shaped to meet the demands of the archetypal source. A spectator does not need in fact to know any of the archetypal tales on which the play is based to appreciate *Birthright*, but knowledge of them invests the action with a primal power and inexorability which allow Murray to endow his peasant characters with a tragic stature. The tensions, the conflicts between them with their focus on possession of what is clearly a small parcel of land, are in consequence never allowed to seem petty. The presence of the archetypal ensures for the reception of *Birthright* an appropriate integrity.

In terms of its dramaturgy, *Autumn Fire* follows many of the techniques that Murray innovated while writing *Birthright*.[16] *Autumn Fire* may justifiably be described as also being 'after *Hippolytus*' but that underpinning archetype only slowly reveals itself. The play shifts between two households in Tobarnabrosna in Munster. The Keegans are becoming comfortably middle class, while the Desmonds, widowed mother and daughter Nance, inhabit a tied cottage below the hill as the dependants of the Keegans' former herdsman. Owen Keegan's is a prosperous household, the result of thrift and hard toil of father, son (Michael) and daughter (Ellen) as the opening dialogue makes abundantly clear: all three characters are continually at work; she is preparing an evening meal while the comings and goings of the two men on returning from market are prompted by the need to stable a horse, move late-born lambs to shelter from an inclement night, or extract a couple of heifers which have strayed into the turnip field. Effortlessly Murray gives an audience a deepening sense of the supposed off-stage geography of the district, and space is carefully related to time in that people are sighted from the Keegans' doorway in the opening act sometime before they enter the action. It is immediately present to a spectator's imagination because it is as if all is taken for granted by the characters: this is credibly their lived space.

On the surface the first act establishes little directly by way of plot. Nance has returned from a stay in the city where she has learned dressmaking and acquired a bright confidence in her appearance and her femininity. She has both material independence and with that an independence of spirit, and both rouse a snobbish, irritable indignation in Ellen, who holds to class difference as compensation for her inability to match Nance's buoyant manner or looks. Nance is indomitable, rising with amusement above Ellen's scorn. Owen and Michael return separately from market and each has a short scene with Nance in which Murray develops in both men a growing fascination with her while simultaneously showing her ability to adapt her witty banter and general style of behaviour to attract each man's notice. While Ellen exemplifies the Munster norm (or in Nance's words: 'the drudge that's made of a labouring woman in the country'),[17] Nance, given her experience in the city, has been transformed from that stereotype into an outsider-figure, a surprising 'other', and it is to her *difference* that all the Keegans quickly respond (the men positively; Ellen critically):

NANCE: Surely to goodness, Ellen, you wouldn't have people for ever talking business? One must have some little fun an' pleasure out of life.

ELLEN: Isn't clean, honest work pleasure enough – work in the fields – in the house – in the dairy? I've never known any other kind of pleasure – and don't want to know it either.

NANCE (*seriously*): And what has all the work done for you, Ellen? What's the good of slaving all your life and having nothing for it but a load o'money in the bank?

ELLEN: I'll tell you what work has done for me. Look at this kitchen and you'll see it. Look at the fowl and the dairy and you'll see it. Look at the farm – north, south, east and west – and you'll see it.

NANCE: When I look at yourself, Ellen, I see it.[18]

That Nance refuses to be *placed* socially but voices a far-from-subservient set of attitudes comes by the end of the exchange to challenge Ellen's ethos and her control within her own space: the kitchen in which she takes such pride. Succinctly the balance of power shifts between the young women from speech to speech, intimating tensions, past resentments and earlier relations that have gone to the nurturing of Ellen's present emotional dissatisfaction and Nance's cheerful sensuality. Two readings of what the stage setting might signify are offered to us; neither reading is privileged or endorsed by Murray. This is deft exposition which ends in unresolved tension; while Ellen's tone is clearly in line with her intentions, Nance's is uncertain and veiled. (Are her last two speeches here framed out of spite or pity?) A growing irritability in Owen is apparent as the act develops, but this similarly provokes an audience's interest by not being immediately motivated: when Ellen at the door later describes seeing Michael chatting with Nance in the boreen below ('Will you watch her now and the way she tosses back the hair from her forehead to show off her lady fingers?'), he curtly instructs his daughter to summon Michael in 'to his tay'.[19] The curtness recurs when Owen finds Nance and Michael alone in the kitchen and he bids his son go out and drive the lambs to shelter.

In the ensuing act (set some six weeks later in the Desmonds' cottage) the ambiguity of Nance's responses is more marked: it is clearly her intent to guard her speech and preserve an emotionally non-committal line of answering when Michael comes trying to develop a hesitant style of courtship. It emerges that there is rivalry for her affections between father and son and that Owen has succeeded; Nance is to become the new mistress of the Keegan household. Murray's carefully framed ambiguities, especially surrounding Nance, prevent audiences drawing too prompt or judgemental conclusions about the lovers' motivations. Owen and Nance are by far the most dynamic of the characters we are presented with, vibrant with energy and daring (the cautious, shy Michael and the curt, self-disciplined Ellen seem solid but predictable and lacklustre creations by contrast) and it seems *right* in terms of dramatic logic that they should be drawn together. But throughout Act I reference has continually been drawn to Nance's lowly origins: Ellen recalls that ' 'Tisn't so long since you saw her without a shoe to her feet and she trailing in here after her mother to get a bit of hot cake or a cup o'tea from us maybe.'[20] How much is her choice of husband directed by ambition? Or by a desire, perhaps, to lord it over Ellen who has continually asserted the social superiority of the Keegans? Given the traditions over land tenure and inheritance among the peasantry in Ireland (with which Murray assumes his audience are familiar), Michael might be a long while coming into possession of the farm, since it would be his only at Owen's death and Owen is palpably in robust health. Has a degree of calculation influenced her decision? Nance has a means of earning her living but marriage to Owen would secure her greater leisure, as is quickly proved in the final act, since Ellen will remain at home to run the house. Till now *Autumn Fire* could simply be interpreted as an essay in peasant realism; but the ambiguities of motivation by the end of Act II have heightened the tensions established in the opening scene such that, while the proposed marriage seems (to take a superficial view) quite a plausible turn of events, it also at a deeper psychological level appears threatening and fateful. Frictions between the characters have been voiced but are held in check; the delicate state of poise is fragile and Nance's coming into a new role in the Keegan household dangerously disturbs the balance of power-relations. It is only in Act III that Murray allows the parallels with the story of Phaedra, Hippolytus and Theseus to emerge as the action moves inexorably towards tragedy.

Nine months have elapsed and Owen, bed-ridden after having suffered an injury to his back while over-exuberantly riding a young horse to market, lies collapsed physically and is mentally defeated. Without the authority of his watchful presence, Nance and Michael have grown more intimate together; Owen's brother and Ellen warn him tactfully to be vigilant and not leave the couple so much alone; Owen insists Michael go away to agricultural college; Michael begs one chaste kiss of farewell when alone with Nance; Owen, managing to gather strength, comes into the room; he observes their apparent guilt, bans Michael the house under his curse; curses himself for marrying late in life; and, though his final words blame son, daughter and wife for what has happened ('They've broken me . . .'), it is his impetuosity that has ultimately *broken* everyone, emotionally and spiritually, in the household.[21] The slow pacing of the first two acts prepares the ground expertly for the final confrontations and bleak outcome. That meticulous pacing in performance conveys the impression that the characters dimly apprehend that some imminent catastrophe is about to overtake them but are searching either for certain confirmation of their intuitions of disaster or for the means to deflect its impact. This is particularly the case with Ellen who, like a latterday Cassandra, repeatedly anticipates as her worse fears precisely what comes to happen (of Owen's hurley-playing, she wrily observes in Act I: 'Making a fool of yourself like that before all the people! 'Twould only serve you right to be hurted or to be put lying on the flat of your back maybe');[22] but when she tries to frame her intuitions in ways that will influence the other characters' actions, she fails in her attempt because they invariably dismiss her dry, surly tone as joyless interfering. There is throughout the first two acts a restless tension surging and building behind the seemingly placid surface of the dialogues and the eventual eruption is the more profound for the preceding suppression. What impresses is how this is not exploited for its potential sensationalism, rather it is all part of the distinct verisimilitude that Murray brings to the representation of his peasant characters, who appropriately do not possess powers of cerebral analysis but who do own intense sensibilities and depth of feeling.

A key scene which shows Murray's dramaturgical artistry at its finest and his control of the strategies that allow him to work so subtly as he does with archetypal material is that between Michael and Nance early in Act II. Michael is shy and rough of speech and can only slowly open his heart to Nance; but he grows more confident, more urgently passionate with her apparent refusals to accept his love; she is being kindly but firm in her rejections (we learn later that she is under oath not to reveal her recent engagement to Owen). The occasion of Michael's visit is to inform her that Owen has plans to send him for training to the Model Farm and he hopes to find support from Nance for his staying:

MICHAEL: You – you wouldn't wish me to go?

NANCE: It's none of my business surely?

MICHAEL (*chilled*): What's that?

NANCE: Surely, your going, Michael, is your own and your father's concern only?

MICHAEL: And wouldn't it make any difference to you, Nance?

NANCE: That's a funny question, Michael. There's no one living, I'm sure, would be wishful to lose a kind neighbour the like of you – but then you'll be improving yourself and having friends *go leor* [galore], and always the best of life.

MICHAEL: What's the good of anything at all to a man that's dead lonely in his heart?

NANCE: O, sure everyone does be lonely at first in strange places. But the spell of home-sickness soon passes.[23]

There is an air of foreboding about the episode that heightens one's attention to the progress of the dialogue, its uneasily shifting tones and the psychological undercurrents to it all. Only in retrospect do we appreciate why the tone was distinctly ominous: Michael's passionate appeals will register in Nance's psyche, though duty to Owen forbids her consciously to cherish them in the present moment; and in consequence the scene becomes crucial in Murray's shaping of the action towards a mythical dimension. It is Nance who invokes the archetype, once she chooses to kindle Michael's affections again. Two men of blood kindred bound by close ties of affection and duty in competition for the same young woman's love have resonances not only of the Phaedra myth from classical lore, but also for Irish audiences of Diarmuid and Finn as rivals for Grania or Tristan and Mark for Isolt from the Gaelic sagas. The rivalry of father and son carries Oedipal intimations too (the Phaedra story, arguably, positions in a new relationship many of the tropes and leitmotifs that structure the myth of Oedipus). As in *Birthright*, intimations of several interrelated archetypes augment the tragic poignancy of *Autumn Fire* while preventing the scrupulously represented peasant experience from being reduced to any form of stereotyping. Murray's dramaturgical strategies achieve both depth and freedom for his subject.

The strategies Murray deploys are exactly paralleled by Eugene O'Neill in his *Desire under the Elms*, an altogether more satisfying, if less challenging, attempt to Americanize classical Greek tragedy than the later *Mourning Becomes Electra*. O'Neill had been deeply moved by *Birthright*, which he saw in New York when the Abbey company included it in their repertory when on tour there in 1911. The play haunted his imagination and in conversation with an Irish friend he questioned why there was no third act to determine the consequences of Hugh's death and its repercussions on the other members of the family. He also questioned why the play had no love interest. When his friend, the actress Eileen Curran, opined that perhaps the relation between Hugh and his mother constituted a typically Irish, romantic element, O'Neill promptly changed the subject.[24] Is it being overly fanciful to ponder whether the intricate waves of loving and loathing that determine the quality of family life in *Birthright* influenced the writing of O'Neill's masterpiece, *Long Day's Journey into Night* (first staged in New York in November 1956)? Here O'Neill had the courage through the discipline of writing to face the private demons that shaped existence as lived by his own family, including a love interest between the mother, Mary Tyrone, and her younger son. Quite how strong the impact of *Birthright* and its dramaturgical artistry was on O'Neill is impossible to determine; nor is there adequate record to prove his continuing interest in Murray's output. The curious fact remains, however, that *Desire under the Elms* was staged at the Greenwich Village Theatre in November 1924, precisely one month after Murray's *Autumn Fire* had been directed by Michael J. Dolan at the Abbey. Is it just coincidence that both dramatists were drawn over the same period of creativity to the myth of Phaedra; that they should both focus on land-hunger as the context for the tragedy, make identical changes regarding circumstantial details in the story, and use the same devices to keep the archetype hidden from precise definition for the audience but leave the knowing spectator to apprehend its presence?

The agricultural and geographical context has changed to New England but the same obsession with ownership of the farmland which fuels the tragedy in *Autumn Fire* is shared by all the men of the Cabot family and by the new wife, Abbie Putnam, in *Desire under the Elms*, though Abbie has a more nakedly defined need for material security than Murray's Nance Desmond ('Waal – what if I did need a hum? What else'd I marry an old man like him fur? . . . This be my farm – this be my hum – this be my kitchen – !').[25] Indeed their desire has intensified to a veritable hunger, verging on desperation. However, O'Neill complicates his portrayal of this consuming lust for possession in order to avoid the simplicities of melodrama by frequently halting the action – even to the moment of Eben and Abbie's final exeunt to prison – while one by one the characters extol the beauty of the encompassing landscape, of sunrise or sunset, the lie of the fields in the light, the exhilaration of physical effort in working the terrain). As in Murray's play, the off-stage world is potently evoked as an object of believable affection and desire to afford O'Neill a firm psychological basis for his characters' motivation. Murray and O'Neill can in time move confidently into handling archetypal material because they have taken care to root their dramas within a meticulously represented and particularized verisimilitude. In neither play does an audience feel it is being required to engage suddenly and confusingly with a different, more symbolic dimension of reality as is the case with Friel's *Living Quarters*, because in both plays the land is the focus of the characters' feelings, the constant, determining factor in their actions and, by virtue of this, the embodiment of their fate. Where O'Neill's play differs from Murray's is in the violence of the conclusion, where Abbie's murder of the child she has conceived by Eben brings resonances of the myth of Medea to fuse with the story of Phaedra. Even then the motivation is still linked with the characters' suspicion of each other's motives: Eben believes Abbie calculatedly conceived the child to oust him from ownership of the farm and she kills it in a misguided attempt to prove to him that her motives were not so crudely materialistic as he supposes. The divisions provoked by the conclusion of Murray's play are profoundly disturbing because they derive from Owen's total misreading of the kissing he witnesses between Michael and Nance: the kiss is the token of a tender and absolute farewell and not, as he interprets it, a sign of incestuous infidelity. The conclusions to both plays turn on a cruel misunderstanding of motive.

Viewing this range of Irish (or Irish-American) plays exploring the Phaedra archetype, one cannot but notice in all a significant alteration from the prototype: in Euripides and Racine's tragedies Theseus comes late into the action as the means of capitulating the tragic climax and its series of terrible deaths; in all the Irish versions of the material the Theseus-figure is a powerful presence throughout and, it could be argued especially of Murray and O'Neill's plays, the chief focus of attention. Where in Euripides and Racine, Phaedra's intimate approaches to Hippolytus are either influenced by, or misread in relation to, both characters' speculations about the future stability of Athens, should Theseus be found to be dead, in Murray and O'Neill's plays (and to some extent in Friel's) there is a deliberate flaunting of his continuing virility by the father before a son he intends to hold in his control.[26] Nance and Abbie are used by their respective husbands as a kind of taunt, a display of male conquest. By altering the positioning of the father's presence and its function in the action, the playwrights effect in the process a further change: the archetypal story of Phaedra and Hippolytus deploys the trope of the older woman lusting for the younger man but in these versions that trope has been replaced by another: the marriage of January with May, of the older man with the younger wife. A consequence of this is that the representatives of Phaedra and Hippolytus are virtually of an age (Abbie is thirty-five and Eben twenty-five, while Cabot is fifty years his senior; Nance is actually younger than Michael, although their precise ages are not given by Murray, while Owen is described as being in his mid-fifties). The effect of this is to accentuate the Oedipal rivalry between father and son in both plays for the woman and for the land (indeed in many ways for the woman as emblematic of the land's fertility and future). Much stage-time in *Autumn Fire* and *Desire under the Elms* is devoted to depicting the sheer dynamism and potency of the father: Owen as champion of the village hurley team, his physical stamina, lively imagination, confidently seductive way with words in courting Nance ('Show me another man, east or west, that plunges into the river in October and runs around the field naked to the skin in the dews o'the morning').[27] Comparable is Cabot's relentless hard work, his spectacularly vigorous dancing at the christening party, his flooring Eben in physical combat. Theseus, as characterized by Euripides and Racine, has political authority but his *sexual* authority is not a dramatic issue of such centralizing importance as in the characterizing of Keegan and Cabot, where its emphatic presence precipitates the tragic crisis. The sexual focus in Euripides' and Racine's plays is inexorably on Phaedra (Phèdre).

In Euripides' *Hippolytus* the tragedy is brought about by two warring goddesses, Aphrodite and Artemis, whose appearances frame the action: they embody certain conflicting feminine principles which demonstrably have the power, if suppressed or neglected, to be destructive in human experience. In Murray and O'Neill's plays the destructive force is a dominant and controlling patriarchy, power-fixated and ungenerous: that is Owen's case even when enfeebled and debilitated because of his accident, since he wishes to frame his will in a manner that circumscribes Michael and Nance's futures from beyond the grave; Cabot is to the last resilient and unrepentant, accepting no responsibility whatever for the tragic climax but seeing the murder and its aftermath as further proof of his own chastening at the hand of his 'hard' God in whose image he models himself: 'I kin hear His voice warnin' me agen t'be hard an' stay on my farm. . . . I kin feel I be in the palm o'His hand, His fingers guidin' me.'[28] Both plays take as the motivating mechanism for their plots the issue of land-hunger and inheritance. *Autumn Fire* in consequence subordinates the Phaedra-figure and her role in the action. By subjecting the father's role and the patriarchal values that inform it to a stern critique, Murray avoids confronting the archetype of Phaedra in its fullness, which examines the mothering instinct run to an erotic excess. It is a matter for debate why the private ideologies shaping Murray's creativity (he was an ardent

Roman Catholic) held him back from sensitively confronting the trope of the older mother-figure as predatory sexual *threat*. Friel side-steps this issue too by engaging with the archetype in a highly cerebral fashion. Only O'Neill has the fearlessness to enter imaginatively into this difficult emotional and psychological terrain, when Abbie takes Eben into the parlour, which he has sanctified in his memory as his mother's *place*, and seduces him into sexual acquiescence by playing the mother's role:

Don't cry, Eben! I'll take yer Maw's place! I'll be everythin' she was t'ye! Let me kiss ye, Eben! (*She pulls his head around. He makes a bewildered pretence of resistance. She is tender.*) Don't be afeered! I'll kiss ye pure, Eben – same's if I was a Maw t'ye – an ye kin kiss me back's if yew was my son – my boy – sayin' good night t'me! Kiss me, Eben. (*They kiss in restrained fashion. Then suddenly wild passion overcomes her. She kisses him lustfully again and again and he flings his arms about her and returns her kisses.*)[29]

O'Neill through this episode enters that dark world of taboo which underpins many archetypes (particularly those which have proved most beneficial to the practice and theory of psychoanalysis); by so daring, he seems to have engaged with the myth of Phaedra and Hippolytus at a level where the distancing effects all too easily implicit in the modern idea of myth (of myth as a fiction, a story) have been shed and a central experience encompassed by this particular myth of Phaedra is apprehended with a consummate immediacy. O'Neill continually writes directly out of the sexual identities of his three main characters, but nowhere with as naked an urgency as here. Until the moment when with her strange logic Abbie explains to Eben that she murdered their child to prove that there was no materialistic motive in her seducing him, her potent sexuality has been represented in deliberately ambiguous terms: by turns antagonistic, cajoling, volatile, openly frank, subtly mesmeric. (Abbie's is a remarkably open role in the freedoms it offers the actress in interpretation.) Even in this scene – and this is the source of its disturbing power – it is difficult to determine whether, or for how long, her fervent eroticism is calculated and predatory. Because they painstakingly eschew the fierce eroticism that, for all her shame, is the core of Phaedra's experience in Euripides' play, there is no scene as intense or as challenging in either Murray's play or Friel's; and no dramatic moment occurs to parallel this which brings an audience so close to seeing the archetype in all its awesome clarity.

Notes

1. James Hillman, *Re-Visioning Psychology* (New York: Harper & Row, 1975), pp. xiii and xiv respectively.
2. James Hillman, 'An Inquiry into Image' in *Dreams and the Underworld* (Spring 1977): 84.
3. In the context of Irish dramatizations of the myth of Phaedra, this is certainly the case with Ulick O'Connor's *The Oval Machine*. O'Connor prefaces the text of his Noh-inspired drama with a summary of Euripides' play commencing with the statement that 'the characters in this play have a relationship with those in ... *Hippolytus*'. That 'relationship' is extremely tenuous; Euripides affords O'Connor a rough plot-structure on which to hang an extensive diatribe about declining values in contemporary professional sport. The Phaedra-figure, Stephanie, is marginalized in consequence of this particular thematic interest. There is no serious attempt to confront issues of passion and one is left with the distinct impression that the myth has been traduced, hijacked for a purpose with which it has no logical affinity. The myth here has become merely a dramatic mechanism, a means of bringing seeming universal importance (because of the attempted association with the archetypal) to what is clearly a highly personal issue. Inevitably such a dubious strategy results in a work that seems rhetorical, inflated and, therefore, banal.
4. Brian Friel, *Living Quarters*, in *Selected Plays of Brian Friel* (London: Faber & Faber, 1984), pp. 171–246.
5. The two devils disguised as Merchants in early drafts of the play dating from 1889 summon 'Unshapen spirits of the / unchristian dead' to help carry away the Countess Cathleen's treasure: 'Hither tivishes,

/ Who mourn among the scenery of your sins, / Turning to animal and reptile forms . . .' See W. B. Yeats, *'The Countess Cathleen': Manuscript Materials*, ed. M. J. Sidnell and W. K. Chapman (Ithaca, NY, and London: Cornell University Press, 1999), pp. 223, 248, 324, which is where the above quotation is sited.

6. See, for example, Dr Trench's attempt to explain the 'hostile influence' that continues to disturb the seances in *The Words upon the Window-Pane*: 'Some spirits are earth-bound – they think they are still living and go over and over some action of their past lives, just as we go over and over some painful thought, except that where they are thought is reality . . . Sometimes a spirit re-lives not the pain of death but some passionate or tragic moment of life . . . In vain do we write *requiescat in pace* upon the tomb, for they must suffer, and we in our turn must suffer until God gives peace.' W. B. Yeats, *Selected Plays*, ed. Richard Allen Cave (Harmondsworth, Mx: Penguin Books, 1997), p. 210.

7. It might be argued that Beckett's *Play* involves more than one dreamer-back, since the drama examines the consequences of adultery and marital breakdown; but, though the dreamers' speeches intersect, the speakers are themselves wholly unaware of each other's existence in their shared purgatorial half-light. Each is concentrating on an inwardly directed confession. Beckett's is not a *social* drama in the sense that the epithet may be applied to Friel's play.

8. See also Marianne McDonald: 'Friel organizes his play around a narrator called Sir who also acts like a stage manager. He consults a ledger which is the "written word" which may be rearranged but not deleted. This narrator can be seen as God, Fate, and/or History, and/or as the collective will of the people involved. . . . On the other hand, "Sir" can be seen as a Greek chorus.' She sees Sir as the author and the play as a transparent view of the writing of plays with a parallel in Pirandello's *Six Characters in Search of an Author*. 'Violent Words': Brian Friel's "Living Quarters: After Hippolytus", *Arion, A Journal of Humanities and the Classics* (Boston University 6(1) (Spring/Summer 1998): 40.

9. Micheál MacLiammoir, *All for Hecuba* (London; Methuen, 1946), p. 147.

10. Hilton Edwards's 'Production' in the Gate Theatre, Dublin, edited by Bulmer Hobson (Dublin: Gate Theatre, 1934), p. 38. Edwards himself played the role of Egosmith.

11. For a fuller discussion of the Pirandellian qualities of *The Words upon the Window-Pane*, see my commentary and notes on the play in Yeats, *Selected Plays*, ed. Cave, pp. 354–6.

12. Ellen's name is recognizably close to Electra's.

13. Far more successful is *The Freedom of the City*, staged at the Abbey Theatre in 1973, where a highly fragmented structure and clashing stylistic juxtapositions none the less achieve a theatrical cohesion and unity, because they illuminate in varying ways a common theme.

14. T. C. Murray, *Autumn Fire*, in *Selected Plays: T. C. Murray*, ed. Richard Allen Cave, Irish Drama Selections 10 (Gerrards Cross: Colin Smythe, 1998), pp. 119–77.

15. T. C. Murray, *Birthright*, in *Selected Plays: T. C. Murray*, ed. Cave, p. 45.

16. Murray had refined the technique further when composing *Maurice Harte* (staged June 1912), in which resonances of the mythical story of Medea underscore a study of a peasant mother's obsession with seeing her son ordained a priest. Mrs Harte's entrenched determination (fuelled by a subtle mix of piety, pride and status-seeking) ultimately destroys the future lives of both her sons (one spiritually and psychologically; the other materially) to her compliant husband's despair.

17. Murray, *Selected Plays*, ed. Cave, p. 122.

18. Ibid., p. 124.

19. Ibid., pp. 131–2.

20. Ibid., p. 131.

21. Ibid., p. 177.

22. Ibid., p. 127.

23. Ibid., p. 148.

24. The account of this discussion is given in Louis Sheaffer, *O'Neill: Son and Playwright* (London: J. M. Dent & Sons, 1968), p. 206. In Sheaffer's later volume of biography, *O'Neill: Son and Artist* (London: Paul Elek, 1974), he writes at some length (pp. 127–8) about resemblances between Cabot and Bat Morrissey and traces potential lines of influence between T. C. Murray's *Birthright* and *Desire under the Elms*.

25. Eugene O'Neill, *Desire under the Elms* and *The Great God Brown* (London: Nick Hern Books, 1995), pp. 24–5.

26. This is also the case in Ulick O'Connor's *The Oval Machine*.

27. Murray, *Selected Plays*, ed. Cave, p. 128.
28. O'Neill, *Desire under the Elms* and *The Great God Brown*, p. 59.
29. Ibid., p. 38.

Antigone in Africa

Athol Fugard

Editors' Preface

In reviewing the revival of *The Island* at the Royal National Theatre in January 2000, Nicholas de Jongh of the London *Evening Standard* ended by saying that it is 'a timeless survivors' guide for political prisoners everywhere, struggling to survive and keep despair at bay'.[1] His point is proven by the use that has been made of this play throughout the world in highly charged political situations, not the least of which was Ireland. The first production of *The Island* was in South Africa (Cape Town) in 1973, and in Ireland it was on Irish television in the 1980s. This was followed by a production at the Gate Theatre in Dublin in 1986, which went on to Limerick and Galway.

Fugard's *Boesman and Lena* with Stephen Rea, Deirdre Donnelly and Des McAleer was put on by Field Day in 1983 at the Guild Hall, in Derry, and then toured. Initially *The Island* had been selected by Field Day, but 'The Northern Ireland Arts Council, however, indicated unofficially that this might not be a very politic choice, so they turned instead to the earlier *Boesman and Lena*'.[2] This play was more oblique in its political comment. Marilynn Richtarick claimed that

Fugard would have appealed to the Field Day directors for a number of reasons. Like them, he was committed to taking theatre out of established venues to reach people who might otherwise have no access to it. Like them, he believed that art and politics had a necessary relationship with each other, and he wrote out of the experience of a society that was, like Northern Ireland's, deeply divided.'[3]

Fugard's *Road to Mecca* and *A Place With the Pigs* have both been performed recently in Ireland.

Fugard's first trip to Ireland was in 1999 (he is a Lanigan on his father's side). In Cork and Listowel he directed a performance of Sophocles' *Antigone* in a translation by Marianne McDonald. Luke Clancy said, 'There may be, Sophocles and McDonald whisper to anyone who will listen, a tremendous moral power in compromise' (*The Times*, 21 July 1999). *Antigone* is still speaking to vital political issues. Gerry Adams personally thanked Fugard for his work.

The parallels between the political theatre of South Africa that Athol Fugard began and that of Field Day are obvious. Field Day was established to give a voice to issues that included those of human rights, rights that had been suspended for a long time in Southern Ireland, and even now in Northern Ireland. Tom Paulin's *The Riot Act*, based on *Antigone*, like Fugard's *The Island*, depicted a tyrannic Creon who was concerned more about enforcing his personal will than the public good. Many productions of *Antigone* do this, when they are performed in places where political abuses occur. This is the reason that many of these productions do not give Creon the justified stature he deserves. This may not do justice to Sophocles' opposition of two people who are justified in defending their positions, but who go hell-bent to their own destruction because they refuse to compromise. Oppressed people gain hope when they see a performance of *Antigone* because the heroine represents them. Although they may not win the immediate battle, at least they are respected for their passionate defence of honour. The Irish and South African blacks are Antigones. In this performance, their voice has been heard.

Marianne McDonald and J. Michael Walton

When John Kani and Winston Ntshona and I created *The Island* in South Africa in 1973, we had no idea of the international resonance that our work would have. However, the story of Antigone in South Africa does not start with *The Island*, but goes back even earlier to the small black drama group of amateur actors that I started in Port Elizabeth in 1963 called the Serpent Players.

At this point in South African history the Afrikaner Nationalist government had been in power for fifteen years, and the monstrous political philosophy which came to be known as apartheid was being defined by one piece of discriminatory legislation after another. In this process, black and coloured South Africans (to use the racial categories of the old South Africa), were being deprived of all their basic human rights. Thus, for example, free political association, freedom of movement, freedom of speech, freedom to have sex with or marry a partner regardless of race, had been taken away.

For the artist in this situation, apartheid brought with it a form of state censorship reminiscent of the worst years of Nazi Germany, and Stalin's Russia: a situation with which the Catholics in Northern Ireland are only too familiar. But this was still only the beginning. In the course of the next thirty-five years the system of apartheid would end up making South Africa one of the most despised nations in the latter half of the twentieth century.

It was in this context that one night in my hometown of Port Elizabeth, to which I had returned after a national tour of the first of my plays to achieve national significance (*The Blood Knot*), a knock on the front door ushered into my life a group of four black men and one woman (Norman Ntshinga, Welcome Duru, Fats Bokhilane, Mike Ngxcolo and Mabel Magada). Soon others would join them. This was the start of one of the most definitive theatrical experiences of my career. This little group had read about my success in the local paper, and had come to ask me to help them start a drama group. None of them had had any previous theatre experience and, very typically, they all had the most menial of jobs: the women were domestic servants, and the men worked as very basic physical labourers. Having worked previously with completely inexperienced would-be black actors up in Johannesburg, I knew just how frustrating this experience would turn out to be. For that group in Johannesburg I had written my first full-length plays (*No-Good Friday* and *Nongogo*) which dealt with life in the black townships.

Apart from the exhausting process of teaching these men and women who came to my door the basics of acting, there would be in addition the problems of a white man associating with black people in the South Africa of that day. The authorities would not allow me to go into the black townships, and these black men and women were running a very considerable risk of police harassment in coming into a white area at night. Because of all of this, my first impulse was to say no. I wanted to devote all my time and energy to capitalize on my success with *Blood Knot* by writing a new play. A totally selfish concern with time and energy is necessary for a serious writer. My guilty white liberal conscience would, however, not allow me this indulgence. I very reluctantly agreed.

In order to capture the interest of the group, and also to test their resources as potential acting material, I chose for our first production Machiavelli's glorious romp, *The Mandrake* (*La Madragola*), which I freely adapted to a black township setting. Our first performance space was scheduled to be the disused snake pit of the Port Elizabeth museum, and this gave the group its name, 'Serpent Players'. Our title for the piece was *The Cure*, and it turned out to be a huge success. I would like to believe that at the end of this exercise, I was no longer the patronizing white liberal that I had considered myself but had become instead a friend of these remarkable and beautiful people. As such, they trusted me, and in our weekly sessions in the little fisherman's shack next to the Indian Ocean, which was my home at the time, I began to learn something about their lives. What I soon realized was that theatre had a much more significant role to play in those lives than just being a source of entertainment.

The Eastern Cape Province of South Africa, where Port Elizabeth is located, from which Nelson Mandela, Steve Biko and the powerful Mbeki family had all come, had a reputation of being the most highly politicized black area in South Africa. It paid a heavy price for the distinction of being in the forefront of black resistance to the apartheid policies of the government.

The black townships in and around Port Elizabeth were the targets of very intense and very brutal police activity. Anything remotely resembling a political conscience or awareness, could lead to the disappearance of the man or woman involved. Thanks to the presence of police informers, it was a climate of fear and suffocating silence. In our talking in that little fisherman's shack, we began to realize that the stage offered us a chance of breaking this conspiracy of silence, and allowing us to talk, albeit in code, about the things which were happening in the daily life of the township. As a result of this, we started looking at plays that would give us the opportunity to start dealing with the very urgent political realities of our situation. In this way we turned to the work of Brecht, Büchner, Beckett, Camus and Shakespeare, among others. I had modelled my earlier one-act play *Klaas and the Devil* on Synge's *Riders to the Sea* because it expressed so well the concerns of the township. With minimal alteration of the established texts, we made it obvious to our eager audiences that what was happening on stage was in fact a reflection of and a comment on our own lives.

It was inevitable that all of this should eventually lead us to the greatest political play of all time, Sophocles' *Antigone*. Whereas the first readings of all the other plays had usually involved a bit of to-and-froing about whether it was the right one for us, the response to *Antigone* was a spontaneous and totally unanimous 'Yes!' The story of that one lone voice raised in protest against what was considered an unjust law struck to the hearts of every member of the group. We were all so in awe of this work that we did not make any attempt to tamper with the text. To the best of our ability, our audiences would get *Antigone* as Sophocles had written it. We used E. V. Rieu's translation.

As had been the case with our other productions, the police harassed us all through the rehearsal period. They interrupted rehearsals to take names and addresses, confiscated scripts and in general did everything possible to intimidate members of the group. When they realized that none of those bullying tactics was going to stop us, they resorted to more brutal measures. I arrived at one of our rehearsals to be told that the young actor Sharkie (Sipho Mguqulwa), playing Haemon, had been taken into police custody. The performance proceeded because I drafted a young factory worker who had just recently joined the group, John Kani, into that role, and we finally got the play on to a stage in New Brighton. The audience response to this production was the strongest yet that we had received to any of our work. And reflecting on it afterwards, I realized even more than the extraordinary character that Sophocles had created in his female heroine: our young theatre group had in fact become the Antigone of New Brighton. It was speaking out against and defying the edicts of the apartheid Creon.

But that was not the end of *Antigone*. Sharkie had in the meantime appeared in a kangaroo court in a remote small town, making it impossible for us to organize a defence with witnesses who could testify on his behalf. There he was falsely accused of various political offences, summarily tried, found guilty and sent to Robben Island for twenty years. This had been a standard procedure with many men and women who had suddenly disappeared off the streets of New Brighton. Serpent Players was to lose a few more of its members in a similar fashion. They would all eventually land up on Robben Island, South Africa's notorious political prison where Nelson Mandela and the top leadership of the ANC (African National Congress) were serving life sentences.

Sharkie had been one of the most passionate members of Serpent Players, and more than anyone else he had recognized and embraced its mission to give the people of New Brighton a voice in those years when they were frightened even to whisper in their own homes. The fact that he had been robbed of a chance to go on stage as Haemon and argue with his father for the life of someone he loved, and for her right to act in accordance with her conscience, was, as he told me in a letter smuggled out of Robben Island years later, an even greater blow than the sentence of twenty years that had been imposed on him. In that same letter he described the extraordinary way that he found to release himself from that frustration.

One of the few treats allowed the prisoners on the island was an annual concert with each of the cell blocks providing a ten- or fifteen-minute item for the programme. Sharkie persuaded his cell block to allow him to provide their contribution to the programme, and one of them to assist him in the staging of a pocket version of the immortal classic. All he had to go on was his memory of the text, and the challenge he faced was the fifteen-minute time limit. With a stroke of genius that as a working playwright I still humbly admire, Sharkie put all his passion, energy and craft into reducing the play to the final confrontation between Creon and Antigone. Sharkie played Creon, and his hapless cell mate, after much bullying and blackmail, was persuaded to put on false breasts inside his khaki shirt, and wear a wig made out of a mop, and risk the ridicule of the entire prison when he appeared as Antigone. As it turned out, there wasn't even a titter when he made his appearance on stage. Sharkie's pre-publicity, which consisted mainly of whispers from cell to cell at night, or in work gangs as they laboured under the sun during the day, had prepared the black audience for what was to come.

The scene in the prison hall where the concert was held directly paralleled the famous production of Anouilh's *Antigone* in Paris during the German occupation. The front row of German army officers had thought they were enjoying French culture, while behind them Parisians received a political message of hope and defiance. So too on Robben Island, the South African warders sat in front of the audience of prisoners, and really admired these Bantus for what they had cooked up for their entertainment.[4] I like to think of that moment of Sharkie's triumph as possibly the greatest fulfilment of this magnificent play's message since Sophocles first staged his *Antigone* in Athens in about 440 BC.

There is a footnote to this occasion. Nelson Mandela, who was in solitary confinement on Robben Island at the time, was not allowed to attend that performance. But he did hear about it. Years later in another prison to which he had been removed, and where the conditions under which he had been kept had been relaxed, he organized a full staging of the text, in which he chose for himself the role of Creon.

In the meantime back home a new development had emerged in the work of the Serpent Players. The group had become increasingly impatient with the oblique commentary on the situation in New Brighton through the established texts we had been staging. Increasingly they pressed me to find some way of dealing directly with the reality of their lives. It is against this background that we embarked on a series of play-making experiments. Regrettably, only one text survives of the first phase of this process (*The Coat*), but it clearly illustrates the process we used.

The Coat was based on an actual incident involving myself and one of the founding members of the group, Mabel Magada. Her husband Norman Ntshinga, one of the five who had trooped into my life years earlier, had also been one of the actors hauled in by the security police dragnet, and ended up on Robben Island, sentenced to ten years' hard labour. In his case, Mabel and I had been able to get to the remote town where he was being tried, in time to give evidence in mitigation of sentence. It made no difference.

While we were saying goodbye to a handcuffed Norman in a police courtyard afterwards, another prisoner, an old man, whose case had preceded Norman's, and who was also bound for Robben Island, came up to us desperately, and asked us to tell his wife and children in New Brighton what had happened to him. He then took off his threadbare coat and said to us, 'This is all I've got. Take it back to my wife. Tell her to use it.'

We told the group about that brief encounter in the police courtyard and it was decided that his few words to us would become the basis of an exercise in play-making. The final product was a very Brechtian analysis of the brutal reality facing millions of black South Africans daily. 'How could the wife use it?' became the key question. With awesome sobriety, realism and passion the group began to try to answer that question, using theatre techniques of improvisation, interior monologues, etc.

The circumstances surrounding the first performance *of The Coat* are worth mentioning. A local amateur white theatre group had for some time been inviting Serpent Players to come to their pretty little theatre and show them something of our work. At first the group thought this would be a wonderful opportunity to give *The Coat* its first airing. But when we learned that one of the conditions involved in visiting the pretty little theatre was that the black actors could not make use of the toilet facilities, and would have to arrive with empty bladders, all hell broke loose within the company. We were confronted yet again with the reality of South Africa, and, with one exception, all the members of Serpent Players said that that condition was too humiliating, and that the invitation should be declined. There was a furious debate over this issue, which ended with nothing resolved. The one person who was prepared to accept that condition, Mulligan Mbikwana, suggested that he and I should take on the reading of the text to the white group, because he felt it was too important an opportunity to make white South Africans realize the reality of life for a black man and woman.

The arrangement I had with the group was that I had to pick them up at the bus terminus, and take them to my little fisherman's cottage for our meetings and rehearsals. On the night in question, when I turned up to pick up Mulligan, one by one all the other members of the group made their appearance and squashed themselves into my old jalopy, and we drove to the pretty little theatre in white Port Elizabeth for the first performance of *The Coat*. It was a stunned and silenced white audience that received our offering. We did not use the toilets and left immediately after the performance. At a suitably deserted spot on the road back to the bus terminus, we got out of the car and relieved ourselves in nearby bushes.

The Coat was followed up by *Friday's Bread on Monday*, the generative image being the black children standing in line outside a bakery on the edge of the black township to buy half-priced stale bread on Monday. That in turn was followed by *The Last Bus*. This dealt with a fifteen-mile walk with all its attendant midnight hazards (police cars and black thugs among them) that faced any black man or woman who missed the last bus.

But that was still not the end of the story of *Antigone* in South Africa. In the years that had passed since Serpent Players' staging of that play, two relative latecomers to the group, John Kani and Winston Ntshona, had emerged as key players.

One day they came to me with one of the most absurd ideas I had ever heard. They wanted to leave their secure but menial jobs and earn their living instead by becoming professional actors. I was supposed to find them a vehicle among the many plays on my bookshelf for this 'Alice-in-Wonderland' notion. To put it bluntly, black theatre simply did not exist at this point in South Africa, and there was nothing even remotely resembling a professional black actor in the country. I tried my utmost to dissuade them of the idea. When I pointed out that there were not proper theatres at our disposal, they countered by saying they would perform as we just had been doing in small private spaces. They would earn their living by passing the hat around afterwards, which is in fact the way they survived during the first year of this experiment. Nothing I could say made any impression on them, and some weeks later I told them I had not been able to find a suitable play to launch their 'professional careers'. They then made the suggestion that we should make such a vehicle for them, using the methods that we had evolved in our play-making experiments in the group.

I threw the challenge back at them by asking them to come up with a suitable idea for such a home-made play. Their responses were as absurd as the idea that they could earn a living by acting professionally. The plots they presented me with would have required a cast of thousands and a budget to match. They were sensible enough to realize this, and when they asked me if I had an idea, I was foolish enough to say I did. The idea was a photograph I had seen in the display of a street photographer at the black bus terminus: a man sitting in front of a crudely painted backdrop of skyscrapers was seated, smiling broadly at the camera, hat on his head, a new suit, shirt and tie to match, and most splendid of all, a cigarette in one hand, and a pipe in the other. John and Winston were dumbfounded at my idiocy. When challenged to tell them how that photograph could end up being a play, I started off by asking, 'Why is he smiling?' It took John's sober realism only a minute to find the answer. 'The only reason a black man smiles these days is if his reference book is in order.' And from that simple beginning, like three subversive spiders, we spun out the story of *Sizwe Banzi is Dead*. It changed our lives, and I believe changed South African theatre in the process.

Some years later the South African Ronald Harwood, author of *The Dresser* and many other plays, asked playwrights and theatre personalities to write essays for a book about 'My most memorable night in the theatre'. I was among those Ronald approached and I wrote him a piece describing the first public performance in New Brighton of *Sizwe Banzi is Dead*. The following is based on what I sent him.[5]

The venue was St Stephen's Hall in New Brighton, Port Elizabeth, and the occasion was our first public performance of *Sizwe Banzi is Dead* in a black township in South Africa. Date: September 1974. The play was already nearly two years old, but it was only after its West End run that we felt sufficiently protected by its overseas success to risk the hazards involved in a township performance. Up until then its life in South Africa had been restricted to private performances before invited audiences, circumstances that theoretically made us safe from censorship and police interference. I say theoretically because even under those circumstances there had been incidents. The last one had been just before a performance at the Space Theatre in Cape Town prior to our departure for London, when we found ourselves confronted by the security police and a warning that if we proceeded with the show we would be charged under the Group Areas Act. They claimed the performance would constitute 'occupation of a building in an area which had been zoned strictly for whites'. We ignored the warning and as it turned out our legal advice was better than theirs. No prosecution followed.

From past experience we knew that what we faced that night in St Stephen's Hall was going to be very different from the appreciative but stunned reception we had enjoyed so far. It is one thing to try to educate a comfortable white audience into what the deeply hated reference book meant to a black man and something else to confront, and in a sense challenge, an angry black audience with those same realities. Because angry and bitter the mood of New Brighton most certainly was. There had recently been a fresh wave of detentions; this time the victims were mostly young student leaders. The militancy among the youth that was to explode later in the 1976 Soweto riots was already very evident and the police were acting with extreme harshness in trying to suppress it. And then finally: *Sizwe Banzi*. For New Brighton that was not just the difficult-to-pronounce name of a character in a play. It is a Xhosa phrase and means quite simply 'The Nation is Dead', so the name itself is a challenge. We were going to try to say a few things – hopefully loudly and clearly – that were normally only whispered in the township shebeens and even then only after the whisperers had made certain that nobody present was suspected of being an *impimi*, a police informer, a supergrass.

When I drove into New Brighton at about half past six that evening it was my first visit in five years. Since 1969 the authorities had consistently refused to give me permission to enter it. The fact that they had relented on this occasion was, I suppose, some measure of the protection that our much-publicized overseas success had given us.

It is impossible to drive into a township without being initially depressed by the appalling conditions in which millions of black people are forced to live in South Africa. This time was no exception. The same soulless monotony of row after row of little one- and two-roomed houses with abandoned attempts at gardens in front of some of them, rutted and stony dirt roads, queues of women and children at the one water tap servicing an entire street, and litter everywhere. New Brighton had not changed. All that had happened in five years was that the squalor had increased. The old catchphrases about the human spirit being able to rise above these conditions didn't work for me this time. Not that I didn't believe it any more, it was just that I couldn't be naive about the realities of township life. The damage to people that I had witnessed was terribly real. Among my friends I had seen strong men defeated by the apparent hopelessness of the situation and ending up wasting away their lives in drunken apathy in the shebeens.

St Stephen's Hall – a square, unadorned brick building attached to St Stephen's Anglican Church – was at that time one of the only two usable halls in New Brighton, population 250,000. A calico banner on the rickety little fence around it announced:

Tonight!
SIZWE BANZI IS DEAD.
The London success comes to New Brighton.
All seats R1.00

Inside the hall Winston was setting out chairs and John was organizing the playing area and a few props needed for the performance. There was a little stage of sorts at one end but because our production relied heavily on audience participation, we had decided to play on the floor with chairs on three sides.

My feelings as I looked around the hall were as predictable as those on entering New Brighton. To describe the facilities as primitive would be an understatement. There were none. Our lighting, for example, was going to be provided by the three sets of fluorescent tubes on the ceiling and our lighting plot consisted of four cues – lights out to indicate the performance was about to start, lights on when the audience had settled down, and then off and on again at the end.

For twenty years I had been involved in attempts to make theatre in South Africa under these circumstances, and I must admit to feeling just a little defeated by the experience as I watched John and Winston. And also resentful. There was a beautiful and very well-equipped little theatre in Port Elizabeth but at that time it was still 'whites only'. The government had not yet made its token concessions that eventually opened theatres to multiracial audiences and casts.

Our few preparations completed, John, Winston and I once again discussed the advisability of censoring a few things in the text, but in the end decided against it. As John put it: 'Why do their dirty work for them?' It was a problem that Serpent Players had faced many times in the past. From the innocent romp of Machiavelli's

The Mandrake, I had seen the political content of our work increase with every production. It was no coincidence that three members of the group had ended up on Robben Island. Security Branch interest in our activities had matched the growth of our political commitment. This performance was to be no exception. At half past seven a car with four well-known faces inside parked on the other side of the road outside the hall. But that is also where they stayed and, as far as trouble from them was concerned, the evening proceeded without incident.

We had always known we would get an audience, but the eventual turn-out was unlike anything Serpent Players had ever had to deal with before. We stopped selling tickets at nine o'clock because even if we had been able to squeeze another body into the hall, he or she wouldn't have been able to see a single bit of the action of the play. People were standing five and six deep behind the last row of seats. Four young men had even managed to scale the walls and were sitting in the fanlights.

The evening got underway with a speech from Welcome Duru, a foundation member of the group. To start with he advised anybody who needed to use the toilets to do so immediately as the play was about to begin and there would be no interval. That was followed by biographical sketches of John, Winston, myself, and Serpent Players. He then told the audience what a marvellous play they were about to see and urged them to clap as often and as loud as they liked. He warned them that there were no women and no singing and dancing in the show and that was because they were in for an evening of something called 'straight theatre'. At this point impatient heckling from the audience forced Welcome to shut up even though, knowing him as I do, I'm sure he still had a lot more to say. I switched off the lights, waited in vain for a very noisy audience to settle down, and then switched them on again. John was in position with his newspaper and ready to start his opening monologue.

I have never yet known an audience that did not laugh its way through the first half-hour of the play, which was the usual time that John took to warm up an audience for the action to follow.

New Brighton was no exception. They knew in a way that no previous audience had the finer nuances of what John was talking about and could recognize and celebrate every local reference. Listening to them, however, I couldn't also help feeling that something more than just a response to a brilliant comedy performance was involved. What Brecht says of crying and lamentation in his *Messingkauf Dialogues* applies equally to the gale of laughter that swept through St Stephen's Hall that night. It was the sound of 'a vast liberation'. To take still further liberties with poor B. B.: New Brighton was mixing laughter into an account of the blows it had received. It was making something out of the utterly devastating.

The opening scene was interrupted by two little incidents. At the end of the story in which John mercilessly lampoons a visit from Henry Ford Jr to the Port Elizabeth plant, a man who had been standing at the back pushed his way through to the front. He entered the acting area and then, as if he was a referee at a boxing match, held up John's arm and announced that '. . . Kani has knocked-out Henry Ford the Junior'. The audience was in total agreement. Then towards the end of the scene when a radiantly smiling Winston posed for his photograph in Style's studio with a cigarette in one hand and a pipe in the other, one of the four men up in 'the gods' was laughing so much he fell out of his fanlight.

Sizwe Banzi is not all comedy and that audience's response to its serious moments was just as Brechtian, if not more so. There were many of them, but there was one that brought the evening to a premature but totally appropriate climax.

For the black people in South Africa there was no more potent symbol of their oppression than the reference book. It completely dominated and dictated their lives and as such was an object of both hatred and dependence. It was most surely the single cause of more misery in my country than anything else. The final scene in the play opens with Buntu (John) switching the photographs in the reference books of Sizwe Banzi (Winston) and a dead man they have stumbled across in an alleyway late at night. The dead man's book has the endorsement which Sizwe needs, but can't get, in order to stay in Port Elizabeth and look for work. At first Sizwe rejects the idea as it involves abandoning his name and taking on the dead man's identity. Winston didn't get a chance to make his protest. After watching the first few seconds of the operation in stunned silence – there are severe penalties attached to tampering with a reference book – a voice shouted out from the audience: 'Don't do it, brother. You'll land in trouble. They'll catch you!' Another voice responded immediately: 'To hell with it. Go ahead and try. They haven't caught me yet.' That was the cue for the most amazing and spontaneous debate I have ever heard. John and Winston tried for a few minutes longer to keep the performance going but in the end had to resign themselves to sitting down and listening to it.

Argument and counter-argument, angry declarations and protests followed fast and furiously. As I stood at the back of the hall listening to it all, I realized I was watching a very special example of one of theatre's major responsibilities in an oppressive society: to break the conspiracy of silence that always attends an unjust social system. And most significant of all: that conspiracy was no longer being assaulted just by the actors. The action of our play was now being matched and equalled by the action of the audience. People were saying directly and forcefully, almost recklessly, what they felt and thought. If the police had been present, I'm sure that would have been the moment when they would have decided to act.

It was Welcome who finally brought the evening under our control again by switching off the lights. After a minute or so of darkness, during which the debate gradually subsided, he switched them on and John and Winston slowly managed to get the performance going.

To my way of thinking what remained of our play came as something of an anticlimax. In discussing it afterwards, John and Winston agreed with me that we should not have interfered with what was happening to the audience, even if it had meant abandoning what remained of *Sizwe Banzi is Dead*. A performance on stage had provoked a political event in the auditorium and there was no doubt in our minds as to which was the more significant. The sense of people wanting to speak, wanting to be heard, had been very urgent and real. As if to confirm that, a very healthy round of applause after my last two lighting cues ended up with everybody standing and singing the banned 'Nkosi Sikelel'i Afrika' ('God Save Africa'), the anthem of the illegal African National Congress.

What my piece for Ronald Harwood does not mention, is that there was a companion play to *Sizwe Banzi is Dead*. But we had decided not to present it at St Stephen's Hall, because its political content was even more explosive. That play was *The Island*, and its story, told with all the humility and truth we could muster, was that of Sharkie's extraordinary fifteen-minute *Antigone* in the prison concert on Robben Island. Over the years since I first read about it in the letters Sharkie smuggled out to me, I had accumulated a huge file of notes and stories about conditions on Robben Island that I had intended using for a play of my own. When John and Winston needed a follow-up to *Sizwe Banzi is Dead*, I laid this file on the table, and it provided us with the raw material for *The Island*.

Once again, using the methods of improvisation and my own writing and structuring of scenes, we set to work. One of the details about imprisonment on Robben Island that had captured my imagination was the cruel ingenuity, useless as it turned out to be, with which the prison guards tried to break the spirit of the prisoners. Among other things, they were subjected to tasks that were impossible to finish, such as emptying the sea into a hole on the beach, or pushing a tree over with your forehead, etc., etc. I strongly believed the necessary tone for the whole piece we wanted to make could only be established by re-creating some such Sisyphean task for the actors who were going to play Sharkie and the cell mate he had dragooned into joining him in his fifteen-minute *Antigone*. It took us several days of harrowing physical explorations before I finally evolved the opening image of the two men trying to shift two mounds of sand that never grew smaller. But I didn't just want to illustrate what happened to men on Robben Island; I wanted to subject the audience to the same experience. To achieve this, I took my cue from the description of a Noh play (*Sumidagawa*) in which a character found it impossible to leave the stage because of her grief and kept circling until a moment of cathartic release was created for the audience. When the play was later done on Broadway the producer said, 'For God's sake don't subject an American audience to that.' We refused to make life comfortable and the opening stayed intact.

To return to creating the play, we thereafter focused on the human drama of two men trying to hold on to their dignity and sanity, who knew absolutely nothing about their future, except that the next day would be a repeat of the hell that they had just lived through, while at the same time they prepared for the prison concert.

Among the stories from Robben Island that we used was the way that prisoners held on to their lives, by story-telling in the cells at night, imaginary telephone calls to families and loved ones, and solo performances of favourite films.

We also decided to create a parallel between the story of Antigone and the two inmates by making the actor who was in fact going to play Antigone in the concert face the same living hell of the heroine in the Sophoclean play by giving him a life sentence on the island. This was made more poignant by his cell mate hearing of his imminent release just before the performance. This imparted a particular resonance and truth to his last line, 'I go now to my living death, because I honoured those things to which honour belongs.'

The first performance took place before an invited audience in the small attic theatre space that Yvonne Bryceland and her husband, Brian Astbury, had created in Cape Town. It was called the Space and it marked the beginning of an alternative theatre movement in South Africa.

It was made memorable to me for several reasons, not the least of which being once again the ubiquitous presence of the South African Special Branch. John and Winston were in their dressing-rooms warming up for the performance when the security men arrived and served us with a notice that we would be prosecuted under the Group Areas Act if we proceeded with the performance. John, Winston, Yvonne, Brian and I went into a huddle to decide what to do. The discussion was very brief. As Yvonne put it, 'Too much is at stake for South African theatre and the country for us to even begin to consider a cancellation of the performance.' A few minutes later, with the three Special Branch officers settled down as part of the audience, the lights went up and John and Winston began the dehumanizing ordeal that starts *The Island*. Something else that contributed to our unwavering and unanimous determination to proceed with the performance is the fact that the windows of the Space looked over Table Bay, with Robben Island in the distance, where Nelson Mandela and Sharkie were no doubt at that moment dreaming about a new South Africa.

Notes

1. Nicholas de Jongh, *Evening Standard* (27 January 2000).
2. Marilynn J. Richtarik, *Acting between the Lines: The Field Day Theatre Company and Irish Cultural Politics*, 1980–1984 (Oxford: Clarendon Press, 1994), p. 204.
3. Ibid. She goes on to say that Kader Asmal (a South African who went into political exile in Ireland, and was recalled to the country by Nelson Mandela to join his new government) in a programme note for the Field Day production 'indirectly drew attention to a broad similarity between South Africa and Northern Ireland when he wrote that "Nothing in South Africa is non-political. Race touches, blights and destroys every aspect of life." In Northern Ireland religion, not race, is used to classify and divide members of the society, but a consciousness of which side people belong on likewise permeates most aspects of life' (p. 209). David Nowlan of the *Irish Times* called the parable 'universal. . . . It has a great deal to say about the abyss of alienation and its resultant loss of identity, a phenomenon not unknown on this island.' (Richtarik, *Field Day*, p. 211). Paddy Woodworth's comment in the *Irish Press* could apply to *The Island*: 'Fugard succeeds in making political lessons emerge unobtrusively from authentic human experience' (Richtarik, *Field Day*, p. 212).
4. The apartheid government went through all sorts of linguistic

manoeuvres to avoid calling black people Africans, and thereby recognizing their prior claim to the land. The term 'Bantu' was used to refer to blacks; in one of the original black languages it simply means 'people'.

5. This version is a revised version of 'Sizwe Banzi is Dead', in A Night at the Theatre, ed. Ronald Harwood (London: Methuen, 1982). The correct spelling of Sizwe Banzi's name in the original language and the original title of the play is with a 'z'; in England, however, the 'z' in Banzi was mistakenly changed to an 's', so Bansi has stuck in all published versions.

Field Day's Greeks
(and Russians)

Seamus Deane

Sophocles has been Field Day's Greek dramatist. In 1984 the company staged Tom Paulin's *The Riot Act*, an adaptation of *Antigone*, directed by Stephen Rea; and in 1990 Rea combined with Bob Crowley to direct Seamus Heaney's *The Cure at Troy*, an adaptation of *Philoctetes*.[1] And as Sophocles was the company's resident Greek, so Chekhov was its resident Russian, also with two adaptations — Brian Friel's *Three Sisters* in 1981 and Frank McGuinness's *Uncle Vanya* in 1995.[2] There is an obvious contrast between the two sets of adaptations. In the Greek plays, catastrophe has arrived at the centre of the political and social system; with the Russian plays, it is occurring, in a premonitory fashion, at the fringes.

Ever since Daniel Corkery induced his famous students, Frank O'Connor and Sean O'Faolain, to look to the Russians to learn the art of the short story and to find in them an echo of Irish experience, it has been an accepted part of the Irish literary repertoire to see in this Corkeronian and Corkonian fascination with stifling provincialism and slow-motion disintegration a model for Irish experience as such. Indeed, the ossification of the community that was cut off from progress, modernity, cosmopolitanism and even revolution became an obsession in the literature of the new Free State (later the Republic) and eventually, after its usual time-lag, of the new Northern Irish statelet. It was not a new preoccupation. Joyce and George Moore and a host of others had either seized or been seized by it in the days of the Irish Revival. But they understood provincialism historically and politically as a condition that was explicable and mutable. In Corkery's pupils, a cohort that extended far beyond O'Connor and O'Faolain, provincialism came to be understood as a racial, even ontological condition, as inescapable in a community that, because of some inner necessity or flaw, had forsworn the modern world and turned inward to die. This was a literary trope that was to assume a secondary life in historical writing and was to claim for itself there an explanatory and apologetic force. According to this, Irish civilization had not been put to the sword by a colonizing and imperial British power. It had failed to survive unstoppable change; or it had resisted enforced change, and fallen into nationalist nostalgia; or if it had welcomed change it was only to recognize that it had greeted its own demise. Whichever way it behaved, it was doomed.[3]

The Russians were taken to be exemplars. They knew how to universalize a provincial condition in a literature that was meditative, exquisite in its psychological nuance, oblique in its political implication, and tragically cadenced in its depiction of the death of a privileged landowning class whose inner torment took precedence as a literary subject over its scandalous oppressiveness. In Ireland, this Chekhovian or pseudo-Chekhovian attitude governed the treatment of the fading Irish landowning classes who became in retrospect highly sensitive possessors of a rich culture tragically lost with the onset of a coarser, more violent, more democratic age. This fantasy has been recycled so often that it is by now fully integrated into that automated system of literary-historical reproduction that has sought to make the perpetrators and beneficiaries of oppression and injustice the victims of a complex fate. For present purposes, the interest of the Irish adaptations of Chekhov or of the Russians in general (especially Turgenev) is that they combined a harsh realism about the impoverished condition of a very specific community along with ghostly intimations of a tragic ending that was desired as much as it was dreaded by its victims.[4] The search for the tragic element as a means of universalizing an historical condition is sometimes undertaken with great subtlety, but once indulged it is unrelenting in its determination to give to the most improbable historical moments the grandeur of an eternal symbol. It historicizes and dehistoricizes simultaneously by stressing the specific circumstances of a time and place as exemplary of a human condition that is *semper eadem*. Moscow can be Dublin or London or any great and entrancing cynosure for the eyes of the desiring provincial in whose miniaturized world the thumbprint of the universal is, nevertheless, visible to all but her or him. Nineteenth- and early twentieth-century Russian fiction and drama, and, in a different but connected manner, Italian opera, had an especial attraction for their Irish admirers and adapters because they too had witnessed an agrarian society transformed by revolutionary nationalism, into which a socialist alloy was blended, from serfdom to a species of modernity at the expense of a former ruling class. In Russian and in Irish writing, the vanishing class was often given the tragic role in this process. Its tragedy was understood to be inescapable, the product of an historical process that had eroded its economic and political base. But such a view of the historical process, especially in its literary manifestations, often became indistinguishable from the traditional conception of an unavoidable human fate. Sometimes this was actually reinforced by the fusion of conceptions of history with adaptations of evolutionary theory. Turgenev and Lermontov in Russia, George Eliot and Hardy in England, George Moore and Somerville and Ross (*The Real Charlotte*) in Ireland, all give us tragic accounts of mundane lives that sometimes seem the more tragic because so mundane, or seem the less mundane because they achieve some kind of tragic status. Novels and short stories of their nature rarely seek for that intensity of confrontation between individual and fate which drama and opera are more equipped, in some of their severer forms, to provide.

Such questions bring us to the Greeks and, as far as Field Day is concerned, to Sophocles. Or almost so. First, the Russians are owed a farewell. It would be difficult, I think, to say that the Friel and McGuinness adaptations of Chekhov have much in common or that there is a particular Field Day 'take' on Chekhov. (There is also the fact that Friel had left Field Day before McGuinness's play appeared.) But it would be possible to say that in several plays and pamphlets, Field Day had opposed prevailing systems of political and cultural authority in Ireland, especially when, like Northern Irish Unionism, they were systems that disguised their criminality behind a façade of legality and/or democracy or even, when desperate, of 'culture'. The problem Field Day pursued and perhaps exemplified was that of understanding the always-changing ratio between the cultural and the political.

All initial efforts at political reform in Northern Ireland, represented by the Civil Rights Association, had been met by state violence; it was obvious then, as since, that Unionism and justice could not coexist. A cultural reshaping of the assumptions that supported the state (and its violence) was a reasonable enterprise on Field Day's part, or on the part of any organization that wanted to see real change. However, if the state could not survive the required changes, what was the relation of cultural renovation to the eventual political demolition of the statelet? One possible rendering of this situation was the tragic one. What began to emerge, both as propaganda and, in some instances, as the product of analysis, was the notion that, once again, the people who were in power, and all their beneficiaries, constituted the embattled community that was fearful of losing its privileges and was therefore the legitimate recipient of sympathy and might even – however improbably – be regarded as worthy of tragic status. This attitude was enhanced by the widespread feeling among the oppressed minority that time was running out for the Unionists, that people who had taken all were bound to lose at least some political and economic-cultural power, and that once begun, that process would continue to a bitter but deserving end. The end of the union was taken by many anti-Unionists as well as by many Unionists to be inevitable once any modification of its initially naked sectarian structures had been conceded. The basic ingredients were there – a specific and provincial history, an inflamed sense of imminent catastrophe, implacable hostility towards inevitable change, and, in some tremulously close future, a transition from the fertile possibilities of historical circumstance to the iron logic of an inescapable fate.

What was most specific in 1984, when Paulin's play was presented, was the transformation of the political world that had been effected by the hunger-strikes of 1981, in which ten republican prisoners had died, and in which the British and Unionist position appeared to have redefined itself yet again as one of 'No Surrender', 'Not an Inch', and other such neo-Creonisms. The reanimation of the British state's failing authority by brutal mini-wars on the coal-miners, on Argentina and on the republican movement in Northern Ireland was one of the transient consequences of Margaret Thatcher's belief that polarizing a political situation was the easiest way to find an ostensibly ethical ground for action within it. Predictably, Northern Irish Unionists welcomed her as a Daniel come to judgement, even though it was her policies that finally transformed the Provisional IRA from a guerrilla movement into a party political organization and laid the basis for its long-term support within the minority community. Still, Thatcher did invoke, in however vicious and suburban a spirit, the idea that the state had to obey ethical imperatives that were senior to all other ethical demands – familial, tribal, religious (sectarian) – by virtue of their universality and impartiality. Other demands might be intuitively more attractive; their satisfaction might be more heartwarming in the short term; but the greater political community's needs must prevail over all. The rule of law must be asserted against capricious behaviour, against locally sanctioned custom, against the extra-territorial demands of the religious spirit. Paulin's version of Sophocles is stylistically alert to these sorts of tension, as well as to the larger tension of invoking Greek tragedy to represent Northern Ireland. The alertness cannot but pass over into embarrassment at times, signalled by the intensification of local dialect effects. The local accent's self-conscious provincialism sometimes parodies the seriousness of the issues which it is otherwise meant to ground. There is also the author's awareness that the pseudo-ethics of the Thatcherite or Northern Irish State cannot bear much scrutiny and must indeed degenerate, time and again, into sheer intransigence. Thus, from the outset, the prevailing political situation has a withering effect on the complexity of Sophocles' play and of most of its famous adaptations. Despite this, the larger questions remain in dispute.

For over a century, Irish revolutionaries and rebels have claimed political status and the British state has repeatedly, but not consistently, denied it to them. It avers instead that they are 'common criminals' and simultaneously says that to admit them to political status would be to acknowledge that the legitimacy of the Ukanian state could be properly called into question. The republican weapon against this criminalization policy has been the hunger-strike – the refusal of food to the point of death for the political and ethical principles involved.[5]

The Riot Act is also an extension of Paulin's quarrel with Conor Cruise O'Brien who had provided a crude and straightforward Unionist reading of *Antigone* in his book *States of Ireland* (1972).[6] According to O'Brien it was the Irish Antigone (Bernadette Devlin McAliskey) who had brought all that woe to the Unionist state. Paulin certainly rebukes this reading: O'Brien's shoddy analysis of the Northern Ireland situation is 'supported by his interpretation of Sophocles' great tragedy, so it is crucial to recognize how badly he misinterprets the play'. Paulin continues:

O'Brien's loyalties are to the 'daylight gods', and he sees the political conflict in the play as one of unequal values and unequal personal responsibilities. Creon, therefore, is both individual and institution, while Antigone, like St Joan, appears as an individual ahead of her supporters. She is 'headstrong' and therefore more responsible because she can supposedly exercise choice. So Creon is rendered almost innocent by his immobile precedence, his simply being there. This is a severe distortion of the tragic conflict.

A worshipper of the state, like O'Brien, is bound to regard Antigone as a troublemaker; more usually, in modern adaptations, it is Creon's position that is liable to caricature. In his essay on O'Brien, Paulin makes it clear that he is attracted to Hegel's reading of the play which denies the absoluteness of either Creon's or Antigone's claims. Hegel reads the play as a contest between

'Instinctive Powers of Feeling, Love and Kinship' and 'the daylight gods of free and self-conscious, social, and political life'.[7]

In Paulin's version of Creon's opening speech, phrases from various Irish, British and American politicians help to highlight Creon's declaration, about the supremacy of loyalty to the state over loyalty to a friend, inverted and echoed in E. M. Forster's famous dictum in *Two Cheers for Democracy*:

However, let me say this, and say it plainly right at the very outset, that if ever any man here should find himself faced with a choice between betraying his country and betraying his friend, then he must swiftly place that friend in the hands of the authorities. That is the only right and proper decision and we must all abide by it.[8]

This rebuttal of a central tenet of liberalism, at least of the Bloomsbury variety, according to which no private relation should take precedence over public obligation, is part of Paulin's political strategy.[9] It is, accordingly, quite easy to see Creon as a Unionist intransigent and Antigone as a republican martyr, one asserting the law of the state as a universal, the other a more fundamental natural law as superior to any created by humans. But this is an unattractive proposition, certainly from Field Day's point of view – although this does not mean that it has to be disavowed. Joe Cleary has pointed up some of the difficulties here; Irish republicanism, as represented by Antigone, may be taken to stand for all that 'feminized' allegiance to natural feeling and ancestral practice that is more properly the historic inheritance of ethnic nationalism.[10] Further, the Hegelian reading is not quite to the point here, since it assumes that Creon represents the just claims of the state as such. Part of the problem in relation to Northern Ireland is that the state is not felt to have any right on its side at all; it is an imposition, a coercive entity founded to sustain injustice and exclusiveness for the sake of one group over another. In that light, there is no question of seeing the Northern Irish problem as one in which the injustices are evenly distributed; it is simply untrue that there is much to be said on both sides. Sophocles' play is not interested in achieving some version of modern TV's notion of 'balance' between two sides. The implication of equal rights already tilts the play politically and certainly would make any reader hesitate to see it as embodying or exploring a collision between Irish republicanism and British/Irish Unionism.

The difficulty is compounded, I believe, if we take into consideration the two views of the hunger-strikes that dominated most of the political debates of these years. One view was that the strikes were heroic and dedicated actions that ultimately won the political recognition the prisoners demanded, and exposed the violence upon which the state depended for its legitimacy. Another was that they were a cultic expression of the victimhood eagerly sought by nationalists which had, in all their somatic excess (the dirty protest, the starvation, the immersion in the stricken and self-immolating bodily suffering), finally been defeated by stern but impartially sane reason. Certainly the United Kingdom as a political system has readily presented itself as a symbolic universe in which English sense has restrained Celtic (and fringe) excess; in which modernity has restrained unhealthy immersions in historical nostalgia and in bitter memories of massacre, genocide, cultural destruction. Yet republicanism resists such mystifications, while acknowledging the power they have established. The hunger-strikes were about the reordering of the symbolic universe that belonged to nationalisms (Irish and British) and the denial of a space outside that (the space of being a 'political' prisoner who refused to consent to or believe in that symbolic universe) by a state that was itself ethnically nationalist and brutally sectarian while pretending to be neither – indeed to be the reverse of these. This is an aspect of the dispute that is not embraced by Paulin's adaptation. The reason may be that it was and is no part of the play's ambition or interest. However, if the play is to be read as a commentary on, or as an allegory of, the prevailing political situation, it scarcely attends to the republican position at all. It may be more centrally about nationalism and Unionism. Perhaps, as Joe Cleary has pointed out, the situation is more introverted than this. According to him, it is more convincingly a play about the internal dynamics of a

Unionism by which Paulin is repelled but to which he would like to find reason to be attracted. Antigone might represent a Unionist culture to which he could give his allegiance were Creon not so irrationally unyielding. In the interval, the only recourse is indeed a form of liberalism that gives priority to friendship and the private life and surveys the debased public life with a Forsterian dismay.

The Riot Act and Derek Mahon's *High Time*, an adaptation of Molière's *L'École des Maris*, appeared together as a double bill in September 1984 at the Guildhall in Derry.[11] The production emphasized the common theme of rebellion against authority, while contrasting the genres. Mahon's work was played in punk costume and was wild and riotous; Paulin's was played in stern greys and silvers, with a claustrophobic stage-set intensifying the sense of inescapable tragedy. In one sense, a political point against established authority was scored; in another, the unresolved dilemma within Paulin's play was not fully addressed. Field Day's Creon deserved all he got, but Paulin's Creon, however 'cack-handed', did not get all he deserved.[12] The production was more decisive than the play, but the play demanded from its director a decisiveness that it could not itself provide. It may be the case, as Clair Wills has argued, that Paulin's belief in the Hegelian idea of the state as the site of reconciliation between civic and tribal rights dominates his version of *Antigone*. Wills sees this belief weakening in later works, like Paulin's volume of poems *Fivemiletown* (1987) and his later collection of essays, *Minotaur: Poetry and the Nation State* (1992).[13] I would modify her view only slightly by saying that there is an irresolution already there in *The Riot Act*. The desire to achieve a resolution is more evident than the achievement itself. Indeed, the achievement is present almost exclusively in the form of a desire.

With *The Cure at Troy*, his adaptation of Sophocles' *Philoctetes*, Seamus Heaney avoided the ready-made reactions that attend upon any dramatic version of *Antigone*.[14] He would have been familiar from his undergraduate days with the account of the story given by Edmund Wilson in the title-essay of his famous collection *The Wound and the Bow* (1941). As with other Sophoclean plays, there is here too a dispute between the ethical requirements of the public and the private life which Wilson believes has been resolved by Neoptolemus' realization of the specifically human (non-political) relationship with Philoctetes:

Yet in taking the risk to his cause which is involved in the recognition of his common humanity with the sick man, in refusing to break his word, he dissolves Philoctetes' stubbornness, and thus cures him and sets him free, and saves the campaign as well.[15]

Wilson's reading allows for no tragic conclusion and, I believe, it is a reading that Heaney follows. He emphasizes, more than Wilson does, that the injustice, pain and suffering endured by Philoctetes demand redress and are not to be appeased by the political expedience of an Odysseus. However, the relationship between expedience and justice is important, for it complicates Odysseus' argument about the priority of the Greek cause over the pain of an individual who has been cruelly maltreated. If anyone other than Philoctetes could use the bow, he would simply steal it as a necessary weapon for state survival.[16] But since it can only be drawn by Philoctetes, he must be persuaded in some way to forgive the wrong done to him, to emerge from his isolation and pain and, in winning redemption from these, to gain success for the Greek political community in the Trojan War. That he will emerge can hardly be doubted; his solitariness, as Lukács pointed out, 'is a specific social fate, not a universal *condition humaine*'.[17]

The process of persuasion has, then, two stages. Neoptolemus, the son of Achilles, is to deceive Philoctetes into surrendering the bow and coming aboard the ship that will bring him to Troy. This done or almost done, Neoptolemus must refuse the Odyssean strategy, return the bow to Philoctetes and keep the promise to bring Philoctetes home, not to Troy to fight for those who abandoned him. Both Wilson's essay and Heaney's play at this point, faced with the impasse that Sophocles had produced, read the intervention of the demi-god Heracles (Hercules) as a moment of emancipation. The supernatural is internalized, Philoctetes hears 'the voice of Hercules in my head',[18] and then the voice of Hercules converges with that of the Chorus. The subjective recognition is socialized and even universalized and the healing process proceeds and spreads apace.

It may be asked, has the impasse really been resolved? The final dispute between Odysseus and Neoptolemus seems beyond resolution. In Alasdair MacIntyre's account, the reconciliation of the chief protagonists

is at the *ad hoc* bidding of Heracles: nothing is learned or could be learned within this framework about how more generally the rival claims of the justice of effectiveness and of the justice of desert are to be evaluated. That those claims can only be rightly evaluated within a theological framework is indeed part of what Sophocles says to his fellow citizens.[19]

It does not solve the issue by saying Hercules' voice is the inner voice of some miraculous revelation; it dissolves it. The words attributed to Hercules and then to the Chorus persuade by incantation and imperatives – hope, believe, call – that sound like advice:

> The longed-for tidal wave
> Of justice can rise up,
> And hope and history rhyme.
>
> So hope for great sea-change . . .
> Believe that a further shore . . .
> Call miracle self-healing . . .[20]

Exhortation is the only resource left; or, in Plato's view, as indicated by MacIntyre, the impasse can only be resolved in philosophical discourse, not in tragic drama. Anyway, there is nothing tragic left. Even Neoptolemus, who had been so torn by the competing demands of effective action on behalf of the community and the appropriate recompense for injustice, finally has it both ways. The stink of suffering yields to the fragrance of justice. He keeps his integrity and Philoctetes is redeemed from pain and the Greek cause is served.

Thus, as in Paulin's case, there would seem to be a moment at which the intractability of the political situation, with its obvious references to Northern Ireland, has to be both acknowledged and refused. In 1991, I reviewed the London production at the Tricycle Theatre and said that if Heaney

were a less powerful writer, he would be ecumenical; hence my insistence on the irenic quality of his work in general and of this play in particular. Ecumenism in this sense is an avoidance of the political. *The Cure at Troy* is not an exercise in deflection, escapism. It may be that there is a certain weariness with Philoctetes and his wound. Heaney, like the rest of us, is fed up with a botched politics, the Green and Orange Lemnos, with Odysseus as visiting Secretary of State. The turn in his poetry that is matched by *The Cure at Troy* is not simply a turn from ground to air; it is a turn from place to time, from a past that was literally grounded – in bogs, in earth, in graves – to a mobile future that refuses locality and localism and risks another kind of language, of perception.[21]

However, in retrospect, the 'turn' I spoke of here seems to be a longing for a harmony that is invoked before or without the actualizing of the local political settlement. It is indeed a play that looks for peace but cannot see how peace is going to come about; instead it declares that, by some future date, peace will have come about and we will all be the better for it. Some of the responses to Heaney's play seem to be governed by the belief that it sponsored the arrival of peace, that it is a play about the change of heart that must accompany the peace process. But it is not. Before peace, it speaks of the arrival of justice – that first. Then war. Then peace. Troy has still to be sacked. The siege – as always in Northern Ireland – continues. Troy's 'meaning' in the play's system of political reference is ostensibly clear; it refers to Northern Ireland. But there is the problem that it also refers to a place that is finally sacked and that this prelude to the final battle, which seems to be about a miraculous change, is not in any coherent sense really about an alteration that will bring reconciliation. Instead, it will bring victory to one side and defeat to the other. This can all be dismissed by denying that the play should be mapped precisely on to the Northern Irish situation. But that would surely be to say that it can be partially mapped in that way only up to the critical moment. Then the allegory or the reference system can be abandoned. This seems unsatisfactory. It's a way of having your cake and then not eating it. The issue has to be faced. Heaney wants to redeem both Neoptolemus and Philoctetes. When they go to Troy, they go as ethically independent of and superior to Odysseus who has attempted to gain an important goal – the success of the Greeks – by deceitful means. But neither Philoctetes nor Neoptolemus can resolve the ethical dilemma they face. Divine intervention is necessary. The miracle is the consequence of an intervention, not of a realization.

Yet, in a strange way, Heaney's play is as much about the intransigence of Philoctetes as Paulin's is about the intransigence of Creon. The suffering of Philoctetes is real; yet it is also indulged and finally becomes tyrannical. Neoptolemus addresses him at times in words that would seem more applicable to Creon:

> The danger is you'll break if you don't bend.[22]

> . . . you're like a brute
> That can only foam at the mouth.[23]

The whole system of political injustice is sustained at this critical moment by Philoctetes' refusal to surrender the suffering by which he has become defined. Creon is similarly entrapped. He is not intransigent for the sake of an ethical or political principle. He will yield almost anything but intransigence itself. Yet what is ethically indefensible in these instances is also what is politically attractive and effective. Paulin and Heaney expose the enormous investment that stereotyping of the self demands in order to sustain the symbolic order that requires the paralysis which makes stereotypical behaviour so effective. Such a system is bound to be archaic; it depends on obsession and repetition. It has the attraction of conferring identity upon those who refuse the labour of creating it. But to maintain the identity, either of tyrant or of victim, it is necessary to preserve the political system (and therefore the symbolic order) that structures these relationships.[24] Little wonder that in both plays, the imminent demise of the political system is heralded by irreversible loss (in Paulin's case) or by an irresistible miracle (in Heaney's case). Neither play truly sees transformation and reconciliation as a process that is activated before catastrophe strikes. It is more the case that this is the condition that is recommended – or that it is hinted will be enforced – after the catastrophe, with Antigone and Haemon dead and with Troy defeated and destroyed. In this respect, both plays enact one of the paradoxes that affected the whole Field Day project. Based on the notion that a transformation of Northern Irish and of all Irish society was necessary and desirable if catastrophe were to be avoided, it also believed that it was only the catastrophe that could bring about the transformation. Russia was one model for the elaboration of this paradox; ancient Greece was the other. Both enabled these writers to think of the relationship between the psychic and the political, although the nature of that relationship remained problematic both for them and for the company that produced their plays.

Notes

1. Field Day wanted to do a production of *The Island*, Athol Fugard's adaptation of *Antigone*; but it could not get financing for this, on the ground that it would be politically too sensitive, from the Arts Council of Northern Ireland. Instead, the company produced Fugard's *Boesman and Lena* (1983), directed by Clare Davidson.
2. Field Day was founded in 1980 by Stephen Rea and Brian Friel. In 1981, Seamus Heaney, Tom Paulin, David Hammond and Seamus Deane joined them as fellow directors. Thomas Kilroy was a director in 1986–90. Brian Friel resigned in 1994 and Tom Paulin in 1995. Of the directors, Friel provided four plays: *Translations* (1980), *Three Sisters* (1981), *The Communication Cord* (1982) and *Making History* (1988); Kilroy provided two: *Double Cross* (1986) and *Madam Macadam's Travelling Theatre* (1991); Heaney and Paulin the plays discussed above. Stephen Rea played the lead role in eleven of the Field

Day productions and directed four. There were fourteen productions in all between 1980 and 1998, nine of them world premières.

3. This is a central theme in Sean O'Faolain's biographies of Daniel O'Connell and Hugh O'Neill, *The King of the Beggars* (1938) and *The Great O'Neill* (1942). These are important works in the genesis of the revisionist school in Irish historical writing, which depended in large part on the claim that modernity accompanied colonialism and that both, while not an unmixed blessing, nevertheless redeemed Irish civilization from tribalism, backwardness, etc. The more benign form of this argument, when applied to the vanishing Anglo-Irish, entered the qualification that the doom attendant upon that particular grouping was tragic since it marked the arrival of modernity, not in its imperial 'improving' version, but in its degenerate, mass-democratic version. Yeats's later plays and poems and all the Big House novels and memoirs of the twentieth century, especially those of Elizabeth Bowen, are the main sources of this interpretation.

4. Among other adaptations of Chekhov are Thomas Kilroy's *The Seagull* (1981) and Frank McGuinness's *Three Sisters* (1990). Brian Friel adapted Turgenev's *A Month in the Country* (1992).

5. An early discussion of this issue, published some years after the Amnesty Act 1885, is George Sigerson, *Political Prisoners at Home and Abroad* (London: K. Paul, Trench, Trübner, 1890).

6. Paulin's attack on O'Brien was included in his collection of essays *Ireland and the English Crisis* (Newcastle upon Tyne: Bloodaxe, 1984); it was initially published as 'The Making of a Loyalist', *Times Literary Supplement* (14 November 1980): 1283–5.

7. Paulin, 'The Making of a Loyalist', p. 1283.

8. Cited by Paulin, ibid. See *Two Cheers for Democracy* (1938; rptd New York: Holmes and Meier, 1979), p. 68: 'I hate the idea of causes, and if I had to choose between betraying my country and betraying my friend, I hope I should have the guts to betray my country.'

9. Tom Paulin, *The Riot Act* (London: Faber & Faber 1985), p. 16.

10. Joe Cleary, 'Domestic Troubles: Tragedy and the Northern Ireland Conflict', *South Atlantic Quarterly* 98(3) (Summer 1999): 501–37. Further treatment of some of these issues and their ramifications is provided in Cleary's 'Modernization and Aesthetic Ideology in Contemporary Irish Culture', in Ray Ryan (ed.), *Writing in the Irish Republic: Literature, Culture, Politics 1949–1999* (London, Macmillan: 2000), pp. 105–29.

11. See Marilynn J. Richtarik, *Acting Between the Lines: The Field Day Company and Irish Cultural Politics 1980–1984* (Oxford: Clarendon, 1994), pp. 216–30.
12. Paulin, *The Riot Act*, p. 62.
13. Clair Wills, *Improprieties: Politics and Sexuality in Northern Irish Poetry* (Oxford: Clarendon, 1993), pp. 132–7.
14. Heaney, according to Paddy Woodworth in 'Field Day's men and the re-making of Ireland', *Irish Times* (5 November 1990): 10, 'disclaimed any Northern Irish allegory in his adaptation of a Greek play'. Woodworth goes on to say that, nevertheless, the play will be seen as Heaney sees the work of O'Casey and Friel: he quotes Heaney thus: 'For them, drama comes to be a factor in the re-reading and rewriting of history, a way of reshaping the audience in posterity, if not in the stalls.'
15. Edmund Wilson, *The Wound and the Bow: Seven Studies in Literature* (1941; rptd. New York: Farrar Strauss Giroux, 1978). The essay is entitled '*Philoctetes*: the Wound and the Bow'. Excerpts from this essay were cited in the theatre programme to the production on 1 October 1990. The first of these reminds us that, according to Wilson, Sophocles 'shows himself particularly successful with people whose natures have been poisoned by narrow fanatical hatreds'. Accompanying these excerpts are others from Bernard Knox, *The Heroic Temper: Studies in Sophoclean Tragedy* (1964; rptd Berkeley: University of California Press, 1983), p. 122; Knox argues that Achilles and Odysseus represent two contrasting ideals for fifth-century Athenians; the Achillean ideal is aristocratic and warlike; the Odyssean ideal democratic, 'insisting on success combined with glory rather than sacrificed for it'.
16. Sophocles is ambiguous on this point. Clearly, the idea that it is the bow and not Philoctetes that the Greeks require increases the force of the argument for effective reason (and action). This is the Odyssean position in its least complicated form. In Heaney's version, it is made plain that it is the bow that Odysseus wants, not Philoctetes; either Odysseus himself or Teucer can bend the bow (see p. 58). Presumably, Heaney wants to intensify the ethical question by reminding us that Odysseus can use the bow and thereby make the position of Neoptolemus, when he returns the bow to Philoctetes, the more exposed to the charge that he is betraying the Greek cause. Ultimately, the process of persuading Philoctetes to surrender himself to the Greek

cause and also to give himself over to the prospect of a future healing is what fascinates. But its evolution remains problematic, especially in Wilson's and Heaney's versions, where the divine intervention dissolves an impasse and then is read retrospectively as a moment of subjective transformation or insight.

17. Georg Lukács, 'The Ideology of Modernism', in *The Meaning of Contemporary Realism*, trans. J. and N. Mander (London: Merlin, 1963), p. 20.

18. Seamus Heaney, *The Cure at Troy: A Version of Sophocles' Philoctetes* (Derry: 1990), p. 78.

19. Alasdair MacIntyre, *Whose Justice? Which Rationality?* (London: Duckworth, 1988), p. 63. For the discussion of the play, see pp. 58–63.

20. Heaney, *The Cure at Troy*, p. 77.

21. Seamus Deane, 'Oranges and Lemnos', *New Statesman* 120 (5 April 1991): 18–19 (18).

22. Heaney, *The Cure at Troy*, p. 75.

23. Ibid., p. 72.

24. Cf. Slavoj Zizek, *The Sublime Object of Ideology* (London: Verso, 1989), especially pp. 153–78, 213–14.

Antigone

Tom Paulin

Early one snowy January morning, in 1984, Stephen Rea phoned me in a dull little town called Charlottesville where I was living – it's a famous town, too, because of Jefferson's twinned master-pieces, the University of Virginia, and Monticello. Stephen asked me would I do a version of *Antigone* for the Field Day by the end of March? I said I would and then asked him had he any advice about how to do it? Go easy on the choruses, Stephen said, they can be a bit of a bore.

Later that morning I crossed the snowy campus of Jefferson's great neo-classical university – I was teaching in the English department there – and borrowed a copy of Jebb's edition of the play. It was a brittle Victorian tome – last borrowed from the library, I noted, in 1903 – but it had marvellously detailed notes accompanying Jebb's stilted translation. Every so often as I worked on my version, this lavishly beautiful stanza of Yeats's chorus on love 'From the "Antigone"' came into my head:

> Overcome – O bitter sweetness,
> Inhabitant of the soft cheek of a girl –
> The rich man and his affairs,
> The fat flocks and the fields' fatness,
> Mariners, rough harvesters,
> Overcome Gods upon Parnassus.[1]

Yeats's anguished lines communicated the tragedy of the play, which is about Creon's refusal to allow the burial of his nephew,

Polyneices, who has fought against Thebes, the city Creon rules. Eteocles, Antigone's other brother, has been killed fighting for Thebes and his body is buried with full honours. Antigone, Creon's niece, buries Polyneices' body, is caught and sentenced to be walled in a cave. The Chorus and the blind prophet, Tiresias, try to make Creon change his mind.

When he does so, it is too late – his son Haemon, who is betrothed to Antigone, has killed himself after quarrelling with Creon and finding Antigone's dead body – she has committed suicide. Eurydice, Creon's wife, also commits suicide.

It was a play that belonged in Ireland. In fact, there were three different versions of *Antigone* produced in Ireland in 1984, or four if one counts Fugard's *The Island*, or five with the film *Anne Devlin*, about Robert Emmet's housekeeper. But as I wrote I didn't know that Brendan Kennelly and Aidan Carl Mathews were hard at work on the play. The only time I'd seen it was in the form of a black-and-white film in modern Greek which I'd watched in a late-night cinema in the centre of Belfast when I was at secondary school in the 1960s. It was before the Troubles but my friends and I were sure it was important, so we went and saw the film at eleven one night and walked back through the dark streets talking about it. All I remember now is Antigone being walled in the cave.[2]

Later, I got to know the play through reading Conor Cruise O'Brien's *States of Ireland*, a study of 'the politics of polarization' which applies the story of *Antigone* to the Northern Irish situation and argues that it was Antigone's free decision 'and that alone, which precipitated the tragedy'. O'Brien sides with Ismene, Antigone's sister, who tries to persuade her not to bury the body of their brother, Polyneices. Ismene is caught in the middle, a classically liberal position, and one forbidden in ancient Greece, where there was *nomos* (an understood law) which made it accepted practice not to remain neutral in a civil war.

Really, Ismene and O'Brien side with Creon. To mount a production of *Antigone* in the North of Ireland all those years ago would be to take on O'Brien's Unionist position and to suggest that the contradictions within the state meant that its politics would always be unstable, violent, tragic, until the border disappeared.

Hegel, I knew, believed that *Antigone* was the perfect exemplar of tragedy. He said that the sacred laws which Antigone revered, and which made her bury her brother, are the instinctive Powers of Feeling, Love and Kinship, not the daylight gods of free and self-conscious social and political life. Hegel argued that neither the right of the family nor the right of the state is denied in the play – what is denied is the absoluteness of the claim of each. Antigone's loyalties are to the *dei inferni,* the gods of the dark instinctual forces of family and tribe, while Creon's are to rational civic life. The great English critic A. C. Bradley has a remarkable essay on Hegel's idea of tragedy in which he argues that Hegel's German nationalism made him too sympathetic to Antigone.[3]

O'Brien's target was Irish nationalism, Bernadette Devlin McAliskey and the Northern Irish Civil Rights Movement, which he saw as responsible for the violent politics of Northern Ireland. He misinterpreted the play, and in doing a version of it I set out to try and prove him wrong again – I say 'again' because I had criticized his account of the play in a review of his Ewart-Biggs lectures in 1981.

Back in Ireland in September that year, I watched nervously as the actors in Derry's Guildhall rehearsed the script I'd written. I imagined Creon partly as a Northern Irish Secretary, and had him give a press conference where he used the usual cliché about doing a great deal of listening. When Douglas Hurd took over as Secretary of State for Northern Ireland that month, I noticed that he duly trotted out the cliché. I wanted Creon to be a kind of puritan gangster, a megalomaniac who spoke alternately in an English public school voice and a deep menacing Ulster growl. I used the Ulster vernacular as far as I could, and slashed away at the choruses to make the play run for fifty minutes and no more.

But there were problems in rehearsal – the cast rebelled against the director who resigned ten days into the three weeks we had to get the play ready for the stage. I had problems with the set – too ethnic Irish I thought – three whitewashed walls splashed with red paint, a bit like a courtyard after a shoot-out in a spaghetti western.

I was going to voice this doubt, but before I could the set designer had resigned in sympathy with the director. Stephen Rea was already playing Creon; now he took over as director. On stage he glowered like Lord Edward Henry Carson, in rehearsal he courteously restored the cast's confidence.

Meanwhile, we had to find a new set designer. While Julie Berber, the Field Day manager, phoned possible designers, I tried to think of an alternative set. The next morning, I woke at five, got out of bed and walked through the silent city. I looked up at the Victorian gothic Guildhall – no joy there. Then something led me down a street I didn't know – Great James's Street – and I found myself in front of a disused Presbyterian church. It was a perfect, neo-classical meeting-house, which represented more than a daylight god. When the new designer, Brien Vehey, arrived, I took him to the church, and then later we got hold of a book of Jefferson's architectural drawings and a new Enlightenment set emerged. *The Riot Act* toured Ireland as one half of a double bill with Derek Mahon's translation of Molière's *L'École des Maris*, which Field Day had also commissioned. I can still hear the intent, concentrated passion with which Veronica Quilligan spoke the lines I wrote for Antigone, and I worry sometimes that I inflicted my views of Hegel and O'Brien on the cast, instead of making more practical suggestions about the script.

As I sat in a packed Oxford Playhouse this winter – a teeming wet night that deterred no one – I naturally recalled my own experience of the play over more than thirty years. Would Declan Donnellan's version have something to do with Ireland? Would it have something to do with living in Blair's Britain? I began to imagine Antigone as Old Labour, Creon as New Labour. The Deputy Prime Minister, John Prescott, former ships' steward and Ruskin student, would be for Antigone, while Peter Mandelson, the then Northern Ireland Secretary, would be for the control freak, Creon. I remembered that the British miners went on strike in 1984, and situations of bitter family conflict happened in many mining communities that year. The former conservative Prime Minister, Harold Macmillan, gave a moving speech about the strike, recalling the miners he'd fought alongside in the trenches and describing them as tigers led by donkeys. He was Tiresias criticizing the miners' leader, Arthur Scargill, and warning the then Prime Minister, Mrs Thatcher's Creon.

Remembering Arthur Miller's *A View from the Bridge*, I knew that the conflict in the play is between what sociologists call *Gemeinschaft* - roughly the family – and *Gesellschaft,* which is civic or public life. It is rare to get this conflict within mainstream white British society, but many members of ethnic minorities appreciate that tension between those two worlds. For more than a quarter of a century I've been a member of an extended Indian family and have gained some appreciation of how opposed the two spheres are.

It is not criticism of Declan Donnellan's production to say that it eschews the topical. This is a highly effective platonic version of the great drama. It sets the play in a kind of rational abstract space and communicates the eternal conflict of principle in a formal and elegant manner. The actor who played Creon did so in a silky, subtle style that made me rethink the part, and I also began to imagine how a classical Roman or French republican might have regarded the ruler of Thebes. I thought of Lucius Junius Brutus who is said to have put one of his sons to death for trying to restore the Tarquins, and I began to see that Bradley had been right about the way in which Hegel's German nationalism made him too sympathetic to Antigone, and so unable to take on the complexity of Creon's actions.

Ismene was subtle and convincing, but Tara Fitzgerald, who played Antigone, failed to draw on the deep well of anguished principle that is at the core of Antigone's character. This may be a defect of the placelessness of the setting, or it may be that Britain just before the millennium was and remains a Teflon society where no principles find a sticking point. The Chorus with their staves and shaved heads were formidable, though at times their essentially undramatic interventions clouded the action. At one point Haemon asks his father, 'Do you love me unconditionally?' This is abstract terminology – the affections do not speak it – and the language has too much of a Shavian rationality ever to be the language of the heart. But this production with its stark, simple set showed that Sophocles' profound drama is still alive.

Reflecting on the production, three months later, I realize even more keenly that it expresses something that worries me about many of the students I teach in their late teens or early twenties; they seem so very far away from the highly political 1960s culture that Stephen Rea and I grew up in. I notice that the culture of individualism which is the result of Thatcher's victory in 1979 has produced a kind of apolitical selfishness and self-interestedness which makes students – English students of English literature – sometimes heavily resistant to learning anything about their own history. Watching another student's involvement in college politics, I am on the brink of saying 'Go and read *Antigone* – life is about tragic choices. Know what side you're on. Know what principles you espouse.' But so far I've kept my mouth shut. I stand before audiences of undergraduates lecturing on Milton, Marvell, Defoe – pillars of English liberty, heroes of free speech in this country, I tell them. Do not forget this. Or I lecture on Conrad's *Under Western Eyes* and recount the plot of *Antigone*. Or I talk to a proctor in full academic dress and try to explain to this academic policeman the racial injustice perpetrated by a certain faculty in the University of Oxford. It is hopeless. Some people are institutionalized – they aren't Creons, but they are his shadows, his clones.

Notes

1. *The Collected Poems of W. B. Yeats*, ed. Richard J. Finnegan, 2nd rev. edn (New York: Scribner Paperback, 1996), p. 276.
2. This was the film by George Tzavellas, *Antigone* (1962), starring Irene Papas.
3. A. C. Bradley, 'Hegel's Theory of Tragedy' (1910), in *Oxford Lectures in Poetry* (London: Macmillan, 1926), pp. 69–95.

The Cure at Troy: Production Notes in No Particular Order

Seamus Heaney

The letter and notes reprinted here were sent to Tony Taccone in April 1995. Mr Taccone was at that time working on a production with the Berkeley Repertory Theater and was due to direct *The Cure at Troy* later in the year at the Oregon Shakespeare Festival.

Dear Tony Taccone,

I hope you got my fax earlier, promising this follow-up. The material is sent on to you here just as it came out of me last night, sitting with my laptop in a cottage in Co. Wicklow. I didn't have your letter in front of me then, but I now see that I have covered in general much that you were asking about . . .

In the meantime, I shall post a copy of the whole document to your home address. (It strikes me that I could almost make it into a 'shelf-interview' – I once saw such thing done by Eugenio Montale, no less.) With all good wishes, from an erstwhile resident of 2444 Carlton Street – the white wooden gabled house in the cul-de-sac beside the supermarket. Spent 1970–1 on the first floor there. Maybe the best year of my life. Heigho!

To some extent I was following advice that my first editor at Faber once gave me: 'Never call a book by a title people are not quite sure how to pronounce.' I myself am still not quite sure if it should be Phil*oc*tetes (chiming with Socrates) or Philoct*e*tes (rhyming with sweeties). A Greek friend (speaker of modern Greek) and another person I know who reads ancient Greek – plus my own sense of the scansion of the English pentameters in the Loeb parallel text – convinced me I should go for the latter, so the sweeties option was the one in my ear all through.

But apart from the difficulties of pronunciation, the title is meant to have a certain thematic promise to it. *Cure* is backlit ever so faintly in Irish usage (or should I say Irish Catholic?) by a sense of miracle. Lourdes and all that. Warts cleared up at holy wells. Seventh son of the seventh son – that kind of thing. (But come to think of it, those faith-healing associations must give the word something of the same aura in 'reformed' English.) Anyhow, I wanted the title to prefigure a benign and unexpected turn of events. Moreover, since the play was first produced and toured all over Ireland (outside the metropolitan centres, in local halls and assembly areas of different sorts), I did not expect that the audiences would be familiar with the plots of the less well-known classical dramas: I was eager to give them a subliminal orientation.

Chorus and Choruses

I suggested three women for the Chorus, in order to give a sense that the action was being invigilated by the three Fates, the Weird Sisters or whoever – this was the mythical dimension to the decision. There was also a gender-politics aspect, insofar as the militaristic, male-bonding world of the Greek army is challenged by the anima (shall we call it?) impulse in Neoptolemus. Of course, the army wins in the end, but there has been a subversion or *bouleversement* or reversal effected by anima-action in Philoctetes also. And finally there was a casting aspect: we wanted to use some of our actresses . . .

The reversal in the original is brought about by the appearance of the *deus ex machina*. I simply had not the nerve to bring on a god two minutes from curtain, so I wanted to prepare for the sudden overturn of attitude in the hero in other ways – while still associating it with the influence of Hercules. Hence, from the beginning, I tried to link the eruption of the volcano with the god's power, so that the synaesthetic climax – flame – streamers of scarlet silk, lurid lights, synthesizer-rumble – would be prepared for and the particular guardianship and command of Hercules over Philoctetes would be well in place. (I seem to remember that in the pause between the first chorus and the beginning of the action proper we had a preliminary growl and rumble and flare-up, the god flexing somewhere off-stage, as it were.) Hercules' speech at the end (which I transpose to the Chorus) is an expression of recognition which Philoctetes has repressed: in other words, the Chorus is the voice of his unconscious.

The extra speeches for the Chorus – at the very beginning and near the end, the one beginning 'Human beings suffer . . .' – were meant to contextualize the action, and not just within a discourse that could apply to Northern Ireland politics. These two speeches also (I see it even more clearly in retrospect) defend the right of poetry/poetic drama to be something other than 'protest'. If you have time or interest, you might want to look at the last couple of pages in the title lecture of my prose collection, *The Government of the Tongue*, where some of the submerged concerns of the opening chorus – especially the lines about poetry being 'in between' – are glossed:

Here is the great paradox of poetry and of the imaginative arts in general. Faced with the brutality of the historical onslaught, they are practically useless. Yet they verify out singularity, they strike and stake out the ore of self which lies at the base of every individuated life. In one sense the efficacy of poetry is nil – no lyric has ever stopped a tank. In another sense, it is unlimited. It is like the writing in the sand in the face of which accusers and accused are left speechless and renewed.

I am thinking of Jesus' writing as it is recorded in Chapter Eight of John's Gospel, my second and concluding text:

And the scribes and Pharisees brought unto him a woman taken in adultery; and when they had set her in the midst, they say unto him, 'Master, this woman was taken in adultery, in the very act. Now Moses in the law commanded us, that such should be stoned: but what sayest thou?' This they said, tempting him, that they might have to accuse him. But Jesus stooped down, and his finger wrote on the ground, as though he heard them not. So when they continued asking him, he lifted up himself, and said unto them, 'He that is without sin among you, let him first cast a stone at her.' And again he stooped down, and wrote on the ground. And they which heard it, being convicted by their own conscience, went out one by one, beginning with the eldest, even unto the last: and Jesus was left alone, and the woman standing in the midst. When Jesus had lifted up himself, and saw none but the woman, he said unto her, 'Woman, where are those thine accusers? Hath no man condemned thee?' She said, 'No man, Lord.' And Jesus said unto her, 'Neither do I condemn thee: go, and sin no more.'

The drawing of those characters is like poetry, a break with the usual life but not an absconding from it. Poetry, like the writing, is arbitrary and marks time in every possible sense of that phrase. It does not say to the accusing crowd or to the helpless accused, 'Now a solution will take place', it does not propose to be instrumental or effective. Instead, in the rift between what is going to happen and whatever we would wish to happen, poetry holds attention for a space, functions not as distraction but as pure concentration, a focus where our power to concentrate is concentrated back on ourselves.[1]

The Northern Ireland Echoes

The first echo is the note to which the writing is tuned. I wanted to have verse that would sound natural if spoken in a Northern Ireland accent. But this is not suggesting that actors should try to *do* Northern Ireland accents: that would be a deplorable distortion. It's just that I knew beforehand that we would be using a number of actors from Ulster, would be opening in Derry, touring the North (as well as the South) and operating under the banner of Field Day; Field Day is a company whose purposes include the revoicing and revisioning of experience by 'talking Irish', as it were (as in 'talking dirty', not as in 'talking French' – the 'Irish' here is adverb rather than noun).

The consequences of this in the diction are, I think, minimal. I was not aiming for a dialect drama. It was more that a local intonation was possible. So, Philoctetes says – a little too often maybe – *Och*. This is a very Irish monosyllable, Scottish too, and meant to make the play at home in the deep ear of its first audience. But I would want an American actor to stick to *Aw*. Otherwise, the whole thing will come out in inverted commas, a performance of an 'Irish' performance rather than a living affect.

Another example: Neoptolemus (or is it the Chorus – I don't have a text near me just now) asks Philoctetes towards the end if he is going to stay there 'saying no forever'.[2] This echoes the Ulster Unionist refusal of the Anglo-Irish Agreement in 1987, when they would not grant that the Irish government had any right to be involved in the envisaging or the conduct of new political arrangements in Northern Ireland. (Incidentally, Thatcher's Tories stuck to their guns – oops, that's what she said about the IRA – and the ultimate result, I would argue, is the relatively hopeful conditions which prevail at present. If the Unionists are still saying no to an Irish dimension, they are doing so with less overbearing and less credibility.) Still, Philoctetes is not meant to be understood as a trimly allegorical representation of hardline Unionism. He is first and foremost a character in the Greek play, himself alone with his predicament, just as he is also an aspect of *every* intransigence, republican as well as Unionist, a manifestation of the swank of victimhood, the righteous refusal, the wounded one whose identity has become dependent upon the wound, the betrayed one whose energy and pride is a morbid symptom.

In other words, while there are parallels, and wonderfully suggestive ones, between the psychology and predicaments of certain characters in the play and certain parties and conditions in Northern Ireland, the play does not exist in order to exploit them. The parallels are richly incidental rather than essential to the version. The essential travail is change; the essential conflict the one that Neoptolemus exhibits, between truth of institution and the demands of solidarity, between personal integrity and political expedience. But still, of course, all that is very complicated: Philoctetes is 'cured' but cured into the very loyalty and solidarity which Neoptolemus had to flout in order to bring the cure about. The play, in fact, could be described in words that Yeats uses about his book *A Vision*: it is 'a stylistic arrangement of experience', an attempt 'to hold in a single thought reality and justice'.

Hope and History

I don't think I would have had the gall to do a play with such a consoling outcome had it not been for the extraordinary events of late 1989. In the autumn of that year, as one watched the Berlin Wall come down, and the philosopher president come to power in Czechoslovakia, and the Romanian tyranny crumble, and so on, it was as if molten and repressed reality were erupting into history in much the same way as the volcanic crisis erupts (with radiant historical consequences for the Greeks) in Philoctetes – the character *and* the play. My own work and my own predisposition had been less sanguine before that: I was and am inclined to 'suspect too much sweet talk' as the final chorus says; and yet, as that chorus also says, one must 'never close one's mind' to the possibility of good as well as bad developments.

Indeed, the poems I was writing in 1989 and earlier had to do with transforming of the given, with preferring the imagined over the endured, with 'seeing things' ('Start seeing things' Neoptolemus enjoins the intransigent Philoctetes). Before my fiftieth birthday I had written 'Fosterling' which talks about 'crediting marvels' and laments a 'poetry / Sluggish in the doldrums of what happens'; and another poem called 'The Settle Bed' maintains that 'whatever is given / can always be remained, however . . . / Plank-thick and hull-stupid and out of its time / It happens to be'.[3] Then too there is a poem in 'Squarings' about a vision which the monks at Clonmacnoise experienced, a boat in the air, which is a little parable of the relationship between the life that must be undergone here and now and the one elsewhere that continues to be dreamt up:

> The annals say: when the monks of Clonmacnoise
> Were all at prayers inside the oratory
> A ship appeared above them in the air.
>
> The anchor dragged along behind so deep
> It hooked itself into the altar rails
> And then, as the big hull rocked to a standstill,

A crewman shinned and grappled down the rope
And struggled to release it. But in vain.
'This man can't bear our life here and will drown,'

The abbot said, 'unless we help him.' So
They did, the freed ship sailed, and the man climbed back
Out of the marvellous as he had known it.[4]

All of this was proceeding in part from a deep impatience with the expected and by now artistically overworked subject-matter of 'the Troubles'. The spirit was wanting more freedom to gambol, tragic circumstances and social obligation notwithstanding. Impatience was getting the better of elegy – and there was a growing inclination not to submit to the mournful evidence but to affirm the marvellous possibility, an inclination which was powerfully and unexpectedly fortified by the events in Europe in '89. I promised a version of *Philoctetes* to my fellow directors at a Field Day meeting in January 1990 and worked on it steadily during that spring at Harvard.

Mary Robinson's presidential campaign was being conducted in Ireland during the rehearsals and first run of *The Cure at Troy* in Ireland in 1990, and the Fianna Fail candidate standing against her was shown up in the course of the election as somebody who had no qualms – indeed he seemed puzzled by anybody else having them – about being 'economical with the truth'. The conflict between personal integrity and political expediency on the stage was thus echoing something going on in the daily life, and many in the audiences were alert to it. I mention it here because this may have been how the lines about how 'Once in a lifetime / The longed-for tidal wave / Of justice can rise up / And hope and history rhyme' got lodged in Mary Robinson's consciousness. At any rate, I was most gratified when later on, as President of Ireland, she quoted these lines – in response to the distresses of famine in Africa, for example, as well as in other contexts. And I was delighted and surprised when, at the opening of the post-cease-fire Forum for Peace and Reconciliation in Dublin last autumn the lines were quoted again, directly, by Dick Spring, the Irish Minister for Foreign Affairs, and when my allusion to hope (in another context, still tied to *The Cure at Troy* chorus) was invoked on that same occasion in the speech that followed – by Gerry Adams, the leader of Sinn Fein.[5]

But gratifying as these after-bonuses are, I again have to emphasize that they *are* bonuses – roll-on, carry-over effects. The play was meant to be a figuring of the whole complication rather than a set of slogans to apply to it. The drama was concentrated inwards towards its own operation rather than outwards towards the current events of its moment. In *Preoccupations*, there is a very relevant epigraph at the front of it from Yeats, where he speaks of how he came to write his play *Cathleen Ni Houlihan*:

At the enquiry which preceded the granting of a patent to the Abbey Theatre I was asked if *Cathleen Ni Houlihan* was not written to affect opinion. Certainly it was not. I had a dream one night which gave me a story, and I had certain emotions about this country, and I gave those emotions expression for my own pleasure. If I had written to convince others I would have asked myself, not 'Is that exactly what I think and feel?' but 'How would that strike so-and-so? How will they think and feel when they have read it?' And all would be oratorical and insincere. If we understand our own minds, and the things that are striving to utter themselves through our minds, we move others, not because we have understood or thought about those others, but because all life has the same root. Coventry Patmore has said, 'The end of art is peace', and the following of art is little different from the following of religion in the intense preoccupation it demands.[6]

What's more, by being an impatient reaction to the burden of dutiful 'commentary'-type drama ('Troubles art'), *The Cure at Troy* seems to me not only a declaration of a need for the imagination to outface the expectations of the topical but also a proof that it can happily and 'relevantly' do so. In other words, the play and *Seeing Things*, the book of poems contemporary with it, are a kind of 'post-cease-fire' writing *avant la lettre*.

Haphazard Information

Photographs of the original production, which would give you some idea of the set and the way the Chorus were often placed on it, should be available from Field Day . . .

Donal Lunny did the music. I don't have a tape, alas. We did make use of it powerfully during the build-up to the first entry of Philoctetes – all that howling, and by the way, Realism was the dominant mode when it came to his foot and his spasms. There may be a tape available of the whole production, as it was done on BBC radio. Produced by Pam Brighton.

Speaking the Choruses

The choruses in metre and rhyme should retain a strong metrical definition. In other words, the 'Human beings suffer' lines should be regularly stressed and end-stopped, with an emphasis on their linear and stanzaic articulation. For the speaking of the blank verse, I can think of no better guide than Robert Frost's notion that one obeys 'the sound of sense'. Which does not entail ignoring the footwork of the verse, but asks that the voice walk or dance or pause in step with it. In general, Frost on 'sentence sounds', on 'tones' and so on, would be an admirable mentor for actors approaching verse dialogue. (Of course, the blank verse is susceptible to a far more 'naturalistic' conversational style.)

The director can divide out the choruses between the three actors (e.g. the first three words of the play we divided between the three women, to let the three central names sing out singly and immediately); director will also probably want to think about choral (not too much, I think) speaking. And repetitions ('His echo was his neighbour' – that did nicely one two three times . . .).

I only say not too much *choral* speaking because in my experience clarity is weakened even if emotive effect is enhanced. I'm afraid I am devoted to the notion of each word being heard clearly by the audience. Bell-bing it into their ear, then carillon to your heart's content. It would be great to get over to see/hear the show. May make it in earliest October.

The 92nd Street Y in New York may have a copy of a tape of a reading directed by Derek Walcott and featuring a couple of members of the original Chorus, done in March 1993.

Enough.

Blessings on your work. 'Believe in miracles . . .'

Notes

1. Seamus Heaney, *The Government of the Tongue, Selected Prose, 1978–1987* (1988; rptd. New York: Noonday Press, Farrar, Straus & Giroux, 1995), pp. 107–8.

2. It is Neoptolemus. Seamus Heaney, *The Cure at Troy: A Version of Sophocles' Philoctetes* (1990; rptd New York: Noonday Press, Farrar, Straus & Giroux, 1995), p. 69.

3. These poems are in *Seeing Things* (New York: Farrar, Straus & Giroux, 1991).

4. Ibid., p. 62.

5. The afterlife of the 'hope and history' phrase continued after April 1995. To mention only two examples: it was picked up by President Clinton on his visit to Ireland later in the year and figured in the title of his book *Between Hope and History: Meeting America's Challenges for the 21st Century* (New York: Random House, 1997). More recently, a collection of essays by the South African Nobelist Nadine Gordimer was called *Living in Hope and History* (New York: Farrar, Straus & Giroux, 1999).

6. Seamus Heaney, *Preoccupations: Selected Prose, 1968–1978* (1980; rptd London: Faber & Faber, 1984), p. 7.

Seamus Heaney and the *Oresteia*: 'Mycenae Lookout' and the Usefulness of Tradition

Helen Vendler

I want to examine, as a contemporary case history of the usefulness of tradition, the unsettling and surprising transformation, in the recent work of Seamus Heaney, of the *Oresteia* of Aeschylus (especially the *Agamemnon*).[1] Never during the quarter-century of hostilities in the North had Heaney written openly inflammatory or recriminatory verse: even the 'bog-poems' – some of which concerned medieval sacrificial victims – refrained from matching the violence of much Irish political sentiment with violence of poetic language. His own intelligence and distrust of propagandistic rhetoric kept Heaney scrupulously away from language expressing the mad exuberance – felt by many, and a temptation to all writers-of those seeking vengeance by violent means.

With the final quelling (as it seemed) of the actual hostilities in the 1994 cease-fire, Heaney felt free at last to write violently of the war as it had been, to show what it had revealed of human nature, not least his own nature. In a totally unexpected move, Heaney published a five-poem sequence of unprecedented linguistic violence called 'Mycenae Lookout'.[2] In an interview with Henri Cole,[3] Heaney described the origins of the sequence in several different traditions: Greek drama, Christian liturgy, Renaissance masque and seventeenth-century lyric:

Instead of being able just to bask in the turn of [cease-fire] events, I found myself getting angrier and angrier at the waste of lives and friendships and possibilities in the years that had preceded it . . .

And I kept thinking that a version of the *Oresteia* would be one way of getting all of that out of the system, and at the same time, a way of initiating a late-twentieth-century equivalent of the 'Te Deum' . . .

I began to read the Aeschylus, and as I did, I also began to lose heart in the whole project. It began to seem too trite – art wanting to shake hands with life. Ideally, what I needed was the kind of poem Andrew Marvell wrote on Cromwell's return from Ireland and what I was setting up for was a kind of Jonsonian masque. At least that's what I began to feel. And then the figure of the Watchman in that first scene of the *Agamemnon* began to keep coming back to me with his in-between situation and his responsibilities and inner conflicts, his silence and his knowledge, and all this kept building until I very deliberately began a monologue for him using a rhymed couplet like a pneumatic drill, just trying to bite and shudder in toward whatever was there.
(pp. 136–7)

Traditions jostle in these remarks: the dramas of Aeschylus; 'Te Deum Laudamus' (the early Christian Latin hymn of thanks); the Renaissance masque of Ben Jonson; Marvell's 'An Horatian Ode: Upon Cromwell's Return from Ireland', which imitates classical Latin elegiacs; the rhymed pentameter couplet as one might find it in the political poetry of Dryden. The mention of the 'Te Deum' suggests that a thanksgiving ought to occur, and that the thanksgiving should be embodied in a ritual native to Heaney (perhaps the Catholic use of the 'Te Deum' on occasions such as a declaration of peace). Heaney's allusion to Marvell's Cromwell shows Heaney reflecting on the grim masculinity of war, and on the rewriting of history by the conquerors. And Marvell's allusion to Horace's *Odes* may have turned Heaney's mind to Latin legend, since we find, in the fifth poem of 'Mycenae Lookout', that Heaney has inserted the fratricidal story of the twin sons of Mars, in which Romulus murders Remus over the proposed border of Rome. Heaney has his visionary Watchman, the 'Mycenae Lookout' of the title, predict the future murder, as he sees

> . . . far-off, in a hilly, ominous place,
>
> Small crowds of people watching as a man
> Jumped a fresh earth-wall and another ran
> Amorously, it seemed, to strike him down. (p. 34)

In this moil of tradition, Heaney feels a poem stirring, a poem of hitherto pent-up historical anger. Heaney's recent description on 'the moment of poetry' illuminates the writing of his sequence: 'The moment of poetry is the moment when all those complications and contradictions of history, politics, culture, fidelity, hostility, inner division, challenge, and change get themselves gathered in words and become available to writer and reader as a mode of self-knowledge'.[4]

To mediate his anger – and indeed all the other emotional complications he listed – Heaney first turns, in 'Mycenae Lookout', to Aeschylus, assuming that the reader will remember the central situation of the *Agamemnon*, in which Agamemnon's sacrifice of his own daughter Iphigenia and his abduction of Priam's daughter, Cassandra, from Troy, end with the murder of both Agamemnon and Cassandra by Clytemnestra and her lover Aegisthus. Yet with all these violent personages to choose from, Heaney's eye lights on two non-violent Aeschylean speakers, the Watchman and Cassandra, to serve as his surrogates.

Aeschylus opens the *Agamemnon* with the Watchman – whose first response, as he sights the victory blazes announcing Agamemnon's return, is one of joy. But then he realizes that he cannot tell his master of the adultery he has observed between Clytemnestra and Aegisthus, that:

> The ox is on my tongue . . .
> I speak to those who know; to those who don't
> my mind's a blank. I never say a word.[5]

Aeschylus' Watchman becomes Heaney's persona, and the epigraph for the sequence is the Watchman's single (probably proverbial) phrase, 'The ox is on my tongue' – a phrase mirroring Heaney's own long-guarded discretion of utterance during the war years. The only other speaking part in Heaney's poem, as I've said, belongs to Cassandra. Heaney reduces Cassandra's many speeches in the *Agamemnon* to her final tragic words, uttered after she has torn off her regalia as Apollo's priestess and stands revealed as a helpless girl. In Aeschylus, Cassandra's closing speech reads, in Fagles's translation:

> Oh men, your destiny.
> When all is well a shadow can overturn it.
> When trouble comes a stroke of the wet sponge,
> And the picture's blotted out.[6]

In Heaney's version, her speech is rendered freely:

> A wipe
> of the sponge,
> that's it.
>
> The shadow-hinge
> swings unpredict-
> ably and the light's
>
> blanked out.[7]

The Watchman's troubled speechlessness and the prophetess's disbelieved speech represent the dilemma of the poet in a time of dishonesty, victimage, murder, infidelity and rape. From these beginnings, Heaney constructed a sequence with five named parts:

1 The Watchman's War
2 Cassandra
3 The Nights
4 His Dawn Vision
5 His Reverie of Water

Heaney's Watchman despairs of translating the truth of history into available language, since language itself is a mark of civilization, while war is pure bestiality:

> No element that should have carried weight
>   Out of the grievous distance would translate.
>   Our war stalled in the pre-articulate.[8]

It is tradition, in the form of the *Agamemnon*, that enables Heaney to give voice to his 'pre-articulate' anger; but the form of the Watchman's accusatory articulacy is shocking, as we hear it in the 'pneumatic drill' (as Heaney has called it) of the Watchman's opening and closing couplets of the first poem in the sequence, 'The Watchman's War':

> Some people wept, and not for sorrow – joy
> That the king had armed and upped and sailed
>   for Troy . . .
> I balanced between destiny and dread
> And saw it coming, clouds bloodshot with the red
> Of victory fires . . .
>
> Up on my elbows, head back, shutting out
> The agony of Clytemnestra's love-shout
> That rose through the palace like the yell of troops
> Hurled by King Agamemnon from the ships.[9]

The Watchman looks on aghast as war-frenzy grips not only the yelling troops but also the civilian population. He hears, shuddering, the 'love-shout' of the adulterous queen as it shakes the house of Atreus. The contamination of slaughter reaches the Watchman's own tongue, which feels like 'the dropped gang-plank of a cattle truck, / Trampled and rattled, running piss and muck, / All swimmy-trembly as the lick of fire, / A victory beacon in an abattoir'.[10] Heaney's distorted diction, as it finally breaks out here, suggests how difficult it was, during the quarter-century of the undeclared war in the North, for the poet to bridle his tongue while his mind felt agitated, polluted, inflamed and appalled.

By the selectivity of his two telling quotations – the Watchman's ox-landed tongue, Cassandra's disbelieving despair – Heaney points up Aeschylus' own emphasis on speechlessness and prophecy, together with the incapacity of either response to stop the momentum of tragic event. By allowing the Watchman's later dawn vision (not in Aeschylus) to see forward (in Dantesque tercets) to the fratricide polluting the foundation of Rome, Heaney enlarges the reach of tradition in the poem, generalizing epic history from Greece to Rome, thence to civil strife in Dante's Florence and any later place. And finally, by bringing the sequence, at the close, home to contemporary Ireland (in the poem called 'His Reverie of Water'), Heaney connects the Aeschylean dream of moral ablution (dramatized at the end of the trilogy in the *Eumenides*) and the historical military struggle over possession of the well below the Acropolis of Athens to his contemporary hope for peace.

Under all allusion to a traditional text lies the fear that the primal cultural text is in danger of being forgotten, and that the poet, in consequence, has a responsibility to bear it out of the ever-threatening fire of oblivion. Resuscitating the Aeschylean myth for Irish purposes, Heaney must make it freshly seeable, transporting the House of Atreus into Irish circumstance. Merely to borrow the Greek plot and reimagine its actors will not suffice; the myth must also be given contemporary language. The rest of this chapter will enquire into the strong measures Heaney took once the cease-fire allowed him, for the first time, a full-voiced anger against the prolonged carnage that took away from him, as from others in Northern Ireland, the possibility of a normal life. Measured eloquence and steady reflective meditation on life had been the staples of Heaney's poems written before the cease-fire; but these are discarded during most of 'Mycenae Lookout', as if only outraged language could suit outrageous acts. By filtering his own anger through the parallels afforded by tradition, Heaney makes his own writing conscious and premeditated, rather than uncontrolled and self-pitying.

How is language made outrageous in 'Mycenae Lookout'? In part by taking seriously the violence of Aeschylus' own language, in which words of sexual violation and words of bloodshed interchange so rapidly that the two categories are shaken into a single dark emulsion. So, too, Heaney's sequence begins and continues in a demotic coarseness relieved only in the closing poem of his sequence. At the opening, as Heaney's Watchman lies on the roof at night, he registers the erotic charge of killing, both in Argos and in Troy. Hearing night after night the wild love-making of Clytemnestra and Aegisthus, he, the confidant of each of them, speaks about their sexual confidence ('it was sexual overload / every time they did it') with the scorn of a soldier contemplating a decadent aristocracy. And the Watchman extrapolates the actions of his earthly rulers to the very heavens, likening himself to Atlas, patron of watchmen, who has to overhear a comparable sort of sexual grossness from the gods ('those thuds / and moans through the cloud cover'). The Watchman's tabloid terms ('every time they did it'; [they] 'made out endlessly') turn bestial when he shows the erotic excitement of war inflaming even the Argives crouched in the Trojan Horse:

> When the captains in the horse
>   felt Helen's hand caress
>   its wooden boards and belly
>   they nearly rode each other.[11]

But instead of indulging their frenzy homosexually, Agamemnon's soldiers take it out in rape: 'In the end Troy's mothers / bore their brunt in alley, / bloodied cot and bed.'[12]

In this violent self-loathing summary, the Watchman includes himself (the 'roof-posted' one) among those whom the war drove mad, joining himself to the bull-like horned Agamemnon and the horsed soldiers, the boasting Argives and the bested Trojans:

> The war put all men mad,
>   horned, horsed or roof-posted,
>   the boasting and the bested.[13]

This adjectival list – *horned, horsed, posted, boasting, bested* – is a scrawled cartoon-version of the epic personae of the Trojan War. Because of the Watchman's 'low' language and his unrelenting rhythms (taking their cue from the heavy trochees of the name 'Agamemnon'), no Heaneyesque softness, whether of exculpation or of human commiseration, can penetrate the language of 'The Nights'. Heaney refuses epic majesty to the Irish slaughter; instead, he brings down Aeschylus to language appropriate to vulgar brawling and war-lust.

But it is not in writing of Agamemnon's battle-frenzy, or Aesgisthus' and Clytemnestra's adultery, or the cavorting gods, or the Argive rapes, that Heaney's invention of a 'low tragic' language for epic material reaches its brutal peak. It is in the second poem of the sequence, 'Cassandra', that tradition is most actively torn from its beginnings and made expressive of the present day. Though a reader of the *Agamemnon* (and of the *Iliad*) knows that Cassandra has been raped not only in Troy by Ajax but repeatedly by Agamemnon, and that she is Agamemnon's personal slave, other items of her Aeschylean presentation – that she appears in the ceremonial robes and wreath of a priestess, that she is King Priam's daughter, that she is a prophetess, that she rides in Agamemnon's chariot – suggest that she appears regal, elevated and exalted, in spite of her status as slave. In a brilliant set of several poetic inventions, Heaney borrows Cassandra from tradition, but re-imagines her as she might appear in Northern Ireland, as one of the sullen young people caught up in sordid events, blurting out truth to bystanders in the midst of civic hatred and hypocrisy.

Cassandra's poem – spoken by the Watchman – is thin, even scrawny, like the raped adolescent's own body: Heaney gives Cassandra soiled punk clothing, an undernourished frame, the shaved head of a girl caught consorting with the enemy, a not-quite-innocent gaze:

> No such thing
> as innocent
> bystanding.

Her soiled vest,
her little breasts,
her clipped, devastated,
scabbed
punk head,
the char-eyed

famine gawk –
she looked
camp-fucked

and simple.[14]

The ostentatiously rhymed but sliced-up dimeter tercets of Cassandra
are themselves a violated form of normal poetry. Heaney here
presses the Watchman's language into an obscenity quickened by
his hatred of the innocent bystanders who watch, erotically
aroused, Cassandra's exposure. On the other hand, Heaney gives
Cassandra her own theatricality; she is not entirely innocent. The
bystanders know she tells the truth, because they recognize it
within themselves as she says it; yet, paradoxically, the Watchman
sees something slightly stagey about Cassandra's bewilderment. As
a prophetess in Apollo's temple, she is used to public appearances;
or perhaps, as a victim, she has learned to play the game of
victimage:

People
could feel

a missed
trueness in them
focus,

a homecoming
in her dropped-wing,
half-calculating

bewilderment.
no such thing
as innocent.[15]

In Heaney's hands, the fate of Cassandra becomes a perennial parable. The poet has his Watchman describe Agamemnon – the slayer of Iphigenia, the rapist of Cassandra – with jeering nicknames, reducing him to type. Cassandra, too, becomes type-cast, as the parabolic lamb readied for slaughter, speaking not her native Trojan but prophetic Greek, resuming her role as the oracle of a revengeful Apollo:

> Old King Cock-
> of-the-Walk
> was back,
>
> King Kill-
> the-Child-
> and-Take-
>
> What-Comes,
> King Agamem-
> non's drum-
>
> balled, old buck's
> stride was back.
> And then her Greek
>
> words came,
> a lamb
> at lambing time,
>
> bleat of clair-
> voyant dread
> the gene-hammer
>
> and tread
> of the roused god.[16]

Finally, Heaney gathers together all these themes – of raped virginity, erotically excited 'innocent bystanders', clairvoyant prophecy, sovereign murder, adultery, vengeance, Fate and historical oblivion – at the obscene climax, binding them in one at the end through the quotation of Cassandra's last Aeschylean words:

> And a result-
>
> ant shock desire
> in bystanders
> to do it to her
>
> there and then.
> Little rent
> count of their guilt:
>
> in she went
> to the knife,
> to the killer wife,
>
> to the net over
> her and her slaver,
> the Troy reaver,
>
> saying, 'A wipe
> of the sponge,
> that's it.
>
> The shadow-hinge
> swings unpredict-
> ably and the light's
>
> blanked out.'[17]

Here, Heaney has his Watchman revert to a different tradition, to the rhythm and manner of folk-ballads. From 'in she went' to 'the Troy reaver' we hear not only the simple sing-song of nursery rhyme but also the abstractions of the twice-told tale – 'the knife', 'the wife', 'the net', 'the reaver'. And the poet's final conspicuous action is to abort – in a Yeatsian move – his final tercet, making its two missing lines enact Cassandra's death.

How much is left of tradition after such violence has been done to it? After all, Heaney has in Cassandra's poem reduced Aeschylean high tragedy to amputated tercets in contemporary dress, tercets voiced in the lowest of styles, with interpolated vulgarity and obscenity. One answer to the question is that everything is left, that to understand Aeschylus today we need to read Heaney. The 'spoiling' of form and language – in a sequence so antithetical to the ceremonious forms of Heaney's earliest writing – reflects accurately the 'spoiling' of life brought about by war. The tragic loftiness that might have served to represent battle and betrayal at their origin falters with the repetitions, in Ireland, of twenty-five years, making epic decline into sardonic balladry, cynically singing the old scandals.

Heaney was unwilling to stop at the devastating amputations of 'Cassandra', the depressed vision of eternal fratricide in the Watchman's dawn vision of the murder of Remus by Romulus, or the cynical view of peace in 'The Nights', where 'peace' is defined merely as the exhausted aftermath of the murderous 'rope-net and . . . blood-bath'. Yet he could not endorse a peace that would remain one of sectarian segregation. When he searches tradition for some equivalent to the restoration of moral equilibrium in the *Eumenides* he finds it in two recollections, one literary and one autobiographical, in the story of the military battle over the memory of the well-digging at his birthplace.

The closing poem-of-wells of 'Mycenae Lookout', called 'His Reverie of Water', is, formally speaking, a brilliant set of three successive linked codas to the Mycenean-Irish war. The first, literary and tragic, coda (in four tercets) closes the Aeschylean borrowings proper with Greek tragic justice. This coda guarantees the literary relevance of the traditional genres of epic and tragedy: there will always be an innocent bath of fresh water, not yet blood-stained; and then the 'far cries of the butchered of the plain' will die into it, ensuring that the war-hero, in the violence begotten by violence, will be murdered, reddening the bath. Though such classical 'justice' closes the *Agamemnon*, it is not what Heaney wants for Ireland, and so he proceeds to a second coda, one derived from historical, not dramatic, Greek tradition.

This second coda (in five tercets) uses the conquest and re-conquest of the water-supply below the Athenian Acropolis to take a long historical view. In this view, all cultural activity of the human species, including the making of war, is repetitive, will recur, and, since biologically determined, is innocent. Though the defenders of the Acropolis thought that only they knew of the secret staircase to the well, the besiegers discovered it:

> secret staircase the defenders knew
> and the invaders found, where what was to be
> Greek met Greek,
>
> the ladder of the future
> and the past, besieger and besieged,
> the treadmill of assault
>
> turned waterwheel, the rungs of stealth
> and habit all the one
> bare foot extended, searching.[18]

The struggle for *Lebensraum* is undifferentiated; land is always and everywhere struggled over, and the strugglers are, in evolutionary terms, 'all the one / bare foot extended, searching'. It is this very repetitiveness of human action, this stoic coda suggests, that guarantees the historical relevance of literary tradition, as a later period can always see itself in an earlier one.

This, however, is to take a view from an Archimedean anthropological distance; and though Heaney recognizes the inarguable truth of the long view, he, like Czeslaw Milosz, also recognizes the necessity of balancing it with a perspective drawn to human scale.

In the final, shortest coda, a personal and hopeful one in three tercets, Heaney considers the fact – and moral solace – of ablution. Yes, he admits the poetic justice of the reddened water in the bath of the first coda; yes, he recognizes the historical treadmill of evolutionary biology in the perpetual territorial struggle of the second coda; but he also wants to assert the simple fact that the coming of peace can perform, on a human scale, the Keatsian 'priestlike task / Of pure ablution round earth's human shores'. Though the idea derives from tradition, in the Eumenides' ritual cleansing of Athens from blood-guilt, Heaney does not summon up the Aeschylean 'Kindly Ones', lest he find himself writing 'a Jonsonian masque' with allegorical personae. (Besides, Eliot had pre-empted the Furies for *The Family Reunion*.) Instead, for the first time in the sequence, Heaney speaks as himself and stands on Irish home ground:

> And then this ladder of our own that ran
> deep into a well-shaft being sunk
> in broad daylight, men puddling at the source
>
> through tawny mud, then coming back up
> deeper in themselves for having been there,
> like discharged soldiers testing the safe ground,
>
> finders, keepers, seers of fresh water
> in the bountiful round mouths of iron pumps
> and gushing taps.[19]

As Heaney brings back the normalcy of his parents' pre-war world and its bountiful water, he uses family memory to 'wash clean' many of the polluted words and images that previously appeared in the poem. The Watchman's anguished nights are exchanged for 'broad daylight': Agamemnon's yelling troops become relieved discharged soldiers; Cassandra the tragic seer gives way to 'seers of fresh water'; the sinister nursery-rhyme of the Troy reaver and his slave is replaced by the innocent rhyme of 'finders, keepers' (its sadder twin, 'losers, weepers', suppressed here); and the blood-reddened water of the archaic murder becomes native water 'in the bountiful round mouths of iron pumps / and gushing taps'.

The closing rural scene of 'Mycenae Lookout' is a retraction, to some degree, of the powerful reactive anger that generated the first four poems of the sequence. And yet, by putting his optimistic coda of ablution within the very same lyric as his other two codas – the tragic one of retributive justice, the stoic of historical repetitiveness – Heaney at the end is (to borrow words from Wallace Stevens) 'of three minds / Like a tree / In which there are three blackbirds'.[20] Heaney has always sought for ways in which to be true to the tangled complexity of his historical situation; and to make three philosophically distinct but 'co-equal' codas occupy his closing lyric is his means of being true to Aeschylus, to history and evolutionary biology, and to his own incorrigible hope.

Literary tradition in the person of Aeschylus has been supplemented in 'Mycenae Lookout' by several other factors: first, by political history, as Heaney views the military contention over access to the Acropolis water-supply with Marvellian *Realpolitik* crossed with anthropological evenness; second, by the poet's secular gratitude for the Anahorish well (replacing his initial impulse toward a religious 'Te Deum'); third, by a vivid sense of the contemporary Irish scene in the figure of Cassandra and her postmodern amputated dimeters. Finally, literary tradition is supplemented by the one necessary thing in all lyric – a sense of the author's own internal predicament. There are many places in 'Mycenae Lookout' where the Aeschylean persona becomes transparent, and we hear Heaney's own voice under that of the Watchman. Czeslaw Milosz whose life was shattered by the Second World War, writes, in 'The Poor Poet', of the young poet's initial wish to celebrate the normal and beautiful:

> The first movement is singing,
> A free voice, filling mountains and valleys.
> The first movement is joy,
> But it is taken away.[21]

Heaney's original joy in nature which, in another time, might have continued unperturbed, is now contaminated by historical circumstance. In a Dantesque moment, he reveals the seepage of that contamination into the most innocent moments of life:

> The little violet's heads bowed on their stems,
> The pre-dawn gossamers, all dew and scrim
> And star-lace, it was more through them
>
> I felt the beating of the huge time-wound
> We lived inside. My soul wept in my hand
> When I would touch them . . .[22]

If Heaney's voice was born to joy, the undeclared war in the North forced him – once the cease-fire gave him permission to unleash his long-suppressed anger and disgust – to take up the 'pneumatic drill' of 'Mycenae Lookout'. When Henri Cole asked Heaney about 'Cassandra', Heaney answered, ' "Cassandra" was written very quickly. It came out like a molten rill from a spot I hit when I drilled down into the *Oresteia* bedrock that's under "Mycenae Outlook".'[23] If we accept Heaney's metaphor of 'bedrock' as shorthand for tradition, we can say, with Stevens, that poets cover the rock with the fresh leaves of the imagination. But if we look to the other half of Heaney's metaphor – to the rill to be found still molten within the fixed forms of the past – we can see that tradition also means, for the poet, access to a pent-up spring of emotion hidden in those apparently monolithic ancestral forms. If Heaney has been, for the past twenty-five years, the most subtle, apt and exacting interpreter of events in the North of Ireland, it is not least because he can bring, to the characterizing of those turbulent events, a set of powerful traditional resources – classical, Christian, Celtic and secular. All of these contexts interrogate and critique each other in Heaney's mind; and 'Mycenae Lookout' is one striking product of that continual interrogation.

Notes

1. This chapter, by the A. Kingsley Porter University Professor at Harvard, was a paper read on 26 May 1998 and published in *Proceedings of the American Philosophical Society*, 143(1) (March 1999): 116–29.
2. Seamus Heaney, 'Mycenae Lookout', in *The Spirit Level* (London: Faber & Faber, 1996), pp. 29–37.
3. This interview appeared in the *Paris Review* 144 (Autumn 1997): 88–138.
4. Seamus Heaney, 'Further Language', *Studies in the Literary Imagination 30* (Autumn 1997): 12.
5. Aeschylus, *The Oresteia*, trans. Robert Fagles (New York: Penguin, 1979), p. 104.
6. Ibid., p. 153.
7. Heaney, 'Mycenae Lookout', in *The Spirit Level*, p. 33.
8. Ibid.
9. Ibid., pp. 29–30.
10. Ibid., p. 29.
11. Ibid., pp. 35–6.
12. Ibid.
13. Ibid.
14. Ibid., pp. 30–1
15. Ibid., p. 3.
16. Ibid., pp. 71–2.
17. Ibid., pp. 32–3.
18. Ibid., p. 37.
19. Ibid.
20. Wallace Stevens, 'Thirteen Ways of Looking at a Blackbird', in *Collected Poems* (New York: Vintage, 1900), p. 92.
21. Czeslaw Milosz, 'The Poor Poet', in *Collected Poems, 1931–1987* (New York: Ecco Press, 1988), p. 61.
22. Heaney, 'Mycenae Lookout', in *The Spirit Level*, pp. 33–4.
23. See *Paris Review*, 144 (Autumn 1997): 137.

Women in Irish Appropriations of Greek Tragedy

Brian Arkins

I

In order to analyse the portrayal of women in Irish appropriations of Greek tragedy, it is necessary to briefly depict the life-style of Athenian women in the fifth century BC and of Irish women in the twentieth century AD.[1] In Athens, aristocratic women were virtually confined to the house (*oikos*), and had no role to play in the city (*polis*) – apart from participating in a number of religious festivals. Women, who entered an arranged marriage at about the age of fourteen, were defined by the social significance of their bodies, by their ability to produce children and especially boys who would continue the citizen line. As the sentence uttered by the bride's father to the groom at the engagement ceremony graphically indicates: 'I give you this woman for the ploughing of legitimate children.'[2] In so far as romantic love existed in Athens, it took the form of a sexual relationship between an older man, who was or would be married, and an adolescent boy between the ages of twelve and eighteen.

Put the other way round, Athenian men controlled everything of importance in the city: politics, the army, the navy, the lawcourts, commerce, agriculture, the Olympic and other Games; women were excluded from all of these activities. It is also probable that women did not attend the theatre (although this is disputed); certainly, in the theatre, the playwrights, directors and actors were all men. Equally well, the vast majority of the Irish appropriations of Greek tragedies are by men (there are three by women).

In reality, therefore, Athenian aristocratic women led extremely restricted lives; in Greek literature, on the other hand, and particularly in tragedy and comedy, women play a very prominent role. This paradox struck Virginia Woolf forcefully in 1929:

If woman had no existence save in the fiction written by men, one would imagine her a person of the utmost importance; very various; heroic and mean; splendid and sordid; infinitely beautiful and hideous in the extreme; as great as a man, some think even greater. But this woman is in fiction. In fact ... she was locked up, beaten and flung about the rooms. A very queer, composite being thus emerges. Imaginatively she is of the highest importance; practically she is completely insignificant. She pervades poetry from cover to cover; she is all but absent from history. She dominates the lives of kings and conquerors in fiction; in fact she was the slave of any boy whose parents fixed a ring upon her finger. Some of the most inspired words, some of the most profound thoughts in literature fall from her lips; in real life she could hardly read, could scarcely spell, and was the property of her husband.[3]

The classicist Helene Foley has remarked on the same paradox in regard to Athenian women:

Although women in fact play virtually no public role other than a religious one in the political and social life of ancient Greece, they dominate the imaginative life of Greek men to a degree almost unparalleled in the Western tradition ... Greek writers used the female – in a fashion that bore little relation to the lives of actual women – to understand, express, criticize, and experiment with the problems and contradictions of their culture.[4]

Halperin explains this paradox by claiming that the silence of actual women in Greek public life and the volubility of fictional 'women', who are invented by male authors, are connected by strict logical necessity: Greek men effectively silenced women by speaking for them on those occasions when men chose to address significant words to each other in public, in the drama, and they required the silence of women in public in order to make themselves heard and impersonate women without impediment.[5] As 'Agathon' says in Aristophanes' *Thesmophoriazusae* (155–6), 'whatever we don't have, we capture by imitation [*mimesis*]'.

The position of women in Ireland during the course of the twentieth century, when Irish writers appropriated the Greek tragedies that are analysed here, changed greatly. From about 1820 to 1960, Irish women had to contend with a patriarchal system that was deeply authoritarian. To a large extent, women were excluded from the male worlds of politics and of work. Because there was no contraception, they were often forced to have large numbers of children, and they, like men, suffered that peculiar form of sexual repression, that arose initially out of the economics of the small farm in the nineteenth century.

The opening up of Ireland from 1960 on to a wide variety of external influences had large consequences for women. They could now work on equal terms with men, gradually began to play a greater part in politics, and became better educated. Women were also enabled to take charge of their sexual behaviour because contraception was legalized. Nevertheless, there was a sense that much remained to be done for women, art being one sphere of activity which could highlight this. So a number of male playwrights made a conscious decision to enact the ongoing drama about the position of women in Ireland by appropriating Greek tragedies that had done the same 2,500 years earlier. The most explicit connection between the conditions of Irish society and Athenian drama is made by Brendan Kennelly: 'The ancient, original Greek infiltrates life in modern Ireland.'[6]

So while the Athenian tragedians portrayed powerful women in a way that bore no relation to the actual lives of women in fifth-century Athens, and used women characters to explore contradictions in their own society, Irish male playwrights reflect a society in which women have increasingly come to enjoy various types of freedom, and set out to advocate further power for women. As the Chorus says in both Euripides' *Medea* and Kennelly's *Medea*, 'There will be / womansongs in the answer to the false / songs of men.'[7]

The programme for women that emerges in these Irish plays includes the following: women are to be independent and free from restraint; women must set out both to change men and to usurp the role of men in the world; women must react to their oppression with rage. For the male playwright, the aim in all of this is, as Kennelly says, 'to be imaginatively a woman'.[8]

2

The Irish tragedies that most obviously deal with the experience of women appropriate, for the most part, the plays of Euripides: *Medea*, *Iphigenia in Aulis*, *Hippolytus*, *Bacchae*, *Trojan Women*. Two plays of Sophocles are also made use of: *Antigone* and *Electra*.

A number of women in Greek tragedy, who act in the absence of their husband or guardian (*kurios*), disrupt the male system and can be termed 'female intruders'.[9] Medea in Euripides' play of that name is a case in point, and is presented in three Irish appropriations: a straight translation by Desmond Egan, a version by Brendan Kennelly, and a loose adaptation by Marina Carr.[10]

Using an emphatic modern register of language that neither adds to nor substracts from Euripides, Egan's translation of *Medea* is paradoxically radical because it forces us to go back and try to fathom the original meaning of the play in 431 BC.[11] The overriding binary opposition in *Medea* is that between woman and man, Medea and Jason; Egan calls Medea 'the first feminist heroine' and Jason 'the prototype of the male chauvinist'.[12] After Medea helps Jason acquire the Golden Fleece and marries him, he abandons her in order to marry Glauke, daughter of the King of Corinth, because he craves the security of marriage into the royal family. Medea waxes eloquent to the Chorus about her position:

> This unexpected disaster that struck me
> Has broken my spirit. I'm devastated.
> I have lost the joy of living, friends, I want only to die.

In that man I could find all that was beautiful
– My husband, now turned into the worst of men.
Of all that has life and intelligence
We women are the most unfortunate ones – we
Who first of all buy – like the highest bidder! – a husband
And end up with a master over our body.[13]

But Medea is not to be trifled with. She engineers the death of her rival Glauke and Glauke's father Creon, kills her own two children, and is then given sanctuary in Athens by the King, Aegeus. Medea has entered the brutal world of men and beaten them at their own game.

In Kennelly's *Medea*, which expands Euripides by more than half, the key word is rage, the rage felt by women at their treatment by men, that of Medea abandoned by Jason: 'The world of rage. / Medea's world. The world of rage.'[14] Kennelly makes his Medea an explicitly feminist figure and an archetypal one at that: her cry 'was the cry / of the first woman / betrayed by the first man'. Seeking to educate men, Medea employs demotic language to describe the sexual domination of women by men:

Men, the horny despots of our bodies,
Sucking, fucking, licking, chewing, farting into our skin,
Sitting on our faces, fingering our arses,
Exploring our cunts, widening our thighs,
Drawing the milk that gave the bastards life.[15]

When the Medea of Kennelly exacts her spectacular revenge on Jason, she is seen to be 'like the cry of Nature itself', for, as Jason says, 'There's a demon in you.' Normal standards do not apply to demonic forces of this order and so when the Chorus ends the play by asking 'Is Medea's crime Medea's glory?' the answer has to be 'Yes'.[16]

Marina Carr's loose adaptation of *Medea*, *By the Bog of Cats . . .*, transfers the action to the Irish Midlands at the present time. After fourteen years of life together and a false promise of marriage, Carthage Kilbride has abandoned Hester Swane (aged forty) by whom he has a child, Josie, and plans to marry Caroline Cassidy (aged twenty). Hester is akin to Medea in a number of ways. Hester's 'tinker blood' corresponds to Medea's foreignness, and Mrs Kilbride's description of her 'whooshin' by on her broom' corresponds to Medea's powers as a sorceress. Like Jason, Carthage owes his position to Hester: 'It was me who tould him he could do better. It was my money that bought him his first fine acres.'[17] Indeed Hester killed her brother with Carthage's help.

When Carthage rejects Hester's pleading and proceeds to marry Caroline, Hester, like Medea, exacts a spectacular revenge: she burns down first Carthage's house and then her own, and kills her child Josie with a knife. But following this infanticide, Carr's Medea does not leave her home in triumph and find sanctuary in another place: Hester is herself killed by the Ghost Fancier with the same knife and uttering the same words as her child: 'Mam – Mam – '[18] The resulting identification of mother and daughter in death suggests that the relationship cannot be unilaterally terminated. Writing as a woman about women, Carr deconstructs the currently dominant reading of Medea as a feminist statement, in which Medea's revenge of infanticide is vindicated. Hester is *not* vindicated, she is killed; she who lives by the knife shall die by the knife. So Carr's ending seems made for Tony Harrison's question in his *Medea*: 'As the sex war's still being fought, / Which sex does a myth support?'[19]

3

Two other important women from Euripides who feature in Irish appropriations are Iphigenia and Phaedra.

Colin Teevan's play *Iph*, which is written *after Euripides' Iphigeneia in Aulis* (sic), portrays a fundamental clash between the demands of the community – the Greeks must sacrifice Iphgeneia (*sic*), daughter of Agamemnon and Clytemnestra, in order to get to Troy – and the demands of the family: Clytemnestra (here Klytaimnestra) defends her daughter.[20] The issue in question is that of primitive violence directed against a vulnerable woman, which Teevan stresses by using Anglo-Saxon language and metre; as Klytaimnestra says to Agamemnon:

> I bore you three children,
> Two daughters and a son.
> But, not content, you now intend
> To rob me of another child.
> And if someone asks you why you kill her,
> What will you reply?
> So Helen might return to Menelaus?!
> It is rich indeed to pay for whores
> With your own children's blood.[21]

Teevan uses material not found in Euripides to stress the bloody fate of Iphgeneia and her loss to Klytaimnestra: Yeats's sonnet 'Leda and the Swan', which is used as an epigraph, deals with the rape of a woman; an additional choral ode portrays the goddess Demeter grieving for her lost daughter Persephone; and the Old Man, who is imported from Aeschylus' *Agamemnon*, wonders 'How we first dipped our hands / In our own children's blood?'[22]

Both Brian Friel's play *Living Quarters* and Ulick O'Connor's play *The Oval Machine* transfer the action of Euripides' *Hippolytus* to contemporary Ireland.[23] But whereas in *Hippolytus* Phaedra is rejected by her stepson Hippolytus and hangs herself, in the plays by Friel and O'Connor the love of the Irish women Anna and Stephanie for their stepsons Ben and Kevin is reciprocated. In the modern world, the fate of women who engage in illicit love is less appalling: it is true that Stephanie in O'Connor's play dies, but we do not know how; Anna in Friel's play remains alive, while her cuckolded husband Frank commits suicide.

4

Two further plays of Euripides – *Trojan Women* and *Bacchae* – feature the experiences of groups of women.

Functioning as the paradigm of the anti-war play, *Trojan Women* depicts the devastating effect of war upon women. The Japanese director Suzuki states of his version of *Trojan Women* that 'I intended to express the disastrous fate of women caused by war, which was initiated by men.'[24] Brendan Kennelly concurs: 'the play is about the consequences of war, it's about the men who win and the women who lose.'[25]

Following Euripides in his focus on the experience of these women as mothers, widows and children of the dead Trojan warriors, Kennelly in his version of *Trojan Women* acutely finds that, although they appear to be 'passive victims at the whimsical mercy of their male conquerors', they in reality exude 'a strong, active, resolute and shrewd note'.[26] So Andromache, wife of Hector, asserts that 'if my body is a slave / an untouched portion of my mind is free', while Hecuba, mother of Hector, wonders, 'May not a woman / win?'[27]

But there is an important way in which Kennelly alters Euripides' portrayal of women: he treats their fate not as abnormal, but as the norm in a patriarchal society – like Ireland.[28] Not only are women 'the spoils of war', but they are also constantly demeaned by men, 'at someone's beck and call'. The answer, Hecuba suggests to Helen, is that women must adopt the callous attitudes of men: 'Pick one, Helen. Pick a man. Fuck him. Let him die. / Stick him in a grave, old, deep, far from the sun. / And remember always – take care of number one.' Which can happen when, as Poseidon foretells, 'women will rule the world'.[29]

Aidan Mathews's loose adaptation of Euripides' *Trojan Women*, called *Trojans*, which is set in Berlin in 1945 at the end of the Second World War, employs modern cynicism to stress the desolation caused by war.[30] The central women of Troy become German and have modern functions: Hecuba is the wife of a *Wehrmacht* officer and Andromache a war-widow of the Reich. Like their ancient counterparts, these women suffer: the sexual submission of the Trojan women to the Greeks is transformed into the sexual desires of both the Allies and the Nazis; Cassandra, who is turned into a Catholic nun, asserts that her community is to be found 'On the altarlist of the dead and the files of the Gestapo'. Furthermore, women can be used to undercut the official German line that there are close links between the achievements of classical Greece and Nazi Germany. Greta 'kept a miniature of the Parthenon on her mantelpiece', but Woman 3 notes that her husband 'went down . . . like Icarus'.[31]

Since Derek Mahon's play *The Bacchae*, which is 'after' Euripides, preserves the invariant core of the plot, it requires us to analyse what Euripides' tragedy *Bacchae* originally was about.[32] The play presents a central clash between the ecstatic, irrational religion of Dionysus and the extreme rationality of the King, Pentheus, which is also a clash between the Bacchae, the female worshippers of Dionysus, and the male King. In Mahon, Dionysus sums up the basic conflict: 'There will be war between the Bacchant wives / and the strict spirit that controls their lives.' Mahon relates these ancient Bacchantes to the modern world by quoting E. R. Dodds's statement that the Bacchante is 'an observed and still observable human type'.[33]

What characterizes the Bacchantes in the choral odes is a yearning for freedom:

> Oh, to be on white
> Aphrodite's isle
> for a brief mortal while
> and a thousand rivers flow
> into the sands below.
> Oh, to be where the airy
> slopes of Olympus sweep
> down to Pieria where
> the nine Muses sleep.
>
> Take us there, Dionysus,
> where ecstasy isn't banned
> and the holy thyrsus
> sprouts from every hand![34]

But Pentheus misreads this desire for freedom and exhibits the typical prejudice of Athenian men about women: 'The whole thing's an excuse for drink and sex.'[35]

Shaw's play *Major Barbara* transposes *Bacchae*'s ancient religious drama into modern dress and into the social sphere.[36] Dionysus becomes a very wealthy manufacturer of arms who has idealistic proposals to abolish poverty. The Bacchae turn into the Salvation Army, which is initially compromised by its acceptance of the *status quo* in society, but when they take money from Undershaft, we witness 'the conversion of the Salvation Army to the worship of Dionysus'.[37] Similarly, their leader Barbara, who began by opposing Undershaft, plays the role of Pentheus.

So Euripides becomes for Shaw an enabling force: it is because Shaw follows the Greek dramatist in insisting on the irresistible power of Dionysus/Undershaft that he is able to move beyond the play's opening categories.[38]

5

Arguably the most influential Greek tragedy in the history of ideas, Sophocles' *Antigone* has recently functioned as dramatic paradigm for a variety of political situations in which a repressive state (Creon) seeks to suppress the rights of the individual person (Antigone).[39] When Antigone insists on burying her dead brother Polyneices in the face of Creon's opposition, one of the binary oppositions that comes into play is a clash between an older man and a younger woman, in which Antigone is proved right (*pace* Hegel).

In the mid-1980s, three Irish writers – Brendan Kennelly, Tom Paulin and Aidan Mathews – appropriated *Antigone*, the first two plays being versions, that of Mathews a loose adaptation.[40] Kennelly's play *Antigone* is the one that most clearly depicts the experience of women, so that it constitutes 'a feminist declaration of independence'.[41] In the face of the implacable male ruler – 'I am determined Creon' – Antigone is equally uncompromising: 'Polyneices is my brother. / I can't be false to him.'[42] When mapped on to contemporary Ireland, this revolt of the Other subtly suggests an attack on a calcified patriarchy by feminists and liberals, who seek less rigid attitudes to issues of gender and sexuality.

In Kennelly, Creon and Antigone classify each other in terms of gender as 'girl' and 'man', but Creon is unwilling to accommodate the resulting concept of difference: 'I would be no man, / she would be the man / if I let her go unpunished.' Antigone says to him: 'You fear the thoughts of difference' and asks: 'What man / knows anything of women?' And yet if Antigone was saved from dying, 'I could change all the men of the world.'[43] Indeed Antigone's willingness to be fair to men is stressed when Kennelly posits romantic love between her and Haemon (not in Sophocles).

In Tom Paulin's play *The Riot Act*, the action is located in Northern Ireland, where Creon becomes a Unionist politician devoted to law and order, and Antigone becomes a republican who wishes to bury her dead brother. Here the alien laws of Creon's Unionist state are opposed by Antigone's devotion to the native ethos of family, kin, tribe. As Antigone says: 'Down in the dark earth / there's no law says, / "Break with your own kin, go lick the State."'[44]

In the end, although Antigone dies, she wins because Creon is eventually forced to change his mind and achieve knowledge (*anagnorisis*). Since Creon's assertion 'I changed it utterly' appropriates a crucial phrase from Yeats's poem 'Easter 1916' that refers to the impact of the 1916 Rising, we infer that Creon's Unionist viewpoint has altered to take account of the republican position. This Irish Antigone is allowed to bury her brother with 'green laurel leaves'.[45]

Set in the Republic of Ireland, Aidan Mathews's play *Antigone* uses the Antigone theme not only to analyse state repression as seen in the Criminal Justice Bill 1984, but also to explore the plight of Irish women. Indeed the power of the state as embodied in Creon is directed against women – 'They'll come for the women down the street' – ordinary women represented by Antigone: 'I represent ordinariness . . . tens of thousands of faceless women. Women who stand in queues, and wait. And their waiting is more busy, more concentrated, than all the bustle of men.'[46] Put in sociological terms, this suggests the fact that women in fifth-century Athens and in modern Ireland lack the sort of power enjoyed by men.

Sophocles' tragedy *Electra* deals with another powerful and lonely character, Electra. Since Frank McGuinness's play *Electra* is a straight translation, we are once more required to analyse what *Electra* was originally about when put on in Athens.[47] Central to Sophocles' play is the desire of Electra for revenge on the killers of her father Agamemnon, Clytemnestra and Aegisthus. Indeed Electra is 'the main figure in the drama, all events being focused on what she feels, thinks and plans',[48] as this extract from one of her speeches indicates:

> First, look at myself and the mother who bore me –
> I hate her.
> Then look at me living in my own home with my
>   father's killers.
> They rule me.
> They decide if I get or I go without.
> How do you think I survive the days when I see him,
> I see Aegisthus sitting on my father's throne?
> He wears every stitch my father wore.
> He pours wine on the same fire where he murdered.
> And the worst – what is worse –
> I see my father's bed, and his killer lies beside my
>   mother.[49]

When Electra's brother Orestes finally reveals himself, he kills Clytemnestra and Aegisthus in accordance with the ancient code of an eye for an eye, a code that is not questioned at all by him or Electra. Accordingly, Electra becomes an integral part of the bloody cycle of killing and counter-killing that besets the House of Atreus. Women can be as destructive as men.

6

The plays by Euripides and Sophocles from the fifth century BC that are analysed here present a series of powerful women characters. Despite the very different sociological position of women in modern Ireland, that portrayal of women in ancient Greek tragedies continues to resonate in the twentieth century. Two at least have become archetypal: *Medea* and *Antigone*. The Greeks had a tragedy for it.

Notes

1. For these Irish plays see M. McDonald, 'When Despair and History Rhyme: Colonialism and Greek Tragedy', in *New Hibernia Review* 1(2) (Summer 1997): 57–70; C. Teevan, *Modern Drama* 41 (1998): 77–89. For Athenian women, see E. C. Keuls, *The Reign of the Phallus* (New York: Harper & Row, 1985). For Irish women, see C. Curtin, 'Marriage and Family', in *Ireland – A Sociological Profile* (Dublin: 1986), pp. 155–72 and P. Jackson, 'Worlds Apart: Social Dimensions of Sex Roles', ibid., pp. 287–306; Joseph Lee, *Ireland: Politics and Society, 1912–1985* (Cambridge: Cambridge University Press, 1990) and Index s.v. 'women'.

2. Cited by Keuls, *Reign of the Phallus*, p. 100.

3. Virginia Woolf, *A Room of One's Own* (London: Harcourt Brace, 1929), pp. 45–6.

4. H. Foley, in *Civilization of the Ancient Mediterranean: Greece and Rome*, ed. M. Grant and R. Kitzinger (New York: Scribner, 1988), pp. 1301–2.

5. D. Halperin, *One Hundred Years of Homosexuality and Other Essays on Greek Love* (London: Routledge, 1990), p. 146.

6. Brendan Kennelly, *Antigone* (Newcastle upon Tyne: Bloodaxe, 1996), p. 51. For comment on Kennelly's *Antigone*, *Medea* and *The Trojan Women*, see K. McCracken in *Dark Fathers into Light*: Brendan Kennelly, ed. R. Pine (Newcastle upon Tyne: Bloodaxe, 1994), pp. 114–47.

7. Brendan Kennelly, *Medea* (Newcastle upon Tyne: Bloodaxe, 1991), p. 34, which echoes Euripides' own thought.

8. Kennelly, quoted in ed. Pine, *Dark Fathers*, p. 22.

9. For the 'female intruder' see M. Shaw, 'The Female Intruder: Women in Fifth-Century Drama', in *Classical Philology* 70 (1975): 255–66; Helene Foley, 'The "Female Intruder" Reconsidered: Women in

Aristophanes' *Lysistrata* and *Ecclesiazusae*', in *Classical Philology* 77 (1982): 1–21.

10. Euripides, *Medea*, trans. Desmond Egan (Newbridge, Clare: Kavanagh Press, 1991); Brendan Kennelly, *Medea*; Marina Carr, *By the Bog of Cats . . .*, in *Plays One* (London: Faber & Faber, 1991).

11. For comment on Egan, see B. Arkins in Egan, *Medea*, pp. 10–14.

12. Desmond Egan, *The Death of Metaphor* (Gerrards Cross: Colin Smythe, 1990), p. 122.

13. Egan, *Medea*, p. 23.

14. For comment on Kennelly see M. McDonald, in *Medea: Essays on Medea in Myth, Literature, Philosophy and Art*, ed. J. J. Clauss and S. J. Johnston (Princeton, NJ: Princeton University Press, 1997), pp. 305–12.

15. Kennelly, *Medea*, pp. 20, 21, 25.

16. Ibid., pp. 72, 75

17. Carr, *Bog of Cats . . .*, pp. 270, 284.

18. Ibid., pp. 339–40.

19. Tony Harrison, *Dramatic Verse 1973–1985* (Newcastle upon Tyne: Bloodaxe, 1985), p. 370.

20. Colin Teevan, *Iph, after Euripides' Iphgeneia in Aulis* (London: Nick Hern Books, 1999).

21. Ibid., p. 50.

22. Ibid., pp. 43–5, 64.

23. Brian Friel, *Living Quarters*, in his *Selected Plays* (London: Faber & Faber, 1984), pp. 171–246; for comment, see A. Peacock in *The Achievement of Brian Friel*, ed. A. Peacock (Gerrards Cross: Colin Smythe, 1993), pp. 113–20. Ulick O'Connor, *The Oval Machine*; I am grateful to Dr Redmond O'Hanlon for providing me with a typescript of this play.

24. Suzuki, quoted in M. McDonald, *Ancient Sun, Modern Light: Greek Drama on the Modern Stage* (New York: Columbia University Press, 1992), p. 35.

25. Kennelly, quoted in Pine (ed.), *Dark Fathers into Light*, p. 139.

26. Brendan Kennelly, *The Trojan Women* (Newcastle upon Tyne: Bloodaxe, 1993). For comment see M. Lloyd, 'Euripides' *The Trojan Women*', in *Classics Ireland* 1 (1994): 54–60.

27. Kennelly, *Trojan Women*, p. 5.

28. Ibid., pp. 40, 14

29. Lloyd, *Classics Ireland*, 56.

29. Kennelly, *Trojan Women*, pp. 8, 74, 58.

30. Aidan Mathews, *Trojans*; I am grateful to Mr Mathews for providing me with the typescript of his play.

31. Ibid., pp. 13, 8, 22.

32. Derek Mahon, *The Bacchae* (Oldcastle: Gallery Books, 1991).

33. Ibid., pp. 12, 9.

34. Ibid., p. 22.

35. Ibid., p. 18.

36. George Bernard Shaw, *Major Barbara* (Harmondsworth: Penguin, 1950); for comment, see F. Macintosh, 'The Shavian Murray and the Euripidean Shaw: Major Barbara and the Bacchae', in *Classics Ireland* 5 (1998): 64–84.

37. Shaw, p. 95.

38. Cf. D. Kiberd, *Inventing Ireland* (Cambridge, MA: Harvard University Press, 1996), p. 61.

39. G. Steiner, *Antigones* (Oxford: Oxford University Press, 1984).

40. Kennelly, *Antigone* (1984); Tom Paulin, *The Riot Act* (London: Faber & Faber, 1985); Aidan Mathews, *Antigone* (1984). For the three Irish versions of *Antigone* see A. Roche in 'Ireland's Antigones: Tragedy North and South', in *Cultural Contexts and Literary Idioms in Contemporary Irish Literature*, ed. M. Kenneally (Gerrards Cross: Colin Smythe, 1988), pp. 221–50, and C. Murray in *Perspectives of Irish Drama and Theatre*, ed. J. Genet and R. Cave (Gerrards Cross: Colin Smythe, 1991), pp. 115–29; for that of Kennelly, see also D. Cairns, 'Sophocles' *Antigone*', in *Classics Ireland* 5 (1998): 141–6.

41. Kennelly, quoted in Roche, *Cultural Contexts*, p. 242.

42. Kennelly, *Antigone*, pp. 27, 9.

43. Ibid., pp. 21, 22, 24, 35.

44. Paulin, *The Riot Act*, p. 27.

45. Ibid., pp. 60, 58.

46. Mathews, *Trojans*, pp. 65, 35.

47. Frank McGuinness, *Electra* (London: Faber & Faber, 1997), p. 9.

48. A. Lesky, *Greek Tragedy* (London: Benn, 1967), p. 119.

49. McGuinness, *Electra*, p. 9.

'Is Medea's crime Medea's Glory?' Euripides in Dublin

John McDonagh

I am convinced that we have two or three poets in France who would be able to translate Homer very well; but I am equally convinced that nobody will read them unless they soften and embellish almost everything because, Madame, you have to write for your own time, not for the past.[1]

As early as 1720 Voltaire had arrived at the heart of a linguistic dilemma that echoes through the work of some of the most influential and popular Irish poets of the twenty-first century. Such diverse talents as Tom Paulin, Seamus Heaney and Desmond Egan have turned their attention to classical Greek drama in an attempt to further examine the complex nature of Ireland's contemporary post-colonial condition. Their chosen texts reflect the violence, betrayal and sense of personal crisis that characterize not only the original Greek play but the context of its contemporary manifestation. The most prolific interpreter of these classical texts, however, has been Brendan Kennelly,[2] a poet characterized by his ability and desires to voice those traditionally marginalized by and excluded from cultural discourses. While his Greek heroines, from Antigone to Medea, rage against their oppressors and exact a terrible revenge on those who cross them, Kennelly's versions are characterized by his ability to bring the texts and the emotions they express into a highly charged, contemporary linguistic realm. The violence experienced by women in contemporary Ireland, from the overtly physical to the sublime elision of their personal experiences, drives Kennelly's versions and injects a passion into the texts that resonates with a sharper contemporary social and cultural critique.

Kennelly is certainly writing for his own time, delving into and becoming energized by the extreme verbal and physical violence of *Medea*, arguably the most successful of his three plays. The sense of betrayal and the ends to which Medea will go to avenge this overwhelming emotional drive are precisely the territory into which Kennelly has often ventured with terrific intensity and emotional bravery. The play easily lends itself to his vituperative, highly personal interpretations, yet exactly what specifically Irish dimension emerges is a more complex question and one that needs to be further explored.

There is, of course, a strong personal attraction between Kennelly and his subject. In 1986, he spent the summer in St Patrick's Hospital in Dublin, recovering from a prolonged period of alcoholism. In the hospital, he listened to the stories of women berating their fathers, sons and, most commonly, husbands, men characterized by their unerring ability to let down almost everybody who relied upon them. As recalled by Kennelly, their phoney declarations of love echo Medea's rejection of the 'plausible' Jason, a cool and calculating promoter of his own self-interest. The men of these women's stories lie, cheat, break promises, physically assault and drunkenly abuse the women and children in their lives. These women are themselves driven to refuge in alcohol, thereby perpetuating their sense of victimization. Their revenge finds expression in their anger, and clearly Kennelly drew parallels with these intensely personal stories and the experience of Medea. While their stories are described by Kennelly as the initial inspiration for his version of *Medea*, there can be little doubt that his own decision to attempt a resolution of chronic alcoholism provided a focal point for his creative energies. He deliberately mentions this crucial juncture of his life in the introduction to the Bloodaxe version of the play,[3] and there can be little doubt that Medea's anger, which gradually hardens to a cool, moral detachment by the end of the play, reflects Kennelly's own difficulties at the time. Interestingly, in the same introduction, Kennelly recognizes in himself the men described by these women, thereby establishing a form of authorial connection with Jason. He recognizes the lies, the deceit and the destruction of family life that go hand in hand with any chronic dependency, be it alcohol, social status or economic power, empathizing with both Medea and Jason, thereby cleverly blurring the distinction between the perception of who is victim and who is victimizer. Few characters emerge from Kennelly's play with any integrity, and the heroine least of all. Medea's final exchange with Jason highlights the fact that his suffering is paramount and Medea's justifications for her actions appear increasingly petty and spiteful. Perhaps for Kennelly this is the only resolution possible, that no life is free from its torment and no action can be wrought without consequences.

Kennelly's stated belief that a marriage 'can be a kind of violent, exclusive intimacy'⁴ certainly rings true in his version of the play and the protagonists play out an all too familiar tragedy. Medea tells the audience that Jason was 'my sun, my moon and my stars, my sacred rivers and holy mountains' (p. 24), only to be revealed, after he has acquired what he needs, as a 'poisonous snake'. Marriage proves to be the 'revelation', a state of free-fall as the man exhibits 'a sudden loss of interest in her body', usually leading to the social exclusion of the woman. Often in the play Medea speaks for women in general, directly appealing to the women in the audience to listen and to respond with their 'silence', what Medea refers to as 'the most powerful weapon of all', and this motif of a communal, protective silence has been often seen in Irish literature. In John B. Keane's *The Field*, for example, the visiting bishop berates Mass-goers over their communal silence regarding the murder of an outsider who sought to buy a valuable local field that was the *de facto* possession of the Bull McCabe. He states:

The church bell will be silent: the mass bell will not be heard; the voice of the confessional will be stilled and in your last moment will be the most dreadful silence of all, for you will go to face your Maker without the last sacrament on your lips . . . and all because of your silence now.⁵

Given Keane's and Kennelly's north Kerry heritage it would appear that this concept of a self-protective silence shared by members of a community is a feature of *Medea* that would have particular resonance within Kennelly's own local community and might again prove to be a source of attraction with the play.

There are, of course, difficult questions that have to be faced in any assessment of a 'version' of another author's work. Kennelly must follow some of the narrative structure of the original Euripidean myth. His Medea will be betrayed by Jason and infamously commit filicide as Euripides' Medea has done, and herein lie both the strengths and weaknesses of this type of drama. His only real freedom within the text is, arguably, the most powerful freedom of all, namely the reconstruction of the words of the characters in an attempt to contemporize the very morality that places these plays in the literary canon in the first place. Kennelly remains relatively faithful to the roles of the Nurse and the Chorus, both of whom retain their roles of moral interpreters of the action. The complex role of Medea as both feminist icon and heartless killer (interpretations which ironically hinge upon each other) cannot be altered by Kennelly to the degree that her actions are changed. Her psyche, however, is open territory and his role in constructing a world vision in which her actions can begin to be understood is crucial. His Medea is a complicated and contradictory character, her confused morality exemplified by the murder of the children. In the intervening twenty-four centuries between Euripides and Kennelly, however, the social, political, sexual and cultural roles of women have radically altered and therefore contemporary interpreters of Medea have to present the play in the light of an audience that is less likely to be impressed by the portrayal of an independent woman than their ancient Greek counterparts.[6] This, however, is not to argue that the cultural situation is unrecognizable; Kennelly has clearly indicated, through his dialogue and plot, that certain human traits, invariably negative ones, have altered only in terms of the context rather than the content. It is these traits (jealousy, revenge, violence) that give the drama its edge and yet curiously it is the plot that restricts real character development. For example, in one of the blurbs on the back of the Bloodaxe edition, Oliver Taplin writing for the Times Literary Supplement rightly acknowledges the 'great verbal virtuosity' of Kennelly's play but curiously also celebrates its 'unpredictable' nature. How unpredictable can a version of Euripides' play be when it largely follows the plot outline and development of the source text? Surely most audiences would be familiar with the original plot and therefore have certain expectations. Kennelly, however, appears to concentrate on making the play relevant to a contemporary audience rather than attempting to make the audience aware of the Greek conventions that the play explores. This crucial distinction is clearly visible in the recognizable Kennellian dialogic interchange between the characters. His Medea is initially humanly unhappy, rightly enraged with her husband, a man she gave up everything for, yet she cascades into an anger that appears superhuman, prepared to subvert all moral conventions in an attempt to satisfy her revenge. This, perhaps, is what most speaks to a contemporary Irish audience, weighed down by the collapse of the institutions which the Irish state had held as central to its perception of the nation. The rapid decline in public respect for the Catholic Church in Ireland in the 1990s, for example, after a series of sexual abuse scandals (ironically given Jason's behaviour) resonates with Medea's resolution that she 'will not continue to live in this house of lies' (p. 22). Her exasperation is born out of the climate of deceit that she has lived with for too long. When Fintan O'Toole wrote in 1992 that, apropos the exposure of the love-child of Bishop Eamonn Casey, one of the options facing the Irish hierarchy was that of 'the bishop as man, fallen, fallible, having no authority but the one that matters: the authority of experience',[7] he could well be describing Jason, a man, as described by Medea, that 'gambled and lost' (p. 74). She labels him a 'poor, sad, pointless man' (p. 74), stripped of the veneer of power and authority that he so valued. Indeed, O'Toole's description of Casey's affair with Annie Murphy reads remarkably like the story of *Medea* itself:

He dazzles her with his power, his confidence, his command of the world. They fall in love and begin a sexual relationship. He promises her nothing, but he doesn't need to, for hurt and abused as she is, she is more than capable of making him into a promise to herself. She gives him pleasure, excitement and adoration. He gives her the first two but probably not the third. She thinks of the future, he thinks of the present, floating on the delusion that he can have the best of all worlds. He makes her pregnant. The baby forces choices on her, choices which, because he is a man and a powerful one, he doesn't believe he has to make. He behaves badly, hypocritically, politically. It ends in tears: first hers, then, after many years, his.[8]

What one associates most with Euripides' Medea, and indeed provides a source of morbid fascination, is the fact that she murders her two children in an act of ultimate revenge on Jason. The act of filicide appears to question one of our most basic human moral precepts, that of the protection and nurturing of children. Of course, it can easily be viewed as a tired misogynistic portrayal of the killer woman, so obsessed with the man in her life that she is prepared to kill her children to avenge his betrayal. Equally, her actions can be viewed as the ultimate act of feminist liberation, freedom from the perceived emotional bondage of motherhood. Kennelly's Medea appears so consumed with her rage that the filicide appears less brutal than it otherwise might, the children almost necessary victims in the cross-fire between husband and wife. Her children were created with Jason, therefore they are a constant reminder to her of his eternal proximity and are thus doomed. Despite the best efforts of the Nurse, Medea damns both the children and their father in the same breath, frighteningly reminiscent of suicidal parents who decide that their children must die with them. In Ireland in the year 2000 six children died at the hands of a suicidal parent[9] and the average murder rate for children (classed as under eighteen years old) in the state over the past four years stands at six. The taking of children by a suicidal parent is an occurrence that brings the often bizarre nature of parental love into sharp focus and can, in certain circumstances, be regarded as an act of ultimate love. In Philip Vellacott's Penguin Classics text, Medea, showing her cool but perverse logic, declares that 'I'll not leave sons of mine to be the victims of my enemies' rage.'[10] Kennelly, on the other hand, has Medea acknowledging that 'passion strangles my love' (p. 66), a position that certainly places a different emphasis on the reasons for the necessity of the children's death. Medea does not kill herself as this would appear as a Jasonic triumph and, indeed, she only embarks on her murderous revenge when an escape route to Athens has been prearranged. However, she is well aware of the effect the death of the children will have on Jason. Equally, a fundamental question of love arises in the case of filicide: to what extent are parents who commit suicide protecting their children by taking them with them? Arguably, parents who commit suicide can show their love for their children by also killing them, either to protect them, or to take them along. At the moment of her children's deaths, Medea exhibits that combination of fierce passion and steely will that characterizes her movement through the play. The love she forlornly seeks from Jason swamps whatever maternal feelings she might have and the children end their life exactly as they began it; directly as a consequence of the tumultuous union of husband and wife. However, whether it can be regarded as Medea's ultimate triumph is a hugely debatable question. While she certainly inflicts her desired revenge on Jason, what is she left with as she escapes to Athens on her fiery chariot? According to the Chorus (in the Penguin Classics text) 'The unexpected God makes possible',[11] and in the final analysis, perhaps this is all we know and all we need to know.

The freedom offered by the 'version' moniker allows Kennelly the opportunity to explore, with some notable exceptions, however, the familiar territory of the marginalized, the socially excluded and those whose behaviour sets them apart from the norms of social discourse. It is precisely in this contentious area of the 'unvoiced' that elements of contemporary post-colonial theory shed fascinating light on new interpretations of those perceived to be at both the centre and margins of cultural, political and sexual discourses. Homi K. Bhabha asserts that it is in 'those moments or processes that are produced in the articulation of cultural differences',[12] such as those between Jason and Medea, the Greek and the outsider, that crucial composite elements in cultural identities begin to emerge. Jason's self-righteousness and, particularly in Kennelly's text, his bumptious self-importance wither when juxtaposed directly with the passion of Medea. He represents a civilized, orderly existence in which marriage has a clear social and economic function. Medea, as a non-Greek, could never be recognized as his wife and she represents the passionate, instinctual barbarian, and it is precisely in the confrontation between Greek and barbarian that Greek society is defined. Jason's eventual tragedy results from his inability to reconcile these opposites, and his incredulous response to Medea's murder of the children highlights his personal removal from the emotional aspects of his psyche. Throughout his poetry, Kennelly has flirted with opposites, his poetic instincts heightened by characters who have to deal with a rational and safe life that is haunted by madness and an unquenched recklessness. Jason and Medea are two clear voices that inhabit every individual, personifying the shifting entity that is selfhood. Kennelly has written that self 'is always open to change and development, what the moral self might call betrayal',[13] and perhaps it is this very lack of openness that seals Jason's fate, and indeed renders Medea unable to cope with the changes in her marital circumstances. Kennelly's poetry is awash with voices, what he refers to as 'prisoners on parole from history', characters desperately seeking articulation beyond the stultifying clichés of self and nationhood. His *Medea* presents a world vision of competing ideologies, and the adherence of both Jason and Medea to their respective beliefs results in the ultimate destruction of their relationship and the deaths of four innocent parties. It is only through the moderating influence of the Chorus at the beginning of Part Two that Kennelly overtly describes the middle ground between these competing ideologies, as usual a middle ground that is most regularly occupied. The Chorus declares that 'to live within limits is to honour the infinite, mysterious potential of excess', a fascinating insight given Kennelly's personal battle with alcohol at the time, a thought that resonates with Patrick Kavanagh's brilliantly simple maxim that 'through a chink too wide comes in no wonder'.[14] Kennelly's play is arguably less concerned with grand national narratives and codes of behaviour than with, as Kathleen McCracken notes, 'the feminist imperatives and, by extension, the broad humanist ramifications'[15] that emerge from the narrative.

Kennelly's text, however, is more complex than a mere rereading of a classic text in a contemporary light. If one accepts Kennelly's traditionally subversive poetic role then Medea's actions cannot be merely explained away as the justifiable actions of a woman scorned. What mention or regard is taken of Jason's undoubted suffering at the loss of his children? Is the experience of men again to be written out of the text as a mere exemplar of their pathological and unquestioned unworthiness? Indeed, it is the two children, significantly both male, who pay the ultimate price for their mother's scorn, begging the question as to the real nature of a sense of victimization in the text. Despite all her acknowledged bitterness, Medea flees at the end of the play; Jason is left in mourning, while her children lie dead. Who else can be regarded as the true victims, other than the children, or is the sentence of living with a loved one's murder a greater punishment, as Medea suggests? Although Medea's rage and sense of betrayal inevitably form the thematic basis of the majority of criticism of the play, Jason and the other men appear as social-climbing, sexually obsessed stooges, mono-dimensional characters who pale into insignificance when juxtaposed with the passionate, determined Medea. Aegeus, for example, is more than happy to overlook Medea's murderous actions on the promise that she will provide him with children, a repetition of her husband's behaviour that Medea, unable to learn from her past experiences, appears content enough to ignore.

Medea's description of Jason as a 'plausible man', skilled in the art of verbal deception, suggests a theme that has concerned Kennelly from his earliest poetic works. In a poem entitled 'Six of One'[16] for example, he exposes the 'barbarian', a man secure in his own self-importance and unafraid to fill the perceived vacuum in the minds of those he meets. Remaining blissfully unaware of his own inadequacies, 'he makes articulate the pitifully dumb', robbing language from the mouths of those he deems as unworthy or incapable of self-expression. Again in *The Visitor*,[17] the ubiquitous house guest struts into a house and, through his own delusions of self-importance and an inability to recognize the needs of those around him, proceeds to 'rob' the children 'of every word they had' by filling their spaces with his stories. In Kennelly's poetry, this form of linguistic violence is perpetrated by teacher against pupil, priest against congregation, parent against child, husband against wife, and almost anybody who is placed in a position of trust by another. 'Love and you will be betrayed' is a constant theme throughout his work and the closer the relationship the deeper the sense of betrayal. In *The Book of Judas*, the betrayal of Jesus involves that most intimate of gestures, a kiss, given by Judas as he stares into the eyes of his victim. When pressed by Hans Christian Andersen as to why he betrayed a man he adored with the ultimate gesture of love, Judas replies: 'One man in all this world understands that kiss.'[18] Kennelly is a skilled demythologizer of language, always prepared to go beyond the semantic surface into the deeper realms of power, control and violence that lie at the heart of linguistic systems. The violence meted out in polite words is the most common violence of all. Medea castigates Jason, accusing him of a 'plausibility' that 'smothers the soul with oily words', preferring 'a passionately meant insult' which, as a consequence of its honesty, acts as 'a kind of compliment' (p. 40). However, this appearance of respectability is unmasked by 'one burning word of honesty', the plausible man uncovered in all his duplicitousness. In much the same way as Roland Barthes lamented the inevitable fate of the farmer Dominici[19] faced with the labyrinthine linguistic constructions of the legal world, so Kennelly's Jason remains neutered by his passionless language, his Greek manners and up-bringing withering in the face of his wife's untamed and ferocious passion. Barthes's brilliant study of Gaston Dominici's 1952 trial for murder concludes that the accused faced the ultimate terror, that of 'being judged by a power which wants to hear only the language it lends us'.[20] Jason undoubtedly suffers that fate at the pen of not only Kennelly but other translators of *Medea*. He is rendered almost mute, unable to move beyond platitudinous defences of his position, defences that are increasingly undermined by Medea's verbal onslaught. Barthes posits the view that 'to rob a man of his language in the very name of language is the first step in all legal murders'[21] and, interestingly, it is Jason and, perhaps more significantly, the two boys who are robbed of their language by Medea. Euripides failed to include the boys' stories in his play, and by extension Jason's story remains partially told, the detail and emphasis provided by Medea. Equally, the murder of the children has traditionally been seen as part of an overall dramatic convention. John Ferguson has written, 'The death of the children is transfigured by being seen as part of timeless sorrow. To understand this is to understand the soul of Greek tragedy; to fail to understand this is to leave empty formalism and dead convention.'[22] Now to use the term 'death' in relation to two children who are consciously and deliberately led to their murder can quite reasonably be assumed in itself to lean towards empty formalism and thus a different and challenging perspective on the play can begin to emerge. The strength of *Medea*, therefore, lies precisely in the text's ability to arouse a variety of responses that depend almost entirely upon the reader's social, cultural and political stance, a classic example of Barthes's notion that the reader is 'simply someone who holds together in a single field all the traces by which the written text is constituted'.[23]

Needless to say, it would also be a travesty to view Jason as some kind of postmodern masculinist icon. His prime motivation in wooing Glauke reflects his desire to move beyond what he perceives to be his lowly station in life. He tells Medea that 'it was not for the sake of a woman that I enter marriage', arguing that he wanted 'royalty to spread through my family', endeavouring 'to distance myself from poverty and shame' (p. 41). His justification resonates with post-colonial Ireland's attempt to distance itself from the poverty of its colonial past, embracing wholeheartedly a neo-colonial economics that brings with it the consequent dilution of a distinctive cultural identity. The architectural prevalence in rural Ireland of the arched hacienda-like bungalow built a few hundred yards from the ruins of the original family home is a contemporary visual manifestation of Jason's desire to be seen to be removed from an inglorious past. He cannot, or at best will not, understand Medea's reaction to his stated desire to improve the social position of his children and, by extension, Medea herself. His shallowness is exposed and ultimately proves to be his undoing. Medea, equally, is a complex mixture of contradictions, an attractive proposition for a poet like Kennelly. Despite the fact that her brother has been murdered in her inevitably vain search for personal happiness, she proceeds to claim that 'I want the happiness that comes from my husband and my children' (p. 41), a claim that appears hollow in the light of the subsequent murder of the very children she mentions as central to her idea of happiness. In many ways, these contradictions lie at the heart of Medea's attraction. She eludes definition or categorization, her words and actions coinciding and diverging with no apparent consistency. driven solely by her vengeful desires. She admits that her one great error was the betrayal of her father, yet she proceeds to kill her two children in an attempt to gain revenge on Jason.

If it is accepted that one of the central features of contemporary versions is the translation of cultures as well as words, then surely the subversive nature of Euripides' original work has to be viewed in the context of intervening social and cultural movements and theories. Given that Euripides' Athens 'was a place in which Pericles proclaimed that the greatest glory of woman is not to be spoken of by men for good or bad',[24] then certainly a play in which a woman is allowed not only to express her emotions but to carry out her revenge to such devastating effect has to be seen as wonderfully challenging of the cultural orthodoxy of its time. Equally, Kennelly's experience of the battered, abused and marginalized women he came across in St Patrick's Hospital in the summer of 1986 finds a powerful expression in the play. His Medea is angry to the point of not caring about the long-term personal consequences of her anger, hinting at a rejection of traditional stoical acceptance of male abuse. Writing at a critical juncture in his own life, Kennelly understands Medea's anger, a vortex of self-loathing that manifests itself in the attempt to destroy all those who come close to her, culminating in the elimination of the only people who are directly of her own flesh. Perhaps she has to kill her children to stand any chance of recovering what little sanity has been afforded her. Attempting to break the grip of alcohol, Kennelly empathizes with a character that is driven to pathological unhappiness, almost relishing the darkness and chaos that typify her existence. Alcoholism is a lonely pursuit, an existence dogged by a paranoia that distrusts all those who seek to help. The concept of a recovery only being possible when the alcoholic realizes his or her own predicament echoes Medea's repeated rejection of the advice of the Chorus, the Teacher and the Nurse. The one person who empathizes with Medea is Medea, as secure as her chaotic mind will allow in her mono-focal drive to avenge.

However, Kennelly's Medea, and for that matter other Irish versions of Greek tragedy, have emerged on the coat-tails of Marxist, feminist, psychoanalytic and post-colonial critical theories and the impact of these ideas on the readers and writers of contemporary versions cannot be underestimated. For example, the elision of the psyche of Jason and the children from the story presents the contemporary reader with grave difficulties. Post-colonial theory in general, and Subaltern Studies[25] in particular, seek out the stories of those whose experiences have formed a central plank of the colonial or post-colonial exercise but who have been excluded from cultural discourses because their articulation would upset traditional and accepted perceptions of history, culture and society. Medea's anger flows freely, her complex character invigorated by an outpouring of revenge virtually un-paralleled in classical or contemporary literature. Her story is told. Jason, despite his infidelity, is the pillar of Greek manners and his story is not told, at least not to the same degree as Medea's. Kennelly's Jason chastises Medea with 'my instinctive wisdom', 'the sanity and rightness of my choice', and refers to the 'noble service' he has rendered his wife and sons. His myopia is confounded when he states, to almost comic effect, that 'women should not exist'. His argument is so fundamentally flawed as to appear mock-tragic and certainly we find out little about his true motivations other than the trite stereotypical male concerns for a better material life for him and his children. As a straight man, he works very well. Medea's response allows Jason no room for manoeuvre in that she decries 'the plausible traitor' as 'the worst scoundrel', strangling Jason's defence at birth and cleverly using her anger to portray him as uncaring and mono-dimensional. Ironically, the majority of the modern Irish versions of classical Greek drama have been written by men, yet the experience of women appears paramount. Are poets still afraid to write about the suffering of men because they may appear to simultaneously elide the experience of women? Is the fear also apparent that in writing about the male characters the poets might appear to tread on the toes of feminist interpretations of the tragedies? Interestingly, the poetic sensitivities are heightened when describing the emotions of the female Other but appear less concerned with the social and cultural pressures that formed the likes of Jason in the first place. Kennelly overtly describes his play as concerned with the 'rage' of women 'mainly against men, Irishmen like myself',[26] and the clear implication in the text is of Medea's being driven to her wits' end by the pathological wanderings of her husband. Indeed, Euripides' play begins at the point of Jason's betrayal of Medea, rather than with the various acts of murderous collusion that characterized their early relationship, including Medea's betrayal of her father Aeetes and the brutal murder of her own brother, Apsyrtus. Is Euripides also refusing to see the entire picture for fear that the creation of his feminist icon might appear more complicated than his play allows? Would the audience's Medean empathy be tarnished by the dramatic scene of Medea's chopping up the body of her brother and scattering it from the back of her fleeing boat? Equally, if the audience imagined the torment of Creon and Glauke as Medea's poisoned crown burns the flesh from their bodies? A critique of the portrayal of men in *Medea* is not a covert Freudian admission of fear or admonishment of Jason's betrayal but rather a filling in of a picture that, occasionally, appears very lop-sided. In *Cromwell* and *The Book of Judas* Kennelly seeks out the nooks and crannies of the psyche condemned to occupy for ever the role of moral scapegoat, so it has to appear unusual that he fails to allow Jason the chance to speak back, other than with hollow admonitions of his betrayed wife. An exception to this portrayal certainly occurs at the end of the play when Jason's obvious and genuine grief for the death of his sons appears to overwhelm him. It is only at this point that he appears to express genuine human emotion rather than the politically driven social-climbing shibboleths of the previous scenes. However, Kennelly leaves his readers no doubt about the real victor in all of this emotional mess by concluding his version with this controversial line: 'Is Medea's crime also Medea's glory?'[27]

The rhetorical nature of this question implicitly suggests that Kennelly's sympathies lie squarely with Medea and that, indeed, the murder of her children has been a literal and symbolic act of liberation. Certainly Kennelly's perception of the liberation of Medea from the traditional shackles of child-rearing and child love is a challenging and stimulating perspective and this final line certainly places Kennelly's version at odds with the standard conclusion of other versions of *Medea*. Is Medea's 'glory' the fact that, unlike Tess of the d'Urbervilles, she ultimately gets away with her murderous revenge? Perhaps it is in this outcome that Kennelly finds the attraction of the play. In drama, as in other forms of literature, an all-pervading Christian morality suggests that all wrongdoers will ultimately pay for their crime, yet Medea triumphantly leaves the broken Jason, takes her chariot and lives out an eventful life in Athens. Alongside Electra, she succeeds in her revenge, emerging from the play like a pre-modern Terminator, leaving behind her the obligatory body-count of discarded mortals who cross her ill-starred path.

The fundamental question of authorial intent inevitably hangs over any version of another author's original work. Kennelly's text is overtly defined as a 'version' and no claims are made to place the text in the genre of the translated edition of the original text. This approach is also adopted by Kennelly in his versions of *Antigone* and *Trojan Women*, Indeed, in his introduction to the text Kennelly makes no reference to any translated text of *Medea* upon which his version is based, contenting himself by referring to 'the Medea that I tried to imagine'[28] as his guiding principle. This arguably gives Kennelly greater freedom over his material in that while remaining faithful to the traditionally accepted outline and development of the plot, he ascribes to himself the ultimate freedom of linguistic interpretation. The shaping of dialogic interchange and the manipulation of words empower Kennelly's Medea to escape the constraints of accepted versions of the original text. For example, in Philip Vellacott's translation for Penguin Classics, Medea attacks Jason on her first encounter with him since his betrayal of her:

> You filthy coward! – if I knew any worse name
> For such unmanliness I'd use it – so, you've come.[29]

For a woman skilled in magic and prepared to go to any lengths to avenge her battered pride, it seems odd that she cannot come up with any words worse than 'You filthy coward!' In Kennelly's version, however, Kennelly's traditional penchant for the venomous *mot juste* comes to the fore as Medea vents her spleen on her traitorous husband:

> Stink of the grave, rot of a corpse's flesh,
> slime of this putrid world,
> unburied carcase of a dog in the street,
> the black-and-yellow greeny spit of a drunk at midnight –
> these are my words for you.[30]

Kennelly's version of the anger of this encounter presents a Medea very different from the somewhat restrained Vellacott version. In Vellacott, her anger is very Anglo-Saxon, restrained, controlled and yet hinting at a fierce retribution to follow. The Irish Medea, however, has no such hindrances. Indeed, the impression is given that Medea could have carried on in this vituperative Falstaffian vein for quite some time, flaunting her insults as her anger increased. The expression of anger is as important to Kennelly's Medea as the practical actions she carries out in the venting of that anger. Consequently, through this manipulation of the dialogue, Kennelly gives a very different portrait of Medea, a woman whose ability to carry out acts of the deadliest ferocity is matched by her desire to express her anger in the clearest possible terms. Therefore, the question arises as to which Medea is most to be feared, the volcanic Medea who openly rants about her hatred for Jason or the more restrained, threatening Medea whose silences are as, if not more, threatening than her words? It is precisely in these areas of contestation that the vitality and imagination of the interpreter come to the fore.

For Kennelly, this voicing of bilious anger is a recurring poetic motif and it comes as no surprise that his Medea should be so adept at expressing her anger in such terms. In an essay dealing directly with the link between poetry and violence, Kennelly asks a seminal question: 'what do we do with the violence of our emotions?'[31] In so many of his poems, Kennelly's characters content themselves with the cathartic power of expression, imploding in violent words and images that in many ways dilute the need for direct reparative action. Medea, therefore, might appear as an unusual choice for Kennelly in that her anger is manifested in the utmost physical violence as well as vituperative rhetoric, and it is in this final act of filicide that the central dilemma over Medea lies. Kennelly ends his version with a highly provocative rhetorical question: 'Is Medea's crime Medea's glory?' His play ends with a question as to the nature of Medea's existence. It is now up to the reader to reply.

Notes

1. André Lefevere, *Translation/History/Culture – A Sourcebook* (London: Routledge, 1992), p. 28.
2. For an extensive bibliographical reference see *Dark Fathers into Light: Brendan Kennelly*, ed. Richard Pine (Newcastle upon Tyne: Bloodaxe, 1994). Kennelly's three classical plays are *Antigone* (1986), *Medea* (1988) and *The Trojan Women* (1993).
3. See pp. 6–8 of the Bloodaxe edn. of *Medea* (Newcastle upon Tyne: Bloodaxe, 1991). References to Kennelly's text of *Medea* are from this version and appear as page numbers in parentheses.
4. From an essay entitled 'Poetry and Violence', in Ake Persson (ed.),

Brendan Kennelly – Journey into Joy – Selected Prose (Newcastle upon Tyne: Bloodaxe, 1994), p. 41.

5. John B. Keane, *Three Plays* (Dublin: Mercier Press, 1990), p. 150.

6. Marina Carr in her version of *Medea* reflects the contemporary status of women in her *By the Bog of Cats . . .*, while at the same time showing their continuing social limitations; in *Plays One* (London: Faber & Faber, 2000).

7. Fintan O'Toole, *Black Hole, Green Card* (Dublin: New Island Books, 1994), p. 137.

8. Ibid., pp. 139–40.

9. Information courtesy of the Garda Press Office (gpresoff@iol.ie), Garda Headquarters, Phoenix Park, Dublin.

10. *Medea and Other Plays*, trans. Philip Vellacott (Harmondsworth, Mx: Penguin, 1963), p. 50.

11. Ibid., p. 61.

12. Homi K. Bhabha, *The Location of Culture* (London: Routledge, 1994), pp. 1–2.

13. *Dark Fathers into Light*, Pine (ed.), p. 171.

14. Peter Kavanagh, *The Complete Poems of Patrick Kavanagh* (New York: Peter Kavanagh Hand Press, 1996), p. 146.

15. Ibid., p. 121.

16. Brendan Kennelly, *The Boats Are Home* (Oldcastle: Gallery Books, 1980), p. 52.

17. Ibid., p. 29.

18. Brendan Kennelly, *The Book of Judas* (Newcastle upon Tyne: Bloodaxe, 1991), p. 236.

19. Gaston Dominici, a farmer, was convicted in 1952 of the murder of Sir Jack Drummond and his wife and daughter, whom he found camping on his land. The essay, 'Dominici or the Triumph of Literature' is contained in Barthes's seminal 1957 collection of essays, *Mythologies* (London: Vintage, 1997).

20. Ibid., p. 46.

21. Ibid.

22. John Ferguson, *A Companion to Greek Tragedy* (Austin: University of Texas Press, 1972), p. 263.

23. Roland Barthes, 'The Death of the Author', in David Lodge (ed.), *Modern Criticism and Theory – A Reader* (London: Longman, 1988), p. 171.

24. John Ferguson, *A Companion to Greek Tragedy*, p. 249.

25. For an excellent examination of the work of the Subaltern Studies group, see an article entitled 'Subalternity and Gender – Problems of Post-colonial Irishness', *Journal of Gender Studies* 5(3) (1966): 363–73.
26. Kennelly, *Medea*, p. 7.
27. Ibid., p. 75.
28. Ibid., p. 8.
29. *Medea*, trans. Vellacott, p. 31.
30. Kennelly, *Medea*, p. 36.
31. Persson (ed.), *Kennelly – Selected Prose*, p. 28.

The Return of Persephone?
Missing Demeter in Irish Theatre

Cathy Leeney

The myth of Persephone and Demeter provides a matrix of archetypal conflicts between opposing values, of freedom and restraint, of separation and connection, of lostness and foundness. The story hinges on the alternation of closeness and separation between mother and daughter. It expresses the emotional landscape of existence without the mother, without the child: the absent child, torn from the maternal haven, and, from Persephone's perspective, the missing mother without whom life becomes an underworld, with Hades the door into the dark.

The myth has been examined as it occurs in the work of writers of fiction, as well as poetry, and in plays. I will suggest briefly what it might mean in the context of some Irish theatre, how (among other things) it draws attention to the role of the mother in contemporary Irish plays. I will look at how the myth relates to Marina Carr's *The Mai*, to work by Teresa Deevy, Abbey playwright of the 1930s, and to newcomer actor-playwright Pat Kinevane's *The Plains of Enna*.

So, to begin with the story: Persephone, also called Kora or Proserpina, is the daughter of Demeter, also called Ceres, the goddess of the earth. The two are inseparable, two-in-one. In some versions of the story a third figure, Hecate, is associated with Persephone as her companion. Hecate stands at the powerful conjunction of the upper and lower worlds. One day Persephone is playing in a summer meadow with her girlfriends when she sees a beautiful narcissus. She runs to pick it, and as she does so, the earth opens in a great chasm under her feet, and Hades, the god of the underworld, carries her away. In his chariot he brings her as his bride to his kingdom of darkness. At the sound of her daughter's cries, a sharp pain seizes Demeter's heart, and she shoots out 'like a bird over land and sea'.[1]

Demeter, the goddess of earth and fertility, is distraught. She searches everywhere for her beloved girl, but no sign. She so mourns the loss of her daughter that the crops fail and the earth is parched and fallow. Zeus pities the starving people and animals, and commands Hades to release Persephone. But before she returns from the underworld, Persephone eats the seeds of a pomegranate given to her by Hades. This ensures that she will return to him for half of every year.

Originary models of the foundation of theatre have an irresistible attraction. The myth of Persephone, as told in the Homeric 'Hymn to Demeter', is associated with the Eleusinian Mysteries which were celebrated in ancient Greece for over 2,000 years. They were organized by and for women before, some say, being taken over by men through the cult of Dionysus. The circularity of the Persephone myth represents an alternative notion of dramatic structure, emphasizing a metaphorical death, the rhythm of existence, and the privileging of compromise and equilibrium over conflict resolved in the obliteration of one force by another.

The story is about cycles, movement from one polarity to another. It is about the trauma of separation, and return, from dark into the light, from absence to presence, from below to above, from the unseen to the seen. The story is about sudden action and extenuated, painful waiting. Its connection with the sources of European theatre suggests a dramaturgy that contrasts with the deep structure of resolution through violence that underlies classic tragedy so powerfully.[2] In contrast, Persephone's story sets a pattern of balance, and proposes equilibrium between forces as opposed to the triumph of one over another. The myth has a temporal meaning too in that it expresses a life-rhythm of dramatic event, in which time becomes alternately extenuated and telescoped as connection is lost and found. In terms of dramaturgy, rhythm replaces plot, and the arc of time overarches mere chronological event to express mythic time.

In theatre the myth of Persephone offers a model of transformation, of process, not a model of conflict and resolution. The
transformation is cyclical, repeated, and resists progress in favour
of balance. The polarities of dark and light, of winter and spring,
of separation and connection have no meaning as conflicting
opposites, but as related, reliant ideas, each violating the other,
each making the other possible.

Mary A. Doll writes: 'Demeter's myth shows us, as does Beckett,
that what must die is the old ego, with its dry, literal way of
seeing.'[3] A most thorough, if oblique, representation in negative of
the Persephone and Demeter relation occurs in Beckett's *Footfalls*
(1976). The association between the myth and Beckett's short play
is invited in the mother/daughter dynamic, in the use of the names
May (and its variation Amy) and Mrs Winter, and most powerfully
in the repetitious circularity of the movement of the piece in
performance. However, a number of aspects of *Footfalls* effect a
parodic image of the Persephone myth: the advanced ages of May
and the Woman's voice; the reduction of cyclical movement to nine
paces right, then left; the ghostly femininity, inexpressive of vitality;
and the bleaching out of masculine presence to the gnomic 'His
poor arm'.[4] Demeter's search for Persephone, in some versions of
the story, took nine days, circling to the left, a *via negativa*, as Karl
Kerenyi describes it, 'to the left, the direction of death'.[5] In
Footfalls, May/Amy walks nine steps in a ritual of finding and
losing of the mother and daughter, 'seven, eight, nine, wheel'
(*Footfalls*, p. 399). The separate identities of May and 'Mother' are
blurred; this blurs any potential for fulfilment in their reunification.
The play presents an action of vestigial life at the edge of an
invasive and, finally, obliterating darkness, culminating in absence:
'*Fade up to even a little less still on strip. No trace of MAY*'
(*Footfalls*, p. 403).

In Marina Carr's *The Mai* (1994) the main character's name
echoes Beckett's pacing semblance. Carr's Mai is both mother and
daughter in a play of four generations of women, of mothers and
daughters. However, Mrs Gaskell's title *Wives and Daughters*
more closely describes the hierarchy of relationship that *The Mai*

dramatizes, for it is the marriage tie that defines a life of value for Mai, as well as for her grandmother, Grandma Fraochlán. The bond between mother and daughter is taken for granted, or twisted and fantasized, to the point of parody or invisibility. The Mai builds a beautiful house in which to wait, Demeter-like, but it is her husband Robert who returns to her, bringing with him a temporary spring. *The Mai* plays out the substitution of romantic hetero-sexuality for the archetypal mother/daughter narrative of separation in winter, and attachment in summer. Carr's play is underpinned repeatedly by altered images of the Persephone story refigured, reversed, or denied.

The narrator, Millie, The Mai's daughter, begins a series of stories which elaborate on the action throughout; she describes The Mai's distress when Robert first left. In the Bluebell Hotel, the woman and the girl drink six whiskeys and six minerals respectively, '[t]hen The Mai turned to me with her sunglasses on, though it was the middle of winter, she turned to me and said, "Millie, would you ever run up to the butcher's and get me a needle and thread." '[6] It is The Mai's first and absurdly abortive effort to find 'that magic thread that would stitch us together again' (*The Mai*, p. 14). It is also a resonant image of the ineffectual solidarity that Millie can offer her mother. The Mai sits, blinded to her daughter's love, and gently yet hopelessly expresses her inability to pursue her search for attachment in the right quarter: 'your Dad'll come back and we will have the best of lives' (p. 14).

Later, when Robert does return, The Mai describes to him a dream she had the night before their marriage, in which she is Persephone to his Hades: 'And I turn to look after you and you're gone . . . and away in the distance I see a black cavern and I know it leads nowhere and I start walking that way because I know I'll find you there' (p. 26). The mythic reference, however, cannot be completed as The Mai's mother is dead. Grandma Fraochlán is no substitute maternal figure either. As the senior representative of the many generations in the play, Carr allows her to emphasize the theme of repetition which is structurally central to the Persephone/Demeter story: Grandma F. says: '. . . because we can't help repeatin'. Robert, we repeah an' we repeah, th'orchestration may be different but tha tune is allas tha same' (p. 23). And what is repeated is not only the passivity of women waiting for absent men, but the neglect of parental love in the face of romantic sexual attachment. As Grandma Fraochlán so unforgettably expresses it, 'I would gladly a hurlt all seven a ye down tha slopes a hell for wan nigh' more wud tha nine-fingered fisherman an' may I roh eternally for such unmotherly feelin'' (p. 70).

The setting of *The Mai* overlooks Owl Lake, and Millie connects protagonists with landscape in her recounting of the legend concerning the lake's origins. Here, Bláth and Coillte are the lovers blissfully together through the spring and summer, until, in autumn, Bláth explains that he soon must go to 'live with the dark witch of the bog' (p. 41). In her grief, Coillte cries 'a lake of tears', in which she is drowned by the witch. The mother/daughter relation is replaced by the romantic attachment between the lovers, and Demeter is refigured as Hades. This reversal of the myth haunts the whole action of *The Mai*. As Millie describes the relation between the story, embodied in landscape, and the characters, 'But . . . in our blindness [we] moved along with it [the story] like sleepwalkers along a precipice and all around, gods and mortals called out for us to change our course and, not listening, we walked on and on' (p. 42). So, the Demeter/Persephone relation is replaced by a heterosexual love relation, and Demeter is redrawn as Hades.

At one point The Mai seems set to play a Demeter role in one of Millie's stories, but emerges instead as a mirroring of Persephone. When The Mai works for the summer in London she befriends an Arab princess 'already betrothed to some sheik or other' (p. 46). Millie is jealous of the closeness between the two, but The Mai's bond with the princess is one of like with like. It has not the complementarity of mother/daughter, for The Mai and the princess are 'two of a kind, moving towards one another across deserts and fairytales . . . enthralled with one another and their childish impossible world' (p. 46). Carr's play returns again and again to narratives and images that invite parallels with Persephone and her story, but Demeter is absent. *The Mai* explores romantic love as the primal bond, and its destructive effect on women as that bond threatens the continuation of the mother/daughter continuum.

Teresa Deevy, writing in the 1930s, uses images of the failure of the myth in all of her full-length plays of the period. In the formulation of feminist psychoanalytic and developmental theory the Persephone myth has been cited as 'a special presentation of feminine psychology'.[7] Carol Gilligan, writing about the place of women in traditional psychological theories of human development, interprets Persephone's story as 'a recognition of the continuing importance of attachment in the human life cycle'.[8] She goes on to describe how the myth expresses attributes and values which developmental theory has eclipsed in 'the celebration of separation, autonomy, individuation and natural rights'. Here the emphasis is on separation; the male child, who is theorized as the norm, must define his identity by recognition and reinforcement of distance and autonomy in relation to the primary (female) carer.

[Freud] considered this difference in women's development to be responsible for what he sees as women's developmental failure . . . a problem in the theory became cast as a problem in women's development, and the problem in women's development was located in their experience of relationships.[9]

The implications of acceptance of the male developmental model as the norm are important for, as a result, the value of the female model is brought into question where it effects moral judgements, and questions of maturity; that is to say, where relationship is privileged over adherence to rules, where connection is favoured over separation.

Teresa Deevy, in her plays of the 1930s, creates a matrix of circumstance, freedom and restraint, of separation and connection, embodying a deep structure of meaning as expressed in the myth of Persephone. Deevy writes about the clash between an ethic of care and community on the one hand, and of autonomy and freedom on the other, between relationship and responsibilities on the one hand, and rights and independence on the other. This is the underlying structure which connects the plays where, on the surface, and from other points of view, each play is singular and discrete. *Temporal Powers* (1932) is about morality, the law and poverty where personal connection gives way under pressure from legal and moral strictures.[10] *Katie Roche* (1936), Deevy's best-known play, is about the failure of the marriage ritual to transform, about power between husband and wife, and the failure of the sublimation of autonomy in favour of connection. In *The Wild Goose* (1936) Martin must choose between ideology (political or religious) and values of cultural continuity and community.

Katie Roche exemplifies the Deevy heroine in that she is mother-less, poor, of low social status, uneducated and brimming with life. She is particularly interesting as a Persephone figure as Deevy draws our attention to Katie's dead mother, and to Katie's close identification with her. Stan is the older man that Katie marries. He was once in love with Katie's mother, Mary Halnan, and when he proposes to Katie there is a momentary and revealing confusion about whether he is speaking in the past tense to Mary, or in the present tense to Katie.[11] In a sense then, Katie embodies her own mother in Stan's eyes, and her failure to be a 'proper' wife to him reflects her mother's failure to achieve the respectability of married motherhood. Katie must mother herself; the only possible substitute mother is the distracted Amelia, whose consciousness of Katie's needs is patchy at best.

Katie's lack of maternal support emphasizes her isolation both socially and theatrically, and underlines how the play represents the failure to complete ritual transformation. The ritual in question is matrimony. Stan and Katie's marriage is a travesty; both parties are trapped in a liminal state, unable or unwilling to cross the threshold from separation to connection.

The strange pattern of Stan's comings and goings throughout the three acts works to remind us of his unfulfilled role as Hades. When, at the end of the play, he finally takes Katie away with him, we are reminded again of Persephone, as Katie mourns her forthcoming separation from the river and trees of her home place.

In the absence of a Demeter figure, the play can present no image of equilibrium on which to end, but only an image of forced courage in the face of overwhelming masculine power.

In her last play for the Abbey Theatre, *Light Falling*, produced in 1948 at the Peacock Theatre, Deevy uses an image of harvest, an image of Demeter fulfilled, *but* the harvest is at night. The fields are lit by moonlight and the men move like shadows as they harvest the corn. The image is in negative, reversed. It reflects how, in all of Deevy's plays of the 1930s, the myth of Persephone fails, equilibrium is not achieved, defeat is almost certain, but the *possibility* of transformation is asserted in the process.

In *The Plains of Enna* (1999), as the title declares, Pat Kinevane makes direct parallels between the Persephone/Demeter myth and the lives of the Denis family in late 1960s rural Ireland.[12]

Kinevane takes the realist theatrical form of a drama of family rivalry over land, and deepens it through complex parallels with Persephone's story. There are direct representations of Persephone (Kora and Julia), Demeter (Nina), Hades (Hady), and Hecate (Hundred).[13] The play concerns the disastrous love affair between Kora and Hady. Hady's father had cheated Kora's out of his farm, which was then found to be rich in mineral deposits. Seamar is Kora's gentle brother, whose masculinity poses a dramatic contrast the socially accepted norms of male behaviour as represented by Hady and his ilk. Meanwhile, Julia Denis, who is studying singing in Italy, breaks the stage action with musical interruptions which function as sun-filled images of Persephone, contrasting with the darkness of Kora's existence.

Kora moves in with Hady, but he is violent and unfaithful. She escapes, but suffers a miscarriage and loses her sanity. In a fury of frustrated rage at Hady, Nina Denis, the Demeter figure, poisons the farm's water supply and cattle lie dying in the fields. The final image of the play is of Kora's electro-shock treatment.

In broad terms the play presents deeply negative images of the exploitation and poisoning of the natural world, which are metaphorical of the breakdown of relationships between the characters. However, the metaphors work also in the reverse direction, so that Hady's failure as a lover, and Nina's failure as a mother, may be read as metaphorical of the corruption of the land, whether for profit or for vengeance.

The Plains of Enna is ambitious in scope and arguably tries to achieve too much. The voice of Kora and Seamar's dead father is introduced, especially in a long dialogue with Kora towards the end of the action. Con Denis speaks to his daughter of her dead baby in benign images of the natural world. His function as a Demeter substitute is perhaps a deliberate re-gendering of the Persephone narrative, but it confuses the already demanding scope of imagery on which the play has been built, and comes too late to succeed in refiguring it. The play works most powerfully in its final images where the realist and mythic levels of meaning combine effectively. The exploration of gender, and in particular the critique of masculinity which lies beneath the surface of the play, is never fully expressed dramatically, but may be felt in the confrontation between Seamar and Hady.[14] The failure of the Persephone myth in the play offers a powerful frame within which to suggest the connections between personal and environmental tragedy. Linked with these is the question of equilibrium between masculinity and the feminine in our inseparable identity with and reliance upon nature.

In relation to Irish theatre, the myth of Persephone draws our attention not only to the presence and absence of mothers and daughters on stage, but also to dramatic forms expressive of the tensions of coexistence, of the energy of equilibrium, and of the paradoxical dependency of light on dark in a Manichaean model of the world. Persephone's story provides a matrix of meaning concerning redefinitions of achievement and maturity in terms of connection and attachment. These redefinitions demand different theatrical forms in which heroes or heroines may be defined by their vulnerability to, and contiguity with, others, rather than by a prized independence. The myth interrogates master dramatic narratives of autonomy through individual achievement; it asks us to question definition of self through separation, and definitions of nature and culture as antithetical.

Notes

1. See 'Appendix A: Summary of the Homeric "Hymn to Demeter"', in *Images of Persephone: Feminist Readings in Western Literature*, ed. Elizabeth T. Hayes (Gainesville, FL: University Press of Florida, 1994), pp. 195–7 (195).

2. René Girard, *Violence and the Sacred*, trans. Patrick Gregory (Baltimore, MD: Johns Hopkins University Press, 1979). See Chapter 3, 'Oedipus and the Surrogate Victim', pp. 68–88, and Chapter 5, 'Dionysus', pp. 119–42.

3. Mary A. Doll, 'Ghosts of Themselves: the Demeter Women in Beckett', in *Images of Persephone*, ed. Hayes, pp. 121–35 (131).

4. Samuel Beckett, *Footfalls*, in *The Complete Dramatic Works of Samuel Beckett* (London: Faber, 1986), pp. 397–403 (402).

5. Karl Kerenyi, *Essays on a Science of Mythology*, quoted by Doll, 'Ghosts of Themselves', p. 128.

6. Marina Carr, *The Mai* (Loughcrew: Gallery Press, 1995), p. 13. Quotations from this point on come from this edition and are followed by page numbers in parentheses.

7. David C. McClelland, *Power: The Inner Experience* (New York: Irvington, 1975), p. 96.

8. Carol Gilligan, *In a Different Voice: Psychological Theory and Women's Development* (London: Harvard University Press, 1982), p. 23.

9. Ibid., p. 7.

10. See Cathy Leeney, 'The Paradigm of Persephone in *Temporal Powers*', *Études Irlandaises* 21(1) (Spring 1996): 81–95.

11. Teresa Deevy, *Katie Roche*, in *Three Plays* (London: Macmillan, 1939), pp. 3–114 (15).

12. In some versions of the myth Persephone's abduction is located on the Plains of Enna.

13. Hecate is a figure of myriad functions, who was associated with Persephone in her mysterious roles in both the upper and lower worlds. She was said to stand at the conjunction of nature, heaven, earth and the underworld, and is hence often represented as dwelling at crossroads, as Hundred does in *The Plains of Enna*. Hecate completes the tripartite representation, with Persephone and Demeter, of the archetypal goddess in triple form. See Alexander S. Murray, *Who's Who in Mythology: Classic Guide to the Ancient World*, 2nd

edn (London: Studio Editions, 1988), pp. 70–1. Hecate is also Medea's aunt.

14. Pat Kinevane, *The Plains of Enna* (unpublished manuscript; 1999). The play was first performed by Fishamble Theatre Company for the Dublin Theatre Festival at the Tivoli Theatre in October 1999.

Unmasking the Myths? Marina Carr's *By the Bog of Cats* … and *On Raftery's Hill*

Eamonn Jordan

I

Marina Carr is the most complicated, confrontational and disturbing writer of the latest generation of Irish playwrights. As a playwright, she has the skills to manipulate the intricate realities of contemporary living, moving the spectator behind and beyond the façade of social norms, mores, conventions and expectations, locating the points of greatest contention and delivering moments of pure savagery, while still creating convincing dramas that are replete with intricate, maimed, destructive, wayward and marginal characters who are full of unrealizable longing.

At a time when many of the male playwrights of her own generation are turning towards a type of parodic violence and towards an ironic knowingness that becomes the shared understanding of the most appropriate way of representing the bonds and connections between characters, Carr radically reaches out for myth and, by so doing, reaffirms the ritualism of theatre and releases an intensity of engagement that many of the other writers are unable either to lay claim to or to sustain. This morbid relentlessness, savage bravery and formidable intensity of encounter and disjunction can be traced back through J. M. Synge's *The Playboy of the Western World* (1907), Tennessee Williams's best plays such as *The Glass Menagerie* (1945) and *A Streetcar Named Desire* (1947), Henrik Ibsen's great works like *John Gabriel Borkman* (1896) and *Rosmersholm* (1886), and back most importantly to classical Greek civilization and to Attic tragedy for structural and thematic precedents – something that a number of critics have already emphasized, in part taking their cue from Carr herself. Clearly, she is her own woman: allowing her writing to be informed by mainly male playwrights is not the same as being shaped, controlled by or dependent on male dramaturgical practices. She does not name specific female playwrights as influences, but the work owes a debt to Emily Dickinson and Emily Brontë.

Since the 1980s many of the leading Irish male playwrights have drawn on Greek myth in various forms, from Brian Friel with *Living Quarters* (1977) and Tom Murphy with *The Sanctuary Lamp* (1975) to the more blatant adaptations of Greek drama seen in Tom Paulin's *The Riot Act* (1984) and Seamus Heaney's *The Cure at Troy* (1990). Both Desmond Egan and Brendan Kennelly offered versions of *Medea,* and versions of *Antigone* are numerous.[1]

Carr started out writing in a Beckettian vein; *Ullallo* was her first play to be written but her third to be performed (in 1991), *Low in the Dark* was first seen in 1989 and *This Love Thing* in 1990. In these works, there is a self-consciousness in operation and a reliance upon a need to use the surreal or the absurd to generate incongruity and dramatic distance. This dramaturgy changed utterly when she began to write plays with Midlands settings, the majority of which were set in the 'present', not in the past, and not in clearly demarcated fantasy or transgressive spaces. This is where the Greek influence is most in evidence. Contrary to the main characters in Greek tragedy, Carr's characters are not so much noble as vagabonds and travellers, and are monstrous in a variety of ways, existing in 'the dungeon of the fallen world'[2] (*Portia, Coughlan* p. 219),[3] as Portia describes it in *Portia Coughlan* (1996). These women are powerful and violent, loving and responsive, they are passionate and relentless, destructive and vengeful.

These Midlands plays exhibit a talent that is courageous, scary and enlivening, and on display is a morbid fascination with the obscure, the bizarre, the extreme and the dark. Behind the veneer, beyond the veneer, no wordplay, no conspiracy of a compassionate or tolerant community exist, just a belligerent animosity and hostile vengeance. Betrayal rather than compassion, savagery rather than empathy dominate. Little pretence is in operation, and few or no social codes are to be observed. Secrecy, shame and indignity run riot across the plays, thereby ensuring that there is not only an absence of morality but also an absence of reciprocal obligations. The characters are on different journeys and little compromise can be reached, unions between individuals are singularly intense and always fleeting: yet an unrealizable faith exists in bonds, however irrational, corrupt and obsolete they may be, while violation and negativity can be as powerful a connection as positive communion. In her work the present cannot be a repetition of the past, even when characters are desperate to make it so.

George Steiner, discussing 'mythical figures' and Jung's 'archetypes', argues that the mystical figure 'would be "a collective personi-fication" giving bearable, joyous, explanatory forms to archaic collective fantasies and phases in the elaboration of the psyche'.[3] As civilization progresses and societies become more rational, this collective figure degrades. But in art these figures survive as we 'revert to "the archetypal analogies", to the primal constellations of gesture and image in art, because the conscious mind, however emancipated and secularized, is both repelled and drawn towards its earliest stages of existence', suggests Steiner.[4] In Carr's work, myth and mask take precedence over the real or the psychological. Victims consistently identify with their persecutors, and victims between themselves can become hostile rivals, vengeful towards each other and misdirecting their anger. Carr does not set in stone clear-cut oppositions between male and female, nor does she reverse previous gender stereotypes where women were weak and ineffective in the shaping of dramatic action in so many plays written by men; instead, in her work, the women characters determine and are shaped by the dramatic action. Portia in *Portia Coughlan* has her unquenchable belief in the bond that existed between herself and her twin and the consolation of the Belmont River; Hester in *By the Bog of Cats* . . . (1998) has her daughter, her mother and her bog; The Mai in *The Mai* (1994) has her belief in the sanctuary of the Owl Lake (Lake of the Night Hag or Pool of the Dark Witch); and Sorrel has a purity of heart that her violation takes away in *On Raftery's Hill* (2000). All the characters have things to value and behave in such a way as to validate their attachments.

Carr understands implicitly the self-destructive intent of her characters, but she does not wish for the spectator to wallow in such destruction, despite its unremitting relentlessness in performance. There is a critique of the self-destructive process that is built into the structures of the drama and into the actions of characters.

That indeterminate space between choice and compulsion, where creativity and destruction blur, and where the community shuts itself away from the vision or trauma of the individual, is the space within which Carr's work functions best. It is a dramatic world where emotions are utterly intense and scary, yet driven by a detailed, impulsive obligation to establish strong connections between cause and effect, where things are named for what they are. While there is some relationship between cause and effect across these Midlands plays, Carr blurs temporal and spatial continuity in *The Mai* and in *Portia Coughlan*. There are no Aristotelian unities on offer here. There is at the core of the work harshness and hardness that are utterly compelling, there is a judgemental structure that invites deliberation and there are formidable, almost irrationally complex demands placed on an audience to engage with the experiences on stage.

Contemporary dramaturgy, like Ireland itself, has undergone radical adjustment over the last number of years. Writing practices have clearly drifted in many respects from being predominantly post-colonial to postmodern, but now are neither fully one nor the other, and thereby benefit hugely from their interstitial status. Marianne McDonald has successfully addressed the relationship between Irish versions of the Greek classics and post-colonialism, particularly how key Attic texts are reworked during moments of political and cultural crisis or transition.[5] Writing practices globally have brought more and more violence and explicitness on stage. And it is not a practice only delivered by male writers; think of Sarah Kane in England or Maria Irene Fornes in America. The violence in Marina Carr's work far exceeds that of many of her male counterparts, a violence not so much in terms of body-count, but in terms of sheer elemental and forceful destructiveness.

Carr has confronted violence on a number of levels; the violence that emerges from society and more importantly the violence and carnage that emerge from families. For instance, in Ireland the issue of sexual violation increasingly has been aired publicly and the longer-term impact of abuse haunts the country in some respects.

Carr's violence, so different from that of her male counterparts who cannot in the main negotiate violence without an attendant irony, emerges from the conflict of relationships, while the reality of the pain on stage must find an accommodating filter. Pain, within a previous dramaturgy, was given substance and obligation, even fulfilment through irony, ritual or dramatic/intertextual precedents. In today's writing there is a serious collapse of the pain/pleasure dialectic. Increasingly, pain is without a context. With that dilution of difference, postmodern practices ensure that more value is placed on simulation, repetition and the sheer instability of identity. Ritual is displaced by spectacle and, with that, deliberations on victimization or violation appear superficial; thus victimization sheds its definitive status.

II

As *By the Bog of Cats* . . . opens, Hester Swane is told that she is going to die and the only way out of this is to risk leaving the bog and all that she holds dear. She has the compulsion and the self-destructiveness to challenge and to face her own doom, with a reckless disregard for her own life and with regard to what she sees as her ineffable right. The play begins with her encounter with the Ghost Fancier (echoes of Ibsen's *Peer Gynt* here), who calls to take her away from the living world. The encounter takes place on a landscape of bog and ice and symbolically captures the tensions of the play. The Ghost Fancier gets his timing wrong, not knowing whether it is dusk or dawn, but he promises to return.

The father of Hester's child, Carthage Kilbride, is about to marry another woman, Caroline Cassidy. He wants Hester to move away to the nearby town so that he can live without Hester's interference in his own life. Carthage thinks that he is being reasonable. He buys Hester the house and he gives her money. He wants compromise of the type that most certainly benefits him. But Hester and Carthage have shared more than intense passion. Their bond is one of blood, of obligation and of promises. All of the community advises Hester to accept her eviction from her house, some for her own good and others for a different good. It is the compromise she needs to make in order to survive, but Hester will ultimately refuse. Hester comments on her exclusion, isolation and abandonment by the community, wondering if they know what it is like 'to be flung on the ashpit and you still alive' (*Bog*, p. 313). The community's opposition towards Hester is seen as monumental by her: she rejects overwhelmingly her disenfranchisement and the rebuff takes the form of intrusion, violence and revenge. Hester regards herself as 'wan big lump of maneness and bad thoughts' (*Bog*, p. 322).

Hester had previously killed her brother, Joseph Swane. Carthage assisted in some way, she claims, and the dead brother's money, his inheritance, was used to set up Carthage in business. Hester could not cope with the bond that existed between her mother and her mother's son, Josie and Joseph – with the son part-benefiting from the mother's name. She talks to the Ghost Fancier of her brother, accusing him of talking as if she 'never existed' (*Bog*, p. 320).[6] When Hester was seven, her mother went away to live with her husband and her son, denying Hester's existence by claiming that Hester was dead. Hester killed her brother out of this obsession for her mother. To be abandoned in that way, to await the return of the mother thirty-three years on, to fear the desertion of a lover and to fear the loss of her own child, more importantly her unwillingness to allow the cycle to continue, all ensure that this play ends in the most painful way. Hester kills her own child and then takes her own life.

From the start everyone wants Hester to relent, but then she arrives at the wedding reception wearing a wedding dress, burns down the house and sets fire to a shed with the cattle locked inside.

Cassidy threatens her, but her self-destructive impulse frightens him away. Because of Hester's performance at the wedding and because she has killed the animals, Carthage tells Hester of his plans to take the child, young Josie, away from her. Caroline offers to intervene, but Hester tellingly remarks that there is 'no need to break' her for she was broken 'a long while back' (*Bog*, p. 337). Hester tells her daughter that she is leaving, but the child promises to wait and to watch out for her. Seeing the pattern between Hester and her own mother repeating again – the symmetry is stunningly replicated – Hester decides to kill herself and the child. She kills young Josie. As others gather to accuse her, Hester dances with the Ghost Fancier and plunges a knife into her heart, dying with the words 'Mam – Mam – ', the same final words spoken by young Josie a little earlier (*Bog*, p. 341). For O'Dwyer, 'Hester and Josie are devoted to each other; they play games and have fun. There is no sense of neglect, as in *The Mai* and *Portia Coughlan*, but of deep love and affection.'[7]

In *By the Bog of Cats* . . . Hester slays the daughter and it is a curiously protective device. Hester knows her own pain and can articulate her mother's absence as the principal source of it. As such, pain becomes some sort of confirmation, even on the back of a repetition compulsion that is indicative of the fact that the pain is unresolved, evidenced by the very need to re-enact. The compulsion to repeat is not a postmodern one of repetition and simulation, rather it is a way of justifying irresolution, a way of ensuring that the pain is perpetuated into the present.

Both Euripides' Medea and Hester resist banishment, both fight rejection and both love intensely the partner who has pushed them from their lives. It is a worthwhile and useful exercise to consider the parallels between *Medea* and *By the Bog of Cats* . . ., and to establish the direct similarity of character and story, such as the following parallels: Hester/Medea, Jason/Carthage, Xavier/Creon, King of Corinth, Caroline/Creon's daughter (Creusa or Glauke depending on the version). Gender-wise, Medea's sons become the young Josie Swane in *By the Bog of Cats* . . . Likewise, indirect relationships are also to be noted, such as Xavier's son dying like Creon and his daughter by touching something laden with poison.

In *By the Bog of Cats . . .* there is no Aegeus figure to offer alternatives and the choric function is taken over partially by Catwoman and Monica. Just as importantly there will be in *By the Bog of Cats . . .* no *deus ex machina* like the one in *Medea*.

Influenced by Aphrodite and Eros, Medea helped Jason, commander of the Argonauts, who promised her undying love. Regarded as a ruthless sorceress, with skills of magic and witchcraft, Medea wreaked destruction almost everywhere she went, whereas Hester's dominant skills are not so much destruction as impulsive survival. As the couple, Medea and Jason, fled Colchis, Medea dismembered the body of Apsyrtus, her half-brother, knowing that her father would pause to pick up the pieces for burial. Medea tricked the daughters of Pelias, King of Iolchos, into boiling their father, who had been responsible for the death of Jason's parents.

Hester protected and built up Carthage Kilbride. When Jason was to take a second wife (as Carthage does in a way), Medea was to be banished, to be made stateless and without home, as she faced eviction from Corinth. Hester is also to be shunted from her own home. Both women feel an irresolvable anger at their rejection. For Jason in *Medea*, the new relationship will be to his advantage, just as he had used Medea to acquire the Golden Fleece. So Jason marries for security, Carthage for land. Medea killed her rival by giving her a poisoned crown and gown. Medea's destructive gifts were disguised as a peace offering, whereas Hester's wedding gift is destruction and carnage. Hester does not kill Caroline Cassidy; the rival woman appears in the Carr text but not in the Greek original. The Chorus in *Medea* reminds us that there are precedents for Medea's actions:

> . . . who cut down her own children,
> Ino, driven insane
> When Hera harried her from home.
> She killed her two children, then herself.
> Poor creature, she went into the sea.
> Drowned herself from guilt.[8]

In Euripides' text Medea kills her children to stop the King of Corinth avenging his daughter's death by killing her sons. She is also avenging her rejection by Jason and his breach of his promises. Other myths suggest that the Corinthians killed Medea's fourteen children.[9] Taplin argues that when it comes to the impact of myth on Greek dramas, 'the constraint is minimal; the scope for artistry enormous'.[10] What had Carthage promised Hester to enrage her so? Why does Hester kill her child and herself? Hester destroys her child for reasons altogether different from Medea's. Is it to avenge herself on Carthage, to avenge herself on her community? Carr rejects the notional fatalism at the core of tragedy, so in many ways her work is a reimagining of the myth and she delivers a revisionist myth. Williamson argues for distinctions in *Medea* between private (*oikos*) and public (*polis*), suggesting that the 'spatial semantics' of the play reveal the 'problematic relationship between public and private', whereby the rage expressed within the inside space cannot be expressed in the public arena, while the public tactics adopted by Medea, such as 'controlled, abstract, intellectualizing', are 'indistinguishable from that of the male characters she confronts' during the early scenes of the play.[11] A similar distinction is at the core of *By the Bog of Cats* . . . The women in *By the Bog of Cats* . . . have access to external spaces, whereas the female characters, apart from Shalome in *On Raftery's Hill*, have no such access.

According to Walton, Euripides wrote about 'the power of the passions, the arbitrariness of fate, and the ambiguity of motive'.[12] Carr scans the same territory. Passion is irrepressible for non-domesticated characters. In Carr, myth makes way for reality, reality for myth. Mystery never becomes mystification. Tragedy's rhythmic unnaturalness seems to rule. It is not so much divine compulsion as the chaos impulse that besets Hester. The curse of the Swanes and its mythology are confrontationally exposed. Hester as woman, Traveller-woman and Bog-woman is excluded triply. Medea had, however, betrayed her own father and killed her own brother, so she is no innocent. Hester had killed her own brother and she is no innocent. Driven by the ecstasy of revenge, she becomes possessed. We witness revenge as blood sport in many

Greek texts and in Carr's work revenge is a central energy that takes the characters beyond rationality, beyond logic and beyond the moral. At what extreme does the revenge impulse kick in whereby nothing matters other than seeing something through to the end? It is the revenge of the dispossessed. Medea plots to kill Jason and his bride; Hester plots in a lesser way and we assume that, as in many of the other Carr plays, the rage will result in the suicide of the character: that Hester may kill herself, but her taking of Josie's life never really enters the equation initially. We can go with the despair of Medea and Hester but can we go with them in their destruction of their children? Lorca's main character in *Yerma* (1935) kills her partner rather than have a child with someone else and the child would have satisfied her maternal craving.

Taplin suggests that 'never, except in mad scenes, are the characters of Greek tragedy portrayed as automata or marionettes. Even when they are viewed as victims of the gods, they remain human and independent.'[13] Lateral thinking and creative solutions are not the stuff of tragedy; extremity and finality are. Carr's great skill is in her ability to tap into that structure. No diplomacy, no counselling, no intervention of social services, the law, religion or myth can take away the pain of the characters. The final line in *By the Bog of Cats* . . . is given to Monica who notes that 'She's cut her heart out – it's lyin' there on top of her chest like some dark feathered bird' (*Bog*, p. 341). The symbol of the swan comes home to roost.

If Carr's desire was to reinscribe women within the social arena, she does not do so by creating positive images of women, attesting to their humanity, but instead she has the tendency to create women who are not so much gruesome as harmed and violated, and not necessarily by patriarchy; women who are acutely alert to their own capacity to violate, hurt, and inspire chaos and dread; women who are not ideal or responsible figures or placed on any pedestal. McGuinness's Pyper in *Observe the Sons of Ulster* (1985) and Caravaggio in *Innocence* (1986) come close to Carr's figures, they are characters that come face to face with their own extreme darkness.

III

In *By the Bog of Cats* . . . we experience a carnivalized wedding celebration like no other, where Catwoman sips champagne from a saucer and the Priest, Father Willow, wears his clothes inside out, mixes up the name of the bride, plans holidays with the Catwoman, and talks of his previous girlfriends, confusing her name with that of his own mother. Further, Mrs Kilbride speaks of her son's childhood in a way that is alarmingly Freudian in its emphasis. She tells of how son and mother shared a bed and of how, in her honour, he prepared an imitation of Calvary in their own back garden. Mrs Kilbride turns up at the wedding in a white dress, and wonders how she was supposed to know that the bride would be wearing white. Josie also wears a white communion dress and Hester arrives at the wedding reception wearing a wedding dress. Hester appears in Act III in a 'charred and muddied' wedding dress (*Bog*, p. 317), its destruction finding a similarity in Sorrel's dress ruined by Shalome. Hester threatens to cut Caroline's dress 'to ribbons' prior to the marriage ceremony (*Bog*, p. 284). By Act II Caroline realizes that the wedding of her dreams is not about to happen. By Act III Hester dreads the fact that Carthage might have Josie taken away from her; she is so desperate in fact that she tries to blackmail the child, threatening that if Josie leaves her mother, Hester will die: 'It's a sourt of curse was put on ya be the Catwoman and the black swan' (*Bog*, p. 327). Then Hester withdraws those threats and instead invites her daughter to dance with her, in order that they might have their 'own weddin'' (*Bog*, p. 327). The dress that brings death to Creon's daughter in *Medea* re-emerges as the wedding dress that brings a different type of death across a range of Carr's plays. For me, 'Carr deliberately plays with the fetishisation of the wedding dress as a significant icon, and by sheer dint of the number of dresses, proliferation is bizarrely unsettling.'[14]

The sense of spatial claustrophobia and the psychological confinement of the play resulted in many spectators feeling uneasy. This, I suppose, is one of the play's great difficulties. To protect an audience Carr attempted to find an alternative reality. When Garry

Hynes directed the play for Druid Theatre Company, the stage design, by Tom Walton, gave the play a strange surreal feel, through a combination of dark green and black colours and a bizarre, blackened staircase, which reflected the peculiar nature of the household's affiliations. Carr litters the play with grotesque details and incidents. For instance, after Isaac's cat dies, he wishes to turn it into a waistcoat. The same man shared a bed with his dead wife, after he was unable to leave the household due to fallen snow. Ded lives with the animals. While the grotesque in *By the Bog of Cats . . .* serves a specific incongruous function, in *On Raftery's Hill* the grotesque is the almost de-humanized reality of the characters living habits: it is the trap and the violation. Even the tender romance between Sorrel and Dara Mood could not counter the overwhelming reality of incest, even as the play calls on Greek myth (*Hill*, p. 43) as a distancing feature.

ISAAC: Zeus and Hera, sure they were brother and sister and they goh married and had chaps and young wans, and the chaps and the young wans done the job wud the mother and father and wud one another, and sure the whole loh a them was ah ud mornin, noon and nigh. I suppose they had to populahe the world someway. Is ud any wonder the stahe a the country and them for ancestry.

In Greek mythology, Zeus and Hera are brother and sister. She is queen of the gods, the daughter of the Titans, Cronos and Rhea. Hera is 'triple Goddess of the three stages of woman's life', the Child Goddess, the Bride Goddess and the Widow Goddess.[15] (So many of Carr's plays rely on these three stages, sometimes with a fourth added: Josie, Hester and Josie in *By the Bog of Cats . . .*; Portia, her mother and her grandmother in *Portia Coughlan*; The Mai, her own daughter, her dead mother, her grandmother in *The Mai*.) For McLean: 'Hera sets the archetype for woman in relationship to man within a patriarchal social order, as ideal wife and companion . . . She is a Goddess of marriage . . . maternity and fidelity, a jealous guardian of the marriage vows and heredity.'[16]

Zeus courted Hera unsuccessfully and then turned to magic, changing himself into a dishevelled cuckoo for whom she had sympathy, holding it to her breast. He then changed form, raped her and out of embarrassment she agreed to marry him, giving birth to six children. Zeus was renowned for his affairs and she avenged many of them.

But Raftery's Hill cannot be Mount Olympus. A myth of origins, of incest and sexual licence fails to help in this instance. There is a difference between a Greek myth about origins and the populating of the world and the reality of the pain of incest, so that the play never has the easy comfort of a mythological dimension. In *By the Bog of Cats* . . . Carr could access *Medea* on three levels and shifts between the worlds of dream, fantasy, reality and the grotesque. Why? In *On Raftery's Hill* all an audience was left with was the precision of the writing, the emerging story and a loose sympathy for some of the characters. Here, there is no escape route, no alternative reality, other than the animal kingdom.

'In her earliest appearance in myth', Hera 'is associated with the cow, showing her connection with fecundity and birth', McLean points out.[17] Here in the play, Red destroys the animals in his own fields, treating the place like an abattoir. Further, the linkage between the human world and the animal world is more pertinent than any ritualistic or dramatic precedent. Dinah attempts to explain circumstances through the animal kingdom: 'Thah's whah we are, gorillas in clothes pretendin' to be human' (*Hill*, p. 30). Her internalization of Red's values is clear here, as Red's comprehension of the world draws on a similar sentiment: 'We were big loose monsters, Mother, hurlin through the air wud carnage in our hearts and blood under our nails, and no stupid laws houldin us down or back or in' (*Hill*, pp. 31–2). And when Sorrel resorts to a similar perspective, stating: 'We're a band a gorillas swingin from the trees' (*Hill*, p. 56), the consolidation of a cycle of violation and internalization is complete.

Not only is *On Raftery's Hill* without serious Irish dramatic precedent, but the cyclical quality of the abuse cycle has its own resonance. Of all the characters, only Isaac and Dara have access to a different moral code. Dara attacks Brophy for his part in his daughter's death and Isaac, despite the quirks, still calls the world to order: for him 'Monsters make themselves. They were hopped into the world clane as the next' (*Hill*, p. 43). The parallel story in *On Raftery's Hill* tells of Sarah Brophy who goes to a grave and attempts to feed her stillborn child, fathered by her own father. She brings the dead child home and dies holding it. Brophy ends up in a mental hospital in Ballinasloe and kills himself by swallowing weedkiller.

After Portia's funeral, Blaize again slanders the Joyces, saying that when 'you breed animals with humans you can only bring forth poor haunted monsters who've no sense of God or man' (*Portia*, p. 229). The similarity of such imagery and language between the plays is striking. In *Bacchae*, Dionysus demands worship from Pentheus. Pentheus refuses and he is dismembered by bloodthirsty women and by his own mother Agave. Zelenak notes the appearance of 'Dionysian rituals of *sparagmos* (tearing apart the sacrificial animal) and *omophagia* (eating the animal's raw flesh)'.[18] In *On Raftery's Hill*, Sorrel is the sacrificial animal, hare-like and harmed. The switch from the concept of a destructive monstrosity to the vulnerability and symbolism of the hare is a constant strategy across Carr's plays, with the symbolism of the hare a bit like the wild duck in Ibsen's *The Wild Duck* (1884). Red is a cruel hunter, killing a hare and then strangling the leverets in the lair. The March hare is associated with Shalome, linking her behaviour and madness, by Dinah. Early in the play Red's brutal interrogation of Ded leaves the father stating to his son 'stop blinkin will ya. You're noh a hare a'ya' (*Hill*, p. 26). In *By the Bog of Cats* . . . Carthage accuses Hester of not being 'the sixteen year auld fool snaggin' hares along the Bog of Cats who fell into your clutches' (*Bog*, p. 288). Late in the play, Xavier threatens Hester, brandishing a gun: 'I ran your mother out of here and I'll run you too like a frightened hare' (*Bog*, p. 328).

In this way the human becomes animal, the animal becomes human as part of the blurring process. Catwoman wears 'a coat of cat fur . . . studded with cats' eyes and cats' paws' (*Bog*, p. 271).[19]

Hester in *By the Bog of Cats . . .* states that she refuses to be 'flung in a bog hole like a bag of newborn pups' (*Bog*, p. 317). In McGuinness's *Innocence*, there is a carnival of the animals. The characters access the animal world, in order to critique the social order. As mentioned earlier, Sorrel's refusal to gut the hare becomes the mode of her own sexual violation, in a way that Sorrel becomes a hare of sorts, prior to her assault, and Hester becomes a swan as part of the desperate process of mythologizing. The presence of swans and geese recurs across *The Mai*, serving as symbols of intense love and innocence, and the black swan, specifically, as a symbol of doom and death. And the story of Sam Brady and his cow, Billy the Black, in *The Mai*, serves as a tale of transgression. Sam was so enraged by Robert's infidelities that he initially let the cow loose in The Mai and Robert's garden and then, later, he took a gun and blew 'the head off the cob feeding innocently near the bank. It's true what they say: swans do keen their mates . . . It's a high haunting sound that sings the once-living out of this world', according to Millie, The Mai's daughter and narrator (*Mai*, pp. 157–8). So in this earlier work, Carr brought together cows and swans.

While we cannot draw on Attic tragedy for confirmation or validation of a dramatic world, likewise we cannot draw on the animal world as a way of rationalizing the self-destructiveness at the core of the Raftery family. The order of the animal kingdom does not ease the burden of human choice. The extent of Dinah's violation of twenty-seven years, from the age of twelve, is put in context by Sorrel's single assault and the devastation that it brings to her. The ferocity of the engagements is deeply unsettling and without the precedent of myth that offers distance, something altogether more disturbing takes place. While The Mai, Portia and Hester kill themselves, the survival of Sorrel suggests some end to a cycle. Catwoman says of Hester that the best thing about her is that unlike most others, she 'knows the price of wrong' (*Bog*, p. 274).

IV

In a sense, Ibsen's tormented adage, that to write is to sit in judgement of oneself, runs riot across the work of Carr. Hers is a relentless and absorbing imagination; hers is a courageous dramatic practice that is not matched by anybody of her generation. In Carr's work it is the battle between woman and man pitched into a world that is locked between obedience and responsibility, fate and circumstances, disobedience and conflicting codes of engagement. Zelenak argues that from fifth-century Athens forward, philosophy, given that it was more easily controlled, 'succeeded tragedy as the central forum of civic discourse'.[20] My fear is that postmodernism will replace a type of drama that was previously known in Ireland, because it is easier to stage and because it is easier to control. Carr bucks that trend. The blatancy, the urgency and the sheer intensity of her dramatic situations hold audiences. Carr's work is narrative-driven; there is a story to be told in as relentless a fashion as possible, while it is informed by a female consciousness over which nobody can claim ownership, authority or dependent precedence. While her early work was structurally and thematically experimental, her later work relies primarily on a misconstrued naturalism.

Carr's plays capture characters that are obsessed and utterly focused. They know what they think they want, but what they want may not always be the best thing for them. Therefore, duties, obligations, debts, antagonisms, vengeance and fears dominate. Her plays gather together characters with ongoing and long-running feuds. No quarter is given or sought. Innocence is no marker against anything. Relationships, in Carr's work, are more often savage and seldom tender. Violation and disturbance are the dominant features. Those in the know are all the more disturbed for it. There is no escape from the terror of existence, the violence of bonds and the sheer madness that is derived from the intensity of connection. Mrs Kilbride openly expresses her need to damage and misshape the child Josie: 'I'll break your spirit yet and then glue ya back the way I want ya' (*Bog*, p. 279). Hester talks of her bond with Carthage in the following way: 'Our bond is harder, like two rocks we are, grindin' off of wan another and maybe all the closer for that' (*Bog*, p. 269). In contrast many of her contemporaries dramatize a world where all that is worth relating to and engaging with is the self. When characters compromise, they appear as if they are ineffectual. Think of Raphael in *Portia Coughlan*, for instance.

How does the violator buy silence: by passing off his or her responsibility or through bribery? Caroline attempts to buy off Hester Swane, as do many of the others in *By the Bog of Cats*... Red offers Dinah money to cheer her up, and he offers Dara Mood and Sorrel, prior to their wedding, the deeds to fifty acres and a cheque for twenty thousand pounds. Dara's refusal to accept enrages Sorrel. Bonds are beyond the rational or the legalistic. Hester says: 'Bits of paper, writin', means nothin', can as aisy be unsigned' (*Bog*, p. 283). There is a need to damage, destroy, hurt and maim. Language is essential in giving credence to this world-view, and for Christopher Murray, 'Carr's use of dialect seems at first reactionary, a whimsical throwback to peasant drama, until its strangeness and bluntness are registered.'[21] In a note to the published text of *Portia Coughlan,* Carr describes the Midlands accents as 'more rebellious than the written word permits' and in another to *By the Bog of Cats*... she declares that the accent 'is a lot flatter and rougher and more guttural than the written word allows'.

Hester's sense of abandonment is constant; she seeks out her mother, looking for her trace or trail, watching for her return, awaiting the reunion of mother and daughter. Carr captures her confusion about her mother, her capacity to idolize the individual who has wounded her most, the need to seek reinforcement and encouragement against that sense of let-down she once was scarred by. Hester's death has been inevitable from the outset. Hester, like Portia, displays all the recklessness and disregard of the nearly dead. Hester puts her mouth over Xavier's gun; Portia defies Fintan's threat of violence. Macintosh comments on and quotes Georg Lukács's idea that the tragic character is dead for a long time before he or she actually experiences death and that 'tragedy proper' begins at the moment when the 'enigmatic forces have distilled the essence from a man', and 'have forced him to become essential'.[22] Carr does not deliver women of a certain class; instead they are marginalized. Monstrous, frightening, intolerant, impetuous, cruel and injurious women are much in evidence. They are content with the destructiveness and the annihilation they leave behind.

To live fully is to be rejected often; to live is to be owned in some way by a name, to be imprisoned within the frame of a tag. Across Carr's work certain tags recur again and again, while people attempt to calibrate difference; 'tinker', 'scrubber', 'bastard' and 'lunatic' are the most obvious. Hester is seen by many in negative and destructive terms. Some liken her to a witch. As Xavier says, 'A hundred year ago we'd strap ya to a stake and roast ya till your guts exploded' (*Bog*, p. 331). This way difference is marginalized, attacked, repressed and violated in many instances. Portia describes the way her mother knocks on the door as a 'witchy ring' (*Portia*, p. 209). In the earlier published version Portia wants to castrate men and rape her mother, but she knows it is not right (*Dazzling*, p. 290). Hester as outsider believes that she can see the others for the 'inbred, underbred, bog-brained shower' they are (*Bog*, p. 289). The sense of doubleness and fragmentation that has haunted male playwriting takes a new twist with Gabriel/Portia. Marianne says: 'The spit, couldn't tell yees apart in the cradle' (*Portia*, p. 211), and in *On Raftery's Hill* is the notion that Sorrel is a 'double Raftery' (*Hill*, p. 46).

Carr hoped to invigorate her work with a suitable intensity by calling on myth and dramatic precedence. *The Mai* is loosely based on Sophocles' *Electra*, and not on Euripides', and *Portia Coughlan* owes a debt to the Egyptian myth of Isis and Osiris and to the story of Byblis and Caunus in Ovid's *Metamorphoses*.[23] The debt to *Medea* in *By the Bog of Cats . . .* is obvious and *On Raftery's Hill*'s acknowledgement of the myth of Hera and Zeus is clear-cut: in the former, murder is ritualized through distancing and dancing, whereas in *By the Bog of Cats . . .*, myth becomes unsanctioned and unviable. It becomes a liability that neither the grotesque nor carnival could alleviate. Frank McGuinness in his programme note to the Abbey's production of *By the Bog of Cats* . . . states: 'I wonder what Marina Carr believes? I can't say for certain, but I am certain in this play she writes in Greek.'

Carr's work captures an inner emptiness, hollowness, echo and shadow, rather than substance. The writing is dominated by a sense of being stalked (and not just literally), possessed, overrun and out of control. Exclusion, expulsion and inclusion are at stake. Abandonment, eviction and violation are repeated. Dispossession and powerlessness not ownership, trauma not confidence, destruction and not desire are consistent, whether applied to dreams, material ownership, or relationships. The characters can't let go of pain or of primal obsessions: identity is consolidated out of pain, not pleasure, as pain is the value system, pain is the reward on some level; pain is not a distraction, but pain is the validation. Hester murders her daughter not out of some irrational impulse but with the calculation and formality that defy the accusation of hysteria or frenzy. Her own destructive agency is in evidence. The articulation of the repetition/compulsion need that drives her characters' revenge is Carr's greatest strength.

Notes

1. For a more complete list, see Marianne McDonald, 'Classics as Celtic Firebrand: Greek Tragedy, Irish Playwrights, and Colonialism', in *Theatre Stuff: Critical Essays on Contemporary Irish Theatre*, ed. Eamonn Jordan (Dublin: Carysfort Press, 2000), pp. 16–26.
2. Page citations for Carr's plays: *Portia Coughlan*, in *The Dazzling Dark*, selec. and intro. by Frank McGuinness (London: Faber & Faber, 1996); *Low in the Dark, The Mai, Portia Coughlan, By the Bog of Cats* . . ., in *Plays One* (London: Faber & Faber, 2000).
3. George Steiner, *Antigones: The Antigone Myth in Western Literature, Art and Thought* (Oxford: Oxford University Press, 1984), p. 126.
4. Ibid., pp. 126–7.
5. McDonald 'Classics as Celtic Firebrand', pp. 18–26.
6. It is the second time that this phrase appears: see p. 315, when she accuses Carthage of the same sentiment.

7. Riana O'Dwyer, 'The Imagination of Women's Reality: Christina Reid and Marina Carr', in *Theatre Stuff*, p. 245.

8. *Euripides: Plays One*, trans. J. Michael Walton, *Medea, The Phoenician Women, Bacchae* (London: Methuen, 2000), lines 1284–9.

9. See Denys Page, *Euripides: Medea* (1938; rptd with corrs Oxford: Clarendon Press, 1967), pp. xxi–xxv. For variations on the Medea myth see Peter D. Arnott, *Public and Performance in the Greek Theatre* (London: Routledge, 1989), p. 126.

10. Oliver Taplin, *Greek Tragedy in Action* (London: Methuen, 1978), p. 164.

11. Margaret Williamson, 'A Woman's Place in Euripides' *Medea*', in *Euripides, Women, and Sexuality*, ed. Anton Powell (London: Routledge, 1990), p. 17.

12. J. Michael Walton, 'Introduction', in *Euripides: Plays One*, p. ix.

13. Taplin, *Greek Tragedy in Action*, p. 165. See also Michael X. Zelenak, 'The Troublesome Reign of King Oedipus: Civic Discourse and Civil Discord in Greek Tragedy', *Theatre Research International* 23(1) (1998): 69–82.

14. Jordan, 'The Theatrical Representation of Incest in Marina Carr's *On Raftery's Hill*', *Irish Journal of Applied Social Studies* 3(1).

15. Adam McLean, *The Triple Goddess: An Exploration of the Archetypal Feminine* (Grand Rapids: Phanes Press, 1989), p. 72.

16. Ibid., pp. 71–2.

17. Ibid., p. 72.

18. Zelenak, 'The Troublesome Reign', p. 80.

19. See Jordan's 'Theatrical Representation of Incest' for an extension of this argument.

20. Zelenak, 'The Troublesome Reign' p. 82.

21. Christopher Murray, *Twentieth-Century Irish Drama: Mirror up to Nation* (Manchester: Manchester University Press, 1997), p. 238.

22. Fiona Macintosh, *Dying Acts: Death in Ancient Greek and Modern Irish Tragic Drama* (Cork: Cork University Press, 1994), p. 78.

23. See Melissa Sihra, 'A Cautionary Tale: Marina Carr's *By the Bog of Cats . . .*', in *Theatre Stuff*, p. 257.

The Sophoclean Killing Fields: an Interview with Frank McGuinness

Joseph Long

ELECTRA: *Is that foul woman dead?*

Frank McGuinness's version of Sophocles' Electra, directed by David Leveaux, received its first performance at the Minerva Theatre, Chichester, on 10 September 1997 with Zoë Wanamaker in the title role, and it opened in London at the Donmar Warehouse on 21 October of the same year. It transferred to Broadway, to the Ethel Barrymore Theater, in November of the following year, where its success was such that the original eight-week run was extended to almost twice that length.

Frank McGuinness is the leading Irish dramatist of his generation. He is Writer in Residence and lectures at the National University of Ireland, Dublin. A significant feature of his writing for the theatre has been the number of adaptations he has done of major playwrights of the modern European canon, from Ibsen and Chekhov to Lorca and Brecht. I asked him what decided him to work on the Greeks.

FRANK MCGUINNESS: It was one of the very few pieces I have ever accepted a commission for. David Leveaux, a director I admire immensely, asked me to do it for Zoë Wanamaker. That was in spring of '97. I went over to see him in London with the express intention of saying that I did not know how to do it. I had never been able to get a handle on Greek theatre. I had, many years before, commissioned a literal translation of *Oedipus*, with a view to writing a version for one of our major Irish actors. That was as close as I had ever come to tackling the Greeks. I did actually teach them for a couple of years and found that it was enormously difficult, for me, to find out what these plays were communicating. I could admire their skill, I could admire their passion, but the heart of them, the beating heart of them, seemed to escape me. I did not believe I would be the right person to tackle *Electra*. Then I met David, who is very intelligent, very approachable, and his enthusiasm for this particular play was infectious. Also, I had always admired Zoë Wanamaker, I had always wanted to do work with her, so that at the end of twenty minutes I had agreed. Then we spent another couple of hours talking about how he saw the play, how he saw the politics of it in contemporary terms.

JOSEPH LONG: *How closely did you work, then, with Zoë Wanamaker?*

FRANK MCGUINNESS: Both Zoë and myself had gone through a very intense period of mourning for our parents. There was a very deep spiritual bond, a very deep emotional bond between us. Even though I had never met the woman personally, I knew, from what David had told me, that we'd both lost a parent within six months of starting this project. I think a lot of our own separate mourning went into the writing and the performing of this particular piece. One of the happiest memories of the whole time comes, para-doxically, from that grief.

JOSEPH LONG: *I know you accept, readily enough, to revisit your text, when you work with actors. Was there much rewriting in this case?*

FRANK MCGUINNESS: Not a line was changed from the draft to the performance text, practically nothing was changed. I think that showed a very deep correspondence between myself, David and Zoë. Normally I am very amenable to looking at texts, to looking at what is speakable and what is not speakable, but Zoë found the text was actually something that she could do, something that she could say, as it was, freshly written. She was clearly an actor who was champing the bit to get this into her mind, to get this around her, and to perform it. We did work terribly hard, terribly intensely. That was the only way that we all got through it. We had to work with the sense of urgency, the sense of necessity, to say what this play is saying.

JOSEPH LONG: *The immediate impulse, then, was an intensely personal one?*

FRANK McGUINNESS: It was drawn from our own lives as much as any version, as much as any performance can be drawn from life. It did really come from the soul. I am not ashamed to say that. It was the only way I could do it. I had looked at that version of *Oedipus* many times over the years and thought: 'How in God's name is one going to do this?' I didn't have that problem, once I realized the creative team I was working with for *Electra*. Once I got down to it, it just came with great urgency.

JOSEPH LONG: *You often follow your plays through rehearsal. Were you involved this time?*

FRANK McGUINNESS: Yes, I was involved for the first couple of weeks. I always leave a rehearsal of any play after two weeks. In this case, I was very happy to leave, because I knew that the responsibility Zoë and David bore to this text was enormous. They have to, by reason of the play, carry enormous responsibility to make it work. At the end of two weeks, they were asking themselves the right, tough questions that they would answer in the course of the previews and in the course of the Chichester run, then bring it into the Donmar. The text went through no changes, really, from the end of these two weeks. My work was done.

JOSEPH LONG: *Zoë herself has paid great tribute to your text. In an interview with Toby Zinman,*[1] *she says that, as an actress, she never really had much interest in Greek drama before, that it was not part of her world or knowledge. She says: 'My interest in acting has been to do new plays. This, to me, was a new play. Frank's adaptation was pared down to its very fishbone; it's clean as a whistle, it's English that I can understand – sometimes slightly crass, sometimes slightly raw, sometimes strange to the ear, but it is accessible to me.' How did you arrive at that text, Frank? You don't know Greek, so did you work from existing translations?*

FRANK MCGUINNESS: I worked with two existing nineteenth-century texts, one prose, one verse, both extremely scholarly. Both extremely helpful, I have to say. I've paid for the rights – OK?! But they were essentially library pieces. They were translations, paradoxically, for those who knew Greek – who knew not merely the language, but who knew lots about Greek mythology. They, if you like, gave me the freedom to leap into a contemporary idiom, and to reduce extremely esoteric images and references to Greek learning. My code was that, if I did not feel an immediate identification with the reference, then I did not put it into the text, because what I wanted to get was to share with an audience the sense of pain, the terrible upheaval, the terrible disturbance, the anarchy that I think Sophocles truly gets in his theatre. That was my prime intention in tackling a play like this. I had no pretensions that it was going to be a landmark in the literary scholarship of investigating Greek tragedy. It was not going to be that. I could not have done that. I make no claims to have done that. But I also wasn't setting out, if you like, to outrage those who did know Greek. They clearly were in a much superior position to me in their comprehension and in their breadth of understanding of what these plays are broadly about. What I wanted to do was to come, as a playwright of the 1990s, and see how did these plays interest me. In doing versions, there's always a selfish element in it, and a necessarily selfish element in it, because that's where the writing of plays comes from: you have to be sufficiently obsessed with yourself to believe that your interest, and your exercise of that interest, will involve an audience as well. And that's the link between doing versions of any play, from any era, and new writing. I did set out to write a play of *Electra*, based on the Greek, but that would be of its time, of the 1990s. That was, I think, a joint intention of everybody involved.

JOSEPH LONG: *It's a play of the 1990s and the production was*

*discreetly Balkanized. The costumes and the set by Johan Engles –
a dirt floor, a fallen slab of white marble – were vaguely modern
and suggested a refugee situation with reference to the Balkan
wars. In his programme note, David Leveaux describes a
documentary film he had seen from Sarajevo, an account of
children who had suffered loss – a father, a mother, a brother, a
sister – as a result of the war. One young girl, whose brother had
been killed in a mortar attack on his school, had been unable to
speak since his death. Leveaux describes a scene, in the film, where
she places a gift of chocolate and a toy on her brother's grave and
whispers to him. He comments that, when Sophocles wrote* Electra
*over two thousand years ago, 'it was precisely to attempt to find
both speech and reason to confront the most fundamental struggles
in the heart of civilization itself'. Had you something like that in
mind, when you were writing the text?*

FRANK MCGUINNESS: The Balkanization of the production was
entirely David Leveaux's. That was how he heard the heart of the
play, how he saw the deep vision of the play. It was from images
that he had observed in newspapers and on television, of that war
that was raging at the time. I think one of the interesting paths that
David took, to mounting a production in that way, was that he had
produced it first in Japanese. He has a theatre in Japan, where he
works with Japanese actors. In a strange way, that removed, if you
like, the rawness or the crudity of such an approach – that he was
working in the Eastern idiom, very deeply in the Eastern idiom, and
that he was talking about a subject that is at the heart of the
Western tradition, which is the Trojan War. So he had, if you like,
this enormous creative objectivity about what he was doing, and
that deeply informed the images on stage, that deeply informed his
directorial approach. My text was there, basically, to serve that
approach. When we had our preliminary conversation, he had
mentioned this to me, how he saw the war, as it was communicated
in the play. I, naturally, could objectively understand that, but, of
course, subjectively, what I was thinking about was the war in the
North of Ireland, the civil war in the North of Ireland, and the
psychic disturbances which that prolonged war had had on *my*

imagination. So that was the access I had to that world of war, that world of recrimination and revenge. That's what drove me forward more than anything.

JOSEPH LONG: *That's not quite the same, is it, as taking the Greeks as a parallel, or metaphor, for the political situation in Ireland?*

FRANK McGUINNESS: I certainly wasn't taking it as being a direct parallel. I wouldn't be interested in doing something like that at all. In terms of personal involvement, there is a line in another interview where David says to Zoë that it was time for her to give a good yell. Probably, in my life, it was time to release a great yell at the reality of losing one parent and at the very real prospect of losing another. My father actually died during rehearsals, ten months after my mother had died. There's where the deep level of commitment and involvement, that *I* had with the play, came through. As I say, you cannot approach a play which centres on something like the Trojan War without having had experience of what war means, of what war is about. In the hinterland of my mind, the Northern conflict was there, but I did not want the play to be looked on as some kind of veiled metaphor for the civil war in the North of Ireland. It was not that.

JOSEPH LONG: *There are details in the text, none the less, which fit as pointers to Northern Ireland. Aegisthus, for example, towards the end of the play, asks, 'Shall there be killing after killing for ever?' The text could be read in that way.*

FRANK McGUINNESS: Absolutely. What David was trying to get, was that the Ancients are realistic. To give that note of realism, I could draw on my own political background. In 1997, when the play was being written, there was certainly no guarantee of any cease-fire, certainly no permanent cease-fire. There had been the break in the cease-fire, so it did look as if it was going to go on and on.

JOSEPH LONG: *There are strongly poetic strands in your writing for the theatre, Frank, and you very often use echoes or imagery drawn from the Bible. When we talked about your play* Observe the Sons of Ulster Marching Towards the Somme, *you commented yourself on the centrality of the Bible to the diction of that play. Your text of* Electra *is full of telling imagery – and many of the critics have picked up on that – such as when the Chorus says:*

> Electra mourns alone.
> She waits for her glory till stone
> Turns to water.

Or again, when Electra herself says: 'My life is a river, it floods with grief.' To what extent did you rework the imagery, to what extent were you bound by the original?

FRANK MCGUINNESS: One of the great problems that I have with Greek tragedy is that it is, obviously, not informed by any contact with the Bible, unlike all the theatre that has deeply affected me. As you can see by looking over there at the bookshelves, I am not short of Bibles. In terms of regular reference, the Bible absolutely runs through everything I have written, not just *The Sons of Ulster*. When I was a child, one of the few books in the house was that family Bible, sitting there on the shelf. It was a source of stories, a source of imagery, a source of poetic material, a source of narrative for me. This meant that there was a great barrier between me and Greek tragedy, that I could not easily comprehend a culture that did not have an Old Testament God and a New Testament Christ at its heart.

JOSEPH LONG: *From time to time, it seems to me that something of a biblical diction seeps through, in turn of phrase, in rhythm. For example, in this passage of the Chorus, after Chrysothemis' second exit:*

> Consider the birds of the air.
> In their fragile nest they sustain
> Those who gave them life and pleasure.

So should we pay to those of our name
That debt, that bond of nature.
As God is just, guardian of all laws,
No mortal escapes punishment.
The day of judgement dawns . . .

FRANK McGUINNESS: In the course of the play, there are quite a few references to God, as well as to 'the gods'. In the literal translations, there are references to 'a god'. I think I made more than there were, I'm not exactly sure, but not many more. That's me, if you like, not Christianizing the play, because you can't do that, but trying to find access, on my own part, into the dark heart of what the Divinity and Divinities do, in this play. What is extraordinary about *Electra* is that, essentially, the gods are dead in it, that God is dead in *Electra*. It is the human beings who inflict these punishments on each other, it is human beings who set out to get revenge. It is the machinations and motivations of humans, of humanity, that lie at the heart of it. The play does not, by any stretch of the imagination, extenuate Man – men and women – from their actions. It holds them absolutely responsible. By reason of that responsibility being visited upon them, it makes their suffering, it makes their triumphs, it makes their loves and their hatreds all the more true, all the more believable, all the more realistic. That was part of the reason why I felt that I could do *Electra*, why I could make a fist of *Electra*, largely because of that humanistic bent in it. It's almost as if Sophocles is lifting two fingers to the gods, in a weird way, in this play. It's almost as if he is saying to his audience that Zeus and the boys – that Zeus and the-boys-and-girls – they're not really what your lives are about. Their power is not really absolute over you, you have absolute power over your own lives. Your mistakes, your crimes, your misde-meanours, your pleasures, your joys – you create what they mean. That, naturally, had an enormous attraction to me, in terms of watching what this early manifestation of this message meant. Suddenly, the theatre, this Greek theatre, was a very mature, complex and threatening place, rather than a place of escapism. I would argue very strongly that it's Sophocles who's saying that, not me.

JOSEPH LONG: *Is that what led you to Sophocles rather than to Aeschylus or Euripides? The idea that, in Sophocles, there are characters who are imposing their will on their own destiny?*

FRANK McGUINNESS: It was purely fortuitous. It was down to the fact that I was asked to do the Sophocles version. But the one thing I did learn, from working with Sophocles, is that I will never again generalize about Greek theatre. What is quite remarkable about the construction of *Electra* is its detail. What is remarkable about its structure is its extraordinary sense of its own purpose, of its own nature. There is so much that is brilliantly specific about the writing in this piece, so much that is, if you like, prophetic as to how modern theatre and modern cinema are going to develop. You get this extraordinary device, at the beginning of the play, where Orestes arrives in disguise and gives out that he is dead. The remainder of the play, up until its last quarter, is a pretence that Orestes is dead, when the audience knows that he is not dead, so you have this sophisticated playing-and-not-playing with suspense. At the heart of the play, you get a long speech by the Messenger, which gives a very graphic, marvellously vivid, retelling of a chariot race. It is done in purely pictorial terms. It is now a cliché to think of the chariot race in *Ben Hur* as one of the defining moments in twentieth-century cinema, in terms of its technique, its sophistication, its mastery of camera. In this Greek play, you find, verbally realized, an equally potent description of just such a race. So you get these terrific games that Sophocles is playing with his audience, clearly indicative that here is an audience learned in the making of theatre, in the manipulations of theatre. In this one play, I've learned to appreciate deeply that level of theatrical knowledge, of writerly knowledge. I would love to go back now and see how *Oedipus* does work, what is his method of bringing that play off, what are the methods of Aeschylus in the *Oresteia*, how does Euripides work. I don't know how, now, but I know how little I do know, from having the practice of working on this play. You can argue, correctly, that if I really want to know that, well, go and learn Greek! I would argue against anyone who might say that to me: Well, if you really want to know, go and write a play!

JOSEPH LONG: *Are there specific liberties you took with the text? What kind of freedoms did you allow yourself?*
FRANK MCGUINNESS: One of the freedoms that I took was in Electra's speech of lament for her brother, spoken to the brother who is actually alive. It was to repeat the word 'pain' five times. I knew that this was going to be a challenge for Zoë, should she decide to do it. If she had asked me to cut that, we might have had an argument, but she didn't want to cut it. And every night she did it differently. Every night I saw it, she did those five words differently, every night. I think that is a reflection of the examination she was putting into the role at every performance, it's why it took so much out of her, that she was, if you like, going on a journey, she knew the end of it, but she didn't know, every night, exactly the pinpointings of where she would pitch a certain line, what she would feel at a certain moment. I gave her, I think, that freedom of creativity in her acting. I deliberately wanted to do that for her as well. She says that she ultimately looked on it as a new play. Well, I wanted it to be a new performance, I wanted this to be an *Electra* that had never been seen before, and I wanted to give her a text that would allow her to do it. And she did it.

JOSEPH LONG: *The imagery of the production, the images on stage, are obviously the work of the director, the designer, the actors. The set is sparse. Electra herself appears as a curiously ambiguous figure. She's wearing a heavy coat, presumably her father Agamemnon's, which can be read as a symbol of what she is carrying with her, into her present situation. To what extent do you feel the imagery of the production corresponded to the vision you had?*
FRANK MCGUINNESS: The imagery was uncannily close to what I was envisaging. The play of my own which is closest to this one is clearly *Baglady*. At the heart of that play, *Baglady*, is a permanently

damaged woman, attempting to make sense out of her life. I give very few stage directions, very few images in *Baglady*. Those that are there are very deliberate, and one of the most deliberate is that she would be wearing a man's heavy overcoat, that she would have boots on her feet, that she would have, if you like, desexed herself, in terms of costume, and that the costume would be a reflection of her own psychic and sexual disturbance, confusion. So I was, actually, at peace when I saw how Electra was to look in this production. It was the way I had mentally prepared for how she would appear on stage and how there would be a connection between one of my plays and this version. In many respects, *Baglady* and *Electra* are both together, go hand in hand. You can call it fortuitous, but I think it was a real sparking of energies between us. I didn't have to spell out how I wanted *Electra* to be or to be seen. I just took it for granted, from the way David had talked previously, that he would have copped on to that. I also believe that he may well have asked me to do it because of *Baglady*.

JOSEPH LONG: *This play has been well received by very different audiences, in Chichester, in London, on Broadway. How do you account for that?*
FRANK McGUINNESS: The one thing this play did for me, it actually broke my heart. I found *Electra* an incredibly moving piece of theatre, even in the literal translation. As I say, I was going through a serious period of mourning at the time. Electra's mourning for her father is a terrible warning against mourning too much, against letting the heart, as Yeats says, turn into a stone. What I found desperately, overwhelmingly sad is the mourning she has for her brother, for Orestes, the true grief that articulates itself there. Also, I think it significant that the imagery in the play is tied in with the natural world. The only other playwrights that have got that extraordinary correspondence between the feelings of the characters and their environment are Shakespeare and Ibsen. I would put Sophocles in the same bracket.

Now this, of course, is a very primitive power, even in this century, even now with the disassociation of our life from the natural world, it still does speak volumes. I think if you give an integrity to Electra's grief for Orestes, an audience will – even the most modern, even the most diverse, even the most sophisticated audience, such as you get in the West End, such as you get on Broadway – this pain touches them, and I think what I really wanted to do was to have this Greek play, this Greek tragedy, speak across the centuries. That still can break an audience's heart. It's not an easy thing to do, but it comes down to, as I say, the integrity of grief, and the playing of that integrity, and the writing of that integrity. That is ultimately the challenge that I set myself: can this play move an audience in the way it has moved me? Because, as I say, Sophocles' enormous skill gives you the discipline to contain the grief. To contain it.

JOSEPH LONG: *There is the intensity of mourning in the play, the intensity of experience, but there is also a political structure in the play. There are distortions inflicted on a whole society by hatred. Then there is the sister, the milder sister, Chrysothemis, who is a figure of rationality, of caution, she wants Electra to 'bow the knee to those in power', to respect the will of Clytemnestra and the will of Aegisthus, who has supplanted Agamemnon. She is a figure of compromise, of prudent acquiescence to the ruling powers. If you pick up the analogy, then, to Sarajevo or to any other modern political situation, there is something of the collaborator there, of the prudent compromise, the willingness to find mid-ways. She is half a free spirit, she is half a collaborator.*
FRANK MCGUINNESS: She is an extremely interesting character, Chrysothemis. You can't pigeon-hole her at all, she shifts with the wind. There are moments when she seems to be on the mother's side, on Clytemnestra's side, there are moments when she seems to be as much obsessed by her father's death as is Electra, there are moments when she is siding with Electra, there are moments when she shows us a depth of emotion that is a parallel to Electra's. They are clearly sisters, they are cut from the same rock. I think that she has been, in her different way, as abused by the events of her father's murder as Electra has been. She has learned to wear the

mask, she has learned to conjure masks. She has also learned the importance of saving her own skin, in a way that Electra not merely has not learned, but has no capacity to learn. There is an ignorance, on Electra's part, which is extraordinarily powerful, but clearly could be enormously destructive to herself. When Electra says 'Kill Aegisthus', which is parallel with Shakespeare's 'Kill Claudio', Chrysothemis knows that she herself is not going to do that. Chrysothemis knows, if Electra does do it, that she has gone into some kind of superhuman state, and not in a healthy way. She makes a very clear statement to her: 'You are a woman, not a man – do you know that?' and it's the man's role in this world to take revenge. Electra sees herself as losing, as having effectively lost, her womanhood. She refers to 'crying bitter spinster's tears'. She talks about her beauty being disfigured by what has happened to her. She wants the male back, she wants Orestes to kill the murderous mother. Her mother's murdering of Agamemnon has effectively exterminated Electra's femaleness. That is something that Chrysothemis fears about herself more than anything else, she does not want to stop being a woman. She does not want to transgress the bonds of gender behaviour, of social behaviour, on that scale. She does not want that degree of commitment to revenge. Electra does. Electra most definitely does. In the parallel universe, if Orestes were really dead, the question you've got to ask is: 'Would she actually do the deed?' And I don't think that there is any doubt but that she would. She would do it. So you can see the terrifying threat Electra would have represented to a Greek audience. That's clear as daylight. If Clytemnestra committed a wrong in murdering Agamemnon, and whether she did or not is again a matter for debate, Electra's passion, her politics are terribly, terribly dangerous. And they still are. The warrior woman is still a figure to be feared.

JOSEPH LONG: *She's a warrior woman, but Leveaux speaks about 'an almost childlike presence' which Zoë Wanamaker brings to the part, an Electra 'who in a sense has remained in the captivity of childhood, because that's literally what Electra is: she has arrived*

*at womanhood without having mediated that'. He says that Electra
suffers like a child, and that's what makes her dangerous.*

FRANK McGUINNESS: I think what is so brilliantly realized in
Sophocles' play, with such an extraordinary psychological grasp,
is that here is a woman who, when she was a girl, saw her father
being brutally murdered, and that this has done dreadful damage
to her, in that it meant that she can never go beyond the events of
that day. She is reliving them, and waiting for the moment to
occur when the events of that day will be avenged and time can
start again. While she is suffering in this dreadful regressive state,
her body has continued to grow, her sexuality has come and gone
and she lives only in a desperate reliving of a past event. Time
itself has effectively deserted her. The whole natural world has
turned against her. The images of the natural world – which I say
the play is permeated in – they are of an alien, aggressive universe
that she really has ceased to be a part of, and she brings all that
rage to bear, almost infantile rage to bear against circumstances
as she sees them affecting her. She sees herself as victimized, she
sees herself as angry, and she sees herself as powerless. All of that
adds up, I think, to what David is saying, to an understanding of
Electra as a child. It's the lack of power which renders her
childlike. It has been her destiny to see that lack of power being
universally, consistently underlined: 'You couldn't stop your
father's murder, you must live with the consequences of that
murder, and you can do nothing to change it.' It maddens her. It
nearly drives her mad. She knows that she is on the edge of going
over the abyss. The killing of Aegisthus is proof of that, the plan
to kill him. Chrysothemis says – it's one of the modernisms in the
play – 'If she had an ounce of sense, she'd shut her mouth.' She
doesn't have it.

JOSEPH LONG: *Well, Chrysothemis says to the Chorus, I've the text
here:*

> *If she had an ounce of sense in her, before she
> opened her mouth,*
>   *She would have exercized caution . . .*

I take your point, but you're not saying, are you, that Chrysothemis thinks Electra is mad?

FRANK MCGUINNESS: Chrysothemis, at this point, realizes the scale of this woman's potential for madness. Electra has said, a few moments earlier in the version, before she declares her plan to kill Aegisthus: 'I'm not insane.' That is the last refuge of a mind on the verge of going insane, to say that. She is saying that to herself as much as to Chrysothemis. You have a raging intelligence at work here, you have a raging imagination at work. She is a deeply imaginative, a deeply intelligent woman, but she is a woman who has been denied any access to adulthood, any access to power, because of the act that was committed when she was a child, and which she was witness to. And which, I think, quite deliberately, she was witness to. That does deeply account for her hatred of her mother, that she did see what happened. Her physical descriptions of the murder of her father are so accurate, so clear, that it is undeniable that she saw what happened.

This mantra of 'I saw' is again a link with *Baglady*: 'I saw, I saw what was done to me.' In this case, it's Electra saying: 'I saw what was done to my father, and I can't grow out of that because it's the defining moment of my life. And if it was done to me when I was a child, then I will hate like a child, and I will be avenged for this abuse, this childhood abuse. I will take a terrible revenge for it, and I will take it against the woman who gave birth to me, I will take it against my mother. She made me watch my father die.'

JOSEPH LONG: *The first image we see of Electra in this production, she is wearing a mask, which suggests the formality of Greek dramaturgy, but she quickly lays it aside . . .*
FRANK MCGUINNESS: Then she puts it on at the end, at the end of the play, and blood starts to come on the mask.

JOSEPH LONG: *There's blood dripping down from the ceiling, you think it's rain, but it's blood, at the end, dripping on the mask. So the formal elements of Greek dramaturgy are referred to, in the production, but not imposed. Similarly, the Chorus is represented simply by three figures, and only one of them speaks. The Chorus is 'sympathetic to the heroine in greatest need, but wise to the eternal truths of time and revenge', as Peter Stothard said with reference to the London production,[2] 'played by Jenny Galloway in the manner of a United Nations aid worker'.*

FRANK MCGUINNESS: It's a good image for it. It was interesting to have two silent members of the Chorus, both younger than the speaking woman. They were clearly two silent victims of war, two women who had lost either husbands or brothers to the war. There were moments in Electra's speech, particularly when she refers to the death of Orestes, dying 'in exile, far from home', when these women would let cries out of them. That was a wonderful touch of David's, that here you were listening to a whole community that had suffered the loss of men in a war. They could deeply identify with Electra's pain. Again, like Chrysothemis, the Chorus show a contradictory approach to their role at times, they advise caution and, at the same time, they know what Electra is going through, they tell her at times: 'You're mourning too much, all the people have lost a father.' They remind her that there have been other deaths. Then, at the same time, they know the tide could turn in other ways, that Electra could become the victor, the predominant political force in this country. They've learned enough from the experience of war to realize that nothing is permanent. Clytemnestra's and Aegisthus' power is not permanent. That's not the way the world works. So they've got that capacity for seeing the two sides of something, which Clytemnestra most definitely does not have. Like Chrysothemis, they stand as radical opposites to Electra and her mother. Clytemnestra is as absolute, in her reading of her own history, as Electra is. They are clearly mother and daughter. Clearly. Clearly women who do not make compromises, clearly women who do not take prisoners. You can see that biological strain, that psychological strain from Clytemnestra to Electra, which makes the hatred all the more profound.

JOSEPH LONG: *Again, to hear you talking like that suggests that there are elements pointing to the situation not only in Northern*

Ireland, but in Ireland as a whole.
FRANK MCGUINNESS: Absolutely. You've got shades of opinion, and then you have those who act decisively for whatever ends they choose to do so. Everything is leading in this play to those last words: 'The deed is done.' There is no judgement made in it. Just that.

JOSEPH LONG: *There is an element of optimism perhaps. There is the phrase of the Chorus: 'Time is a gentle god, he heals'. Is that a sign of some optimism you might have about Northern Ireland?*
FRANK MCGUINNESS: No, that is a direct reference from the original text. Again, it is the cajoling of the Chorus, of the dominant member of the Chorus, always making sure that two sides are represented. The Chorus cannot stand absolutely accused of entirely backing Electra in her protest. Aegisthus identifies them as supporters of Electra and Orestes. He says: 'They're the ones who sided with you.' The play proves that he's wrong in making such a simplistic estimation of what the Chorus is about. You can never be sure, as I say, of which way the wind is going to blow, in the Chorus.

JOSEPH LONG: *The Greeks have been appropriated in different ways, by modern Irish playwrights. Translation isn't the right term. A translator has to respect the word, the texts have to be comparable, line by line. A version, then, is a dramaturgical exercise. It's remarkable, in Irish theatre over the past fifteen years or so, that a number of poets like Brendan Kennelly, Seamus Heaney and others have become dramatists for the specific purpose of adapting a Greek tragedy into an Anglo-Irish idiom. Others again, other playwrights, use a framework which echoes classical Greek themes or structures. One thinks of Marina Carr,* By the Bog of Cats . . ., *in which there is a* Medea *structure in the background, but the play is by no means a version, in our sense, of* Medea. *How do you understand that tendency in Irish theatre? Is there something specifically Irish about it, in the contemporary theatre world?*

FRANK MCGUINNESS: No, it's happening in America as well, actually. If you look at the recent production at the Gate Theatre, here in Dublin, *bash* by Neil LaBute, there are very deep Greek roots there, with the Iphigenia myth coming through powerfully. Or look at a writer like Sarah Kane who, God rest her, is no longer with us, she was deeply influenced by the structure of Greek plays, deeply influenced by the mythology of the Greeks. Sarah is probably the most important English writer of the past twenty years. The body of work is not great, she died so young, but she will be looked on as a key voice. Younger writers are immersing themselves in the violence of Greek theatre, the enormous violence of Greek theatre. *Electra* is not a pretty play, by any means. The passions that are stirring are very strong meat. I think, in that respect, they are probably doing work that is on a parallel with Marina Carr's. It seems to be happening through the English-speaking world, that the Greeks are emerging as the dominant international force in our theatre. Possibly because we are living at a time of apocalypse. The strong meat is the diet they want to feed on.

JOSEPH LONG: *Across Europe, too . . .*
FRANK MCGUINNESS: Never forget Ariane Mnouchkine's *Oresteia*. As usual, I pay homage to her. As usual, she was ahead of the posse.

I would say that, if you want a specific reason for its emergence in the last twenty years with poets, not playwrights, but poets like Brendan Kennelly and Seamus Heaney, you're dealing with a poetic theatre, a theatre that doesn't shy away from passion, that doesn't shy away from politics – both Seamus and Brendan, and indeed Derek Mahon, who has done versions of the Greek plays. It's a wonderful opportunity for them to extend the range of their voice and also to make some money. Never forget that. The Greeks knew it. You can make a few bob in the theatre.

JOSEPH LONG: *Well, Frank, let's hold that one over, for another day's discussion. You've given us fascinating insights into your own creative processes, your writing, your theatrical practice. Thank you for that. You've opened up the whole world of passion and politics in Greek tragedy. Most of all, you've shown how you addressed the vexed question of bringing a modern audience to the point of sharing your own engagement with a classical text.*

We'll leave the last word with the poet, not with the bank manager. It does seem to me that you have extended the range of your own voice with this play. The text you give us in Electra *is extraordinarily rich and suggests a highly poetic form of theatre. Over and beyond dialogue and situation, you marshal a whole range of prosodic effects – assonance, alliteration, rhythms – with great power and impact. I'd like to end with the passage where the Chorus evokes the workings of Justice and Fate. You use rhyme sparingly in the play as a whole, but you use it at telling points. Here, within the passage, you move from assonance to rhyme, and you build a progression of rhythm, tempo and patterns of sound, which develops into something close to a strophic form. We'll leave the last word with the poet:*

CHORUS: May I not bear false witness,
But through the darkness,
I see the workings of Justice.
She knows what has to be.
She will plant her fatal kiss
On the lips of your enemies.
And soon she will be here.
My mind is dancing.
That dream's destroyed my fears.
I heard that and my heart took wing.
Your father, leader of the Greeks,
He will always remember,
And the axe that bloodied his brave cheek
Waits the call from its bronze lair.
Bronze too are the terrible claws
Of the god who devours the lawless.
She has seen the bed where adulterers sleep,
Seen the wedding clothes, the wedding feast,
And her gift will be a pit so deep
No cry of comfort from man nor beast

Shall reach their ears who did the deed
And sinned against the mighty gods.
It's clear as day for all to read
Revenge will never spare the rod.
If there's not truth in that woman's dreams,
Our prayers are lost and dying screams.
The founder of this house,
Pelops, long ago,
You began this sorrow.
Thrown from his chariot,
Martilus died, brought
Down by your deceit,
And sorrows meet
With sorrow since in this unhappy house.

Notes

1. *The New York Times*, 29 November 1998, p. 7.
2. *The Times*, 7 November 1997.

Index

Abbey Theatre, Dublin 29, 103, 108, 126, 232, 261
Adams, Gerry 129, 178
Adaptation of Greek text to Irish context *see also* Translation for translocation 186–95
Aeschylus 7, 11–14, 39, 89
  Agamemnon 44, 80, 181–97
  Eumenides 80, 103
  Oresteia 13–14, 40, 44, 46, 280
  Prometheus Bound 41, 54–57
Aisling (poetry concerned with dream or vision) 51, 84
Anouilh, Jean 39
  Antigone viii, 134
  Beckett 21
Aristophanes 7, 20
  Frogs 41–42
  Thesmophoriazusae 200
Aristotle 4, 91–92
Arkins, Brian xi, 198–212
Arnott, Peter D. 262
Artaud. Antonin 31
Asmal, Kader 146
Auden, Wystan Hugh 16

Bardic poetry vii, xiii
Barker, Harley Granville 5
Barthes, Roland 222–23
Beckett, Samuel 105–06, 108, 125, 132, 241
Benjamin, Walter 7
Berber, Julie 168
Bhabha, Homi K. 219
Biko, Steve 131
Billington, Michael 27
Bokhilane, Fats 130
Bradley, Andrew Cecil 167, 169–70
Brecht, Bertolt 39, 132, 142, 263
Brenton, Howard xii
Brighton, Pam 179
Brontë, Emily 244
Brough, Robert 35
Brutus, Lucius Junius 169
Büchner, Georg 132
Burke-Kennedy, Mary Elizabeth 81
Bury, John Bagnell 98
Byron, George Gordon, *Lord* 54

Camus, Albert 132
Carr, Marina 11, 21, 81, 230, 232, 234
  By the Bog of Cats . . . 29–30, 78–79, 202–03, 243–62, 279
  Low in the Dark 85
  Mai, The 234–37, 245–46, 254
  On Raftery's Hill 243–62
  Portia Coughlan 85, 244, 246, 254
Carson, Edward Henry, *Lord* 168

Casey, Eamonn, *Bishop* 217
Cave, Richard xi, 101–27
Céitinn, Seathrún
    Foras Feasa ar êirinn viii
Chekhov, Anton Pavlovich 33,
    148–50, 162, 263
Chorus, representation of 48, 57,
    67, 69, 169, 172–74, 179–80,
    278–79, 281–82
Civil Rights Association, Northern
    Ireland 151
Clancy, Luke 129
Clark, David R. 10
Cleary, Joe 154–56, 162
Clinton, William Jefferson 180
Cocteau, Jean
    La Machine infernale 3, 49–50
Cole, Henri 181
Conrad, Joseph
    Under Western Eyes 170
Constantine, David 30–31, 34
Corkery, Daniel vii, 88, 148–49
Craig, Edward Gordon 5
Cromwell, Oliver 32, 37
Crowley, Bob 148
Cultural resonances 32
Curran, Eileen 119

Dante Alighieri 186, 196
Da Ponte, Lorenzo
    Don Giovanni 21
Davidson, Clare 161
Deane, Seamus xi, 50, 148–64
De Brún, Pádraig, Monsignor 40,
    82, 87–88, 90–91, 93–94, 96,
    98
De Jongh, Nicholas 128, 146
Deevy, Teresa 232, 237–40
Defoe, Daniel 170
Delanty, Greg 81
Devlin McAliskey, Bernadette
    153, 167

Dickinson, Emily 244
Dinneen, Patrick, *Rev.* 99
Dionysus, changing perceptions of
    21–22
Dolan, Michael J. 119
Doll, Mary A. 234
Donellan, Declan 81, 168–69
Donmar Warehouse, London 263,
    265
Donnelly, Deirdre 128
Druid Theatre Company 254
Dryden, John 182
Dublin Drama League 108
Duru, Welcome 130, 141
Duse, Eleanora 5

Economou, Thomas 5
Edwards, Hilton 107, 125
Egan, Desmond 6, 81, 201, 213,
    244
Eliot, George 150
Eliot, Thomas Stearns xiii, 3,
    5–6
Engles, Johan 267
Erasmus, Desiderius 3
Eriugena, John Scotus 37
Euripides 7–8, 19–29, 32, 41,
    89–90
    Alcestis 44
    Bacchae 204, 206–07
    Hippolytus 40, 41, 51, 80,
        103–24
    Iphigenia in Aulis 203–4
    Iphigenia in Tauris 90
    Medea 8, 29–33, 35, 61–67,
        201–03, 213–31, 243–62
    Trojan Women 28, 41, 204–06

Fanning, Ronan 83
Feminine perspective *see* Women,
    representation of
Ferguson, John 223, 231

Field Day (theatre company founded by Brian Friel and Stephen Rea) 38, 53, 128–29, 148–70
Fitzgerald, Tara 169
Fo, Dario 8
Foley, Helene 199
Ford, Henry, Jr 142
Fornes, Maria Irene 246
Forster, Edward Morgan 154
Freud, Sigmund 55s
Friel, Brian xii, 11, 81, 161, 163
  Communication Cord, The 161
  Gentle Island, The 46–47
  Living Quarters after *Hippolytus* 47–51, 103–10, 204, 244
  Making History 161
  Month in the Country, A (trans. from Turgenev) 162
  Three Sisters (trans. from Chekhov) 148, 150, 161
  Translations viii, 38, 46–47, 161
Frost, Robert 179
Fugard, Athol viii, 17, 128–47, 161, 166
  Blood Knot, The 128
  Boesman and Lena 130
  Coat, The 135, 136
  Cure, The 131
  Friday's Bread on Monday 136
  Island, The 52, 128–30, 144–46, 161, 166
  Klaas and the Devil 132
  Last Bus, The 136
  No-Good Friday 131
  Nongogo 131
  Place with the Pigs, A 129
  Road to Mecca 129
  Siswe Bansi is Dead 138, 140–44, 147
  Space, The 145–46

Gaskell, Elizabeth 234
Gate Theatre, Dublin 107
Geilt, Suibhne (pseud.) 82, 90
Gilligan, Carol 237
Girard, René 241
Goethe, Johann Wolfgang von 54
Gray, Terence 5
Greek canon, attractions of 8
Gregory, Isabella Augusta Persse, Lady 9
Guildhall, Derry (Londonderry) 53, 156
Guthrie, Tyrone 5, 33, 103–04

Halperin, David M. 199–200
Hammond, David 161
Hardy, Thomas 150
Harwood, Ronald 138, 144, 147
Heaney, Seamus 11, 61, 213, 279–80
  Cure at Troy, The: A Version of Sophocles' Philoctetes 15–17, 43, 46, 67–74, 81, 148, 156–64, 171–80, 244
  'Mycenae Lookout' in *Spirit Level, The* 181–97
Hedge schools viii, xii, 37
Hegel, Georg Wilhelm Friedrich 154, 167
Herodotus 92
Hillard, Albert Ernest 98
Hillman, James 102, 124
Hofmannsthal, Hugo von 3, 5
Hölderlin, Friedrich 67
Holland, Mary 75
Homer ix, 92–94
Hugo, Victor 54
Hurd, Douglas 167
Hynes, Garry 253–54

Ibsen, Henrik 243, 247, 256, 258, 263

Irish language translation *see* Translation into Irish

Irish setting *see* Setting, Irish

Jebb, Richard C., *Sir* 42, 165

Jonson, Ben 182

Jordan, Eamonn xi, 243–62

Joynt, Maud 97–98

Joyce, James ix-x, 37, 50, 65–66, 148

Jung, Carl Gustav 245

Kane, Sarah 246

Kani, John 129, 133, 137–38, 140–146

Keane, John B.
  Field, The 215

Keats, John 194

Kelly, Patricia 87–100

Kennelly, Brendan 11, 21, 59–68, 81, 213, 279–80
  Antigone 18–19, 52, 59–60, 166, 207–08
  Boats Are Home, The 230
  Medea 8, 21, 29, 32–33, 61–67, 200–02, 213–31, 244
  Trojan Women 21, 28–29, 67, 205
  Visitor, The 221, 230

Kerényi, Karl 234

Kerry (county) 215–16

Keuls, Eva C. 210

Kiberd, Declan vii-xiii, 39

Kilroy, Thomas 161–62

Kinevane, Pat 232, 242

Knox, Bernard 163

LaBute, Neil
  Bash 280

Latin paraphrases of Greek materials 87

Lee, Joseph 210

Leeny, Cathy xi, 232–42

Lefevere, André 229

Lermontov, Mikhail Iurevich 150

Leveaux, David 263–78

Long, Joseph 263–82

Longford, Christine 80

Longford, Edward, Lord 44, 81

Lorca Federico, Garcia 263

Lucian of Samosata 94–95

Lukács, Georg (György) 157, 164, 259–60

Lunny, Donal 179

McAleer, Des 128

Mhac an tSaoi, Máire 87–88, 94

McClelland, David C. 241

McCracken, Kathleen 220

McDonagh, John 213–31

McDonald, Marianne viii, 32, 37–86, 125, 128–29, 210–11, 246, 261

Mac Giobúin, Cathal, *Rev.* 97

Mac Giolla Eoin, Art C., *Rev. Fr* 90

McGuinness, Frank 14, 260–61
  Electra 75–78, 81, 209
  Innocence 252
  Interview with 263–82
  Observe the Sons of Ulster Marching Towards the Somme 252, 269
  Three Sisters 162
  Uncle Vanya 148, 150

McGuire, James B. 10

McHale, John *see* Mac Hale, John, *Archbishop of Tuam*

Mac Hale, John, *Archbishop of Tuam* 92–93

Mac Héil, Seán *see* Mac Hale, John, *Archbishop of Tuam*

Machiavelli. Niccoló
  La Mandragola 131

McIntyre, Alisdair 158
MacLagm(h)ainn, Seoirse *see*
    Thomson, George
McLean, Adam 262
McLeish, Kenneth 29
MacLiammóir, Micheál 107, 125
MacMillan, Harold 168–69
MacNeice, Louis 21, 44–46, 60,
    77, 81, 83
Mac Tomáis, Seoirse *see*
    Thomson, George
Magada, Mabel 130, 135
Mahon, Derek 81
    Bacchae, The: After Euripides
    21–27, 74–75, 206
    High Time 156, 168
Mandela, Nelson 131, 133, 146
Mandelson, Peter 168
Manning, Mary
    Youth's the Season 107
Marvell, Andrew 170, 182, 195
Marx, Karl 54–55
Masqueray, Paul 43
Mathews, Aidan Carl 6, 21, 61,
    28, 81
    Antigone: A Version 52, 58–9,
    166, 207–09
    Trojans 28, 205–06, 211
Mbikwana, Mulligan 136
Medieval 'translations' 87
Metre and rhyme 179
Mguqulwa, Sipho 133–34, 146
Miller, Arthur 169
Milosz, Czeslaw 193, 195, 197
Milton, John 170
Minerva Theatre, Chichester 263,
    265
Mnouchkine, Ariane 280
Molière, Jean Baptiste Poquelin de
    L'école des maris 156, 168
Moore, George 148, 150
Murphy, Annie 217–18

Murphy, Pat
    Anne Devlin 52, 166
Murphy, Tom
    Sanctuary Lamp, The 11, 46,
    81, 244
Murray, Christopher 52, 262
Murray, Gilbert 5
Murray, Thomas C.
    Autumn Fire 47, 110–11, 113–21
    Birthright 111–13
    Maurice Harte 126
Myth, calling on 260–61
Myth of Ireland 51

Ní Êimhthigh, Mairghéad 98
Ní Mhurchú, Síle x, 87–100
Nietzsche, Friedrich Wilhelm 27
Noh plays, Japanese 145
North, Michael Arthur 98
Northern Ireland
    Arts Council 128
    Political situation 11, 37–38,
    55–60, 69–71, 151–55,
    159–60, 167, 173, 181, 196,
    267–68, 279
Norwood, Gilbert 20
Nowlan, David 18
Ntshinga, Norman 130, 135
Ntshona, Winston 129, 137,
    140–46

O'Brien, Conor Cruise viii, 53,
    153, 162, 166
O'Casey, Sean 11, 163
    Juno and the Paycock 44, 80
Occupation of Ireland by the
    British 37–39
O'Connell, Daniel 162
O'Connor, Frank 148–49
O'Connor, Ulick
    Oval Machine, The 81, 124,
    126, 204

Ó Doibhlin, Breandán 93
O'Donovan, John 92
O'Dwyer, Riana 249
O'Faolain, Sean 148–49, 162
Ó Fiannachta, Pádraig 96, 97
Ó Mathghamhna, Domhnall 95–96
Ó Meachair, Pádraig 97
O'Neill, Eugene 3
    Desire under the Elms 119–24,
    126–27
    Mourning Becomes Electra
    102–03
O'Neill, Hugh 162
Ó Rinn, Uilliam 95
Ó Súilleabháin, Muiris x, 88, 100
O'Toole, Fintan 217–18
Ovid
    Metamorphoses 101

Page, Denys 262
Paisley, Ian 53
Papas, Irene 170
Paulin, Tom 11, 41, 81, 162, 213
    Fivemiletown 156
    Minotaur: Poetry and the
    Nation State 156
    Riot Act, The 52–4, 129, 148,
    152–56, 161, 165–70, 168,
    207–08, 244
    Seize the Fire: A Version of
    Aeschylus's Prometheus
    Unbound 12, 41, 55–58
Pearse, Pádraig 39
Pirandello, Luigi 108–09
Plato 95–96
Plutarch 96
Political motives 47, 53–54, 159
Post-colonial condition of Ireland
    213
Prescott, John 168

Quilligan, Veronica 168

Racine, Jean, 49, 104–05, 110–11,
    122
Raftery, Anthony viii–ix
Rame, Franca 8
Raphael, Frederic 29
Rea, Stephen 128, 148, 161, 165,
    168, 170
Reinhardt, Max 5
Republicanism, Irish 154–55
Revival, Irish 148
Revivalist writing 89
Richtarik, Marilynn J. 146, 162
Rieu, Émile Victor 132
Robinson, Mary 177
Roche, Anthony 52–53
Ross, Martin see Somerville, Edith
    Oenone, and Ross, Martin
Royal Court Theatre, London 5
Russian literature 148–50

Sartre, Jean-Paul 39
Savory, Theodore 3, 35
Scargill, Arthur 169
Scott, Michael 81
Semele, story of 101
Setting, Irish 10
Shakespeare, William 21, 132
Shaw, Fiona 29, 75
Shaw, George Bernard 20, 170
    Major Barbara 80, 207
    St Joan 21
Shelley, Percy Bysshe 54
Sheridan, Thomas, Rev. 40, 80
Sigerson, George 162
Sihra, Melissa 262
Smith, Sidney Bernard 81
Somerville, Edith Oenone, and
    Ross, Martin
    Real Charlotte, The 150
Sophocles x, 7, 14–19, 21, 41,
    90–91, 150
    Antigone 42, 51–54, 58–60,

128–48, 165–70, 207–09, 244

Electra 75–78, 209, 260, 263–82

King Oedipus (Oedipus Tyrannus, Oedipus Rex) 40, 43, 80, 91

Oedipus at Colonus 43–44

Philoctetes 67–68, 163–64, 171–80

Spring, Dick 178

Steiner, George 245

Stevens, Wallace 195–97

Synge, John Millington ix-xi, 11, 42, 44, 80, 110–11, 132, 243

Taccone, Tony 171

Tacitus, Cornelius xii

Taplin, Oliver 216–17, 251–52

Teevan, Colin 6, 210

Iph 81, 203–04

Thatcher, Margaret 152, 169

Theocritus 97

Thomson, George x-xi, 82, 88–90, 92, 95–96, 98

Thucydides 28, 97

Tragedy

origins of 6–9

relevance to Ireland 34–35, 37–8, 40

Roman 3

Translation

difficulties in 6, 9, 30–33, 266

for translocation *see also* adaptation of Greek text to Irish context 30, 33, 213

into Irish vii, 40, 87–100

Tricycle Theatre, London 159

Turgenev, Ivan Sergeevich 149–50

Tzavellas, George 170

Ua Laoghaire, Peadar, *Rev.* 94

Ua Nualláin, Tomás 91–92

Vedrenne, John Eugene 5

Vehey, Brien 168

Vellacott, Philip 218, 228

Vendler, Helen 181–97

Virgil, Irish language translation of *Imtheachta Aeniasa* vii

Voltaire (Arouet, François Marie) 213

Wall, Maureen viii

Walton, J. Michael viii, 3–36, 128–29, 251

Walton, Tom 254

Wanamaker, Zoë 75, 263–78

Warner, Deborah 36

Wilding, Longworth Allen xi-xii

Williams, Tennessee 243

Williamson, Margaret 262

Wills, Clair 156, 162

Wilson, Edmund

Wound and the Bow, The 156–57, 163–64

Winchester, Simon 83–84

Wisdom, *'sophia'* 25

Women, representation of 19–20, 60, 77, 198–212

Woodworth, Paddy 163

Woolf, Virginia 5, 9, 199

Xenophon 97–98

Yaari, Nurit 32

Yeats, William Butler 9–10, 18, 21, 32, 42–44, 66–67, 77, 81, 83, 105, 108–09, 125, 162, 165–66, 170

Cathleen Ni Houlihan (Countess Cathleen, The) 44, 105, 178

Zelenak, Michael X. 256

Zinman, Toby 265

Zizek, Slavoj 164